Saving South Beach

Florida History and Culture

Florida A&M University, Tallahassee
Florida Atlantic University, Boca Raton
Florida Gulf Coast University, Ft. Myers
Florida International University, Miami
Florida State University, Tallahassee
University of Central Florida, Orlando
University of Florida, Gainesville
University of North Florida, Jacksonville
University of South Florida, Tampa
University of West Florida, Pensacola

∫AVING
SOUTH
BEACH

M. Barron Stofik

Foreword by Gary R. Mormino and Raymond Arsenault

University Press of Florida
Gainesville ~ Tallahassee ~ Tampa ~ Boca Raton
Pensacola ~ Orlando ~ Miami ~ Jacksonville ~ Ft. Myers

Copyright 2005 by M. Barron Stofik
Printed in the United States of America on acid-free paper
All rights reserved

10 09 08 07 06 05   6 5 4 3 2 1

Library of Congress Cataloging-in-Publication Data
Stofik, M. Barron.
Saving South Beach / by M. Barron Stofik ;
foreword by Gary R. Mormino and Raymond Arsenault.
p. cm. – (Florida history and culture series)
Includes bibliographical references (p.) and index.
ISBN 0-8130-2902-3 (alk. paper)
1. South Beach (Miami Beach, Fla.)—History—20th century.
2. Miami Beach (Fla.)—History—20th century. 3. Historic
preservation—Florida—Miami Beach—History—20th century.
4. Historic buildings—Conservation and restoration—Florida—Miami
Beach—History—20th century. 5. South Beach (Miami Beach, Fla.)—
Buildings, structures, etc. 6. Miami Beach (Fla.)—Buildings,
structures, etc. I. Title. II. Series.
F319.M62S76 2005
975.9'381—dc22   2005053160

The University Press of Florida is the scholarly publishing agency
for the State University System of Florida, comprising Florida A&M
University, Florida Atlantic University, Florida Gulf Coast University,
Florida International University, Florida State University, University
of Central Florida, University of Florida, University of North Florida,
University of South Florida, and University of West Florida.

University Press of Florida
15 Northwest 15th Street
Gainesville, FL 32611-2079
http://www.upf.com

to Jerry and Libby

Contents

Series Foreword

Saving South Beach is the latest volume in a series devoted to the study of Florida history and culture. During the past half century, the burgeoning growth and increased national and international visibility of Florida have sparked a great deal of popular interest in the state's past, present, and future. As the favorite destination of hordes of tourists and as the new home for millions of retirees, immigrants, and transplants, modern Florida has become a demographic, political, and cultural bellwether.

A state of vast distances and distant strangers, Florida needs more citizens who care about the welfare of this special place and its people. We hope this series helps newcomers and old timers appreciate and understand Florida. The University Press of Florida established the Florida History and Culture Series in an effort to provide an accessible and attractive format for the publication of works related to the Sunshine State.

As coeditors of the series, we are deeply committed to the creation of an eclectic but carefully crafted set of books that will provide the field of Florida studies with a fresh focus and encourage Florida researchers and writers to consider the broader implications and context of their work. The series includes monographs, memoirs, anthologies, and travelogues. And, while the series features books of historical interest, we encourage authors researching Florida's environment, politics, and popular or material culture to submit their manuscripts as well. We want each book to retain a distinct personality and voice, but at the same time we hope to foster a sense of community and collaboration among Florida scholars.

Saving South Beach is a stirring tale of one of America's most celebrated places and of how a dedicated core of volunteers managed to preserve the historic district from developers' schemes and political opponents. Today, South Beach glitters as one of America's—indeed, the world's—most exotic locales. It was not always so, and how South Beach evolved from a barrier island to Miami Beach to a district celebrated for its Depression-era Art Moderne hotels to a haven for elderly Jews and to its present reincarnation as the most desirable address in Florida is the story of M. Barron Stofik's remarkable book.

The Great Depression may be best known for bread lines, apple sellers, and national doubt, but to middle-class Americans fortunate enough to be working, Miami Beach was alluring—and cheap. In an area called South Beach, along Collins Avenue and Ocean Drive, local architects designed scores of Streamline-style hotels with magical names: the Carlyle, the New Yorker, and the St. Moritz. In contrast to the ornate, boom-era hotels, the sleek 1930s structures incorporated glass block, stainless steel, and chrome into their modest interiors and exteriors.

By the time the term *Art Deco* entered the English lexicon in 1966, South Beach had sadly declined. Scorned by developers and embraced by thousands of poor, elderly Jews, the area south of Sixth Street was designated "blighted" by the Miami Beach City Commission. Old South Beach was doomed, or so it seemed. A remarkable series of characters saved South Beach, and Stofik's chronicle is captivating. Barbara Capitman, a widow when she first viewed South Beach in 1976, became the driving force who foiled developers determined to level the 230–block district and replace it with luxury apartments and office buildings. Stofik's book includes an extraordinary cast of characters: Cuban exiles who fell in love with the lovely buildings, volunteers who profiled and compiled lists of 1,200 buildings deemed significant, and local and national preservation officials who realized the importance of these buildings, many not even a half-century old. Stofik tells the story with a style as graceful and as streamlined as the Art Deco hotels she loves.

Gary Mormino and Raymond Arsenault
University of South Florida, St. Petersburg
Series Coeditors

Preface and Acknowledgments

First, let's get the geography straight. Miami Beach is not the sandy side of the city of Miami. Miami Beach is an independent city, one of thirty-one municipalities that lie within Miami-Dade County. Making this distinction clear is a thankless task that has bedeviled local tourism officials since 1915. Miami Beach lounges along seven miles of the Atlantic coast, between the cruise ships sailing through Government Cut on its south and the little town of Surfside on its north. Miami is on the other side of Biscayne Bay to the west. Miami Beach parochially has been divided into North, Middle (or Central), and South Beach since the early 1920s. The lines of demarcation steadily shifted northward as the city grew. South Beach used to be south of Fifth Street. Today, most people think of South Beach as everything south of Dade Boulevard, about twenty blocks north of its earlier boundary.

The first time I remember visiting South Beach was in 1960. Lincoln Road Mall was new and an attraction. Miami Beach was promoted as "America's Riviera." The entire neighborhood was painted white and sparkling as if it were scrubbed clean every night.

This book begins sixteen years later. The decline in South Beach in that short time was shocking. The tourists had discovered new destinations. South Beach, along with its population of elderly Jews, became largely ignored except during election years. It became tired, shabby, and its new nickname was "God's Waiting Room." Then it got worse.

Crime frightened most residents off the streets in the 1980s. They were replaced by drug dealers and prostitutes and people who shot each other. Part of the neighborhood was declared blighted, and a major social services agency classified the oldest part of South Beach as a "slum."

Fast forward another ten years, and there was another astounding transformation. The place sizzled with nightlife, celebrities, and young people seeking excitement and each other. In 1992, *Travel and Leisure* magazine called South Beach "the hippest hangout on earth."

These dramatic shifts could give a neighborhood whiplash. A sundries store trying to serve the needs of its customers had to stock beach towels for sunburned tourists in the sixties, extra-strength arthritis medicine for senior citizens in the seventies, a gun under the counter in case of robbery in the eighties, and designer bottled water for supermodels in the nineties. Residents, property owners, and seasonal visitors were carried along the waves of change with seemingly little say over their destiny.

It didn't happen by accident. Today's South Beach is the unanticipated result of a lot of well-intentioned people tinkering with the neighborhood. Almost all of them blame someone else for the decline and suggest that he or she is a person without whom its resurgence never would have happened. They're all correct. This was an ensemble performance. Each decision, each incident, each person affected the outcome in a meaningful way.

People who have visited South Beach or seen it on TV and in the movies have different images of the neighborhood, from an idyllic tropical resort to an Art Deco architectural treasure to a celebrity-sprinkled party scene.

In fact, South Beach is an ordinary neighborhood where people get up in the morning and read the newspaper and have a cup of coffee before going to work. It is a neighborhood where people shop at the market for milk and laundry detergent, run errands, go to the doctor, attend church or synagogue. It is a neighborhood where kids go to school and play baseball, where the cable guy doesn't show up on schedule, where the house has to be cleaned and the garbage taken out. It is a neighborhood filled with lawyers and musicians, Jews and Hispanics, salespeople and teachers, straights and gays, TV producers and ad executives, actors and waiters (often the same).

It is a neighborhood that also is an idyllic tropical resort, an architectural treasure, and a celebrity-sprinkled party scene. This is its story.

The author would like to thank the following persons and organizations who provided information and assistance in the research for this book: Stanley Arkin, Les Beilinson, Lynn Bernstein, Black Archives History and Research Foundation of South Florida, Inc., Matti Bower, Diane Camber, Andrew Capitman, Ph.D., John Capitman, Ph.D., Charles Citrin, City of Miami Beach, Dade Heritage Trust, Florida Governor's Office of Film and Entertainment, Gaslamp Quarter Association, Greater Miami Convention and Visitors Bureau, Historical Museum of Southern Florida, Richard Hoberman, Michael Kinerk, Las Vegas Convention and Visitors Authority, Nancy Liebman, Marty Merkley, Ernie Martin, Ph.D., Miami Beach Chamber of Commerce, Miami Design Preservation League, Aristides Millas, Monroe County Tourist Development Council, New Orleans Metropolitan Convention and Visitors Bureau, Ferdie Pacheco, M.D., David J. Phillips, Linda Polansky, Jimmy Resnick, Randall Robinson, Ivan Rodriguez, Denis Russ, Gerry Sanchez, Ellie Schneiderman, Bruce Singer, Vincent J. Trunzo, Dennis Wilhelm, Dona Zemo, and Elan Zingman-Leith.

Special thanks go to Sam Boldrick and the staff of the Florida Room at the Miami-Dade Public Library, Susan Arthur Kemppainen, Beth Lyons, the Miami-Dade Historic Preservation Division, and the people of South Beach. I am in debt to the army of journalists who wrote the first draft of the story in newspapers and magazines and who created a record of people's lives that does not exist anywhere else. My deepest gratitude goes to my family, who endured the final months of this project, not without complaint, but with loving tolerance.

Chronology

1915	The Ocean Beach hotel, first in Miami Beach, opens on Washington Avenue. Town of Miami Beach is incorporated by John Collins, Carl Fisher, and J. N. and J. E. Lummus.
1925	Art Deco style is introduced at the *Exposition Internationale des Arts Decoratifs et Industriels Modernes* in Paris.
1926	Category 5 hurricane hits Miami Beach.
1973	City commission creates the Miami Beach Redevelopment Agency.
February 1975	Miami Beach, south of Fifth Street, is declared "blighted."
August 1976	The Miami Design Preservation League is formed.
January 1977	First cursory visual survey of the Art Deco district by league volunteers.
October 1978	First Art Deco Week festival.
May 1979	Miami Beach Architectural District is listed on the National Register of Historic Places.
April 1980	Mariel boatlift begins.
May 1980	Riots in Miami's African-American neighborhoods.
January 1981	The New Yorker Hotel is demolished.
February 1981	Metro-Dade County adopts a historic preservation ordinance.
1981	Miami Beach Development Corporation is formed.
June 1982	Miami Beach adopts a municipal historic preservation ordinance.

September 1982   Moratorium is lifted from South Shore redevelopment area.

September 1984   *Miami Vice* premiers on fall television schedule.

April 1985   First Ocean Drive Developers' Conference hosted by the Miami Beach Development Corporation and Dade Heritage Trust.

March 1985   South Florida Arts Center opens on Lincoln Road.

July 1986   City commission designates the Espanola Way and Ocean Drive/Collins Avenue Historic Districts.

August 1986   Miami City Ballet moves to Lincoln Road.

March 1987   The Biscaya is demolished.

1987   South Pointe Tower is completed, the first new building in the former South Shore redevelopment area.

November 1987   Abe Resnick is elected to Miami Beach City Commission.

May 1988   The Senator Hotel is demolished.

October 1989   The Lincoln Theater becomes home of the New World Symphony.

June 1990   City commission designates the Flamingo Park Historic District.

August 1992   Hurricane Andrew hits the greater Miami area.

October 1992   National Trust for Historic Preservation holds its annual conference in Miami.

November 1992   City commission completes designation of the local historic districts to bring the National Register Art Deco district under city regulation.

May 1993   Fifth Street Gym is demolished.

November 1993   Nancy Liebman is elected to Miami Beach City Commission.

February 1996   Ocean Beach Historic District extends preservation controls into the area south of Sixth Street.

July 1997   Gianni Versace murdered on steps of Casa Casuarina.

1997   The 44-story Portofino Tower ushers in a new wave of high-rise construction in the South Pointe area.

1998   Bass Museum of Art embarks on four-year expansion project.

1999   MiMo (Miami Modernism) movement begins to save 1950s Beach hotels.

CHAPTER 1

The Shtetl

Benjamin Levy started each day at 5:30 a.m. He cleaned up, dressed in his fine white suit, and set out walking.[1] A few shopkeepers already were working brooms against cigarette butts and gum wrappers that had been cast recklessly on the sidewalk the previous day. Hotel lobbies were showing their first signs of activity as maintenance men checked at the front desk for overnight complaints of burned-out lightbulbs and stubborn plumbing. Platoons of domestic workers and hotel chambermaids were landing at bus stops. There always were a few other pedestrians—some walking with dogs, more of them walking with canes.

Stanley Worth had opened the doors for the breakfast crowd by the time Benjamin Levy arrived at the Concord Cafeteria on Collins Avenue. Orthopedic shoes shuffled across the terrazzo floor toward the food line where Broadway Charlie was sliding pans of his freshly scrambled eggs and fried potatoes into their assigned spaces on the stainless steel steam table.

Levy took a tray and pushed it along the serving line, assembling his usual breakfast of cereal, eggs, a soft onion roll with butter, Jell-O, and coffee.[2] The cashier took his $3.50 with a smile and her customary "How're you feeling today?" Other customers had the breakfast special on their trays: juice, two eggs, potatoes, just-baked bread, and coffee for a buck sixty-five. They examined each item with the intensity of a radiologist reading an X-ray, much to the amusement of Broadway Charlie, whose voice was as raspy as his spatula against the hot griddle.[3]

The 250 seats in the dreary dining hall quickly filled. The sounds of clattering dishes, clanking silverware, and chair legs scraping against the scuffed floor echoed off the faded green walls and mixed with the chatter of voices heavy with accents of Russia, Poland, Romania, and Brooklyn.

The Concord had been a neighborhood institution since Stanley Worth's father-in-law opened it in 1947. Stanley had managed the cafeteria for almost twenty-five years. The food was good and fresh, the portions generous, and the prices inexpensive. It became a popular spot for celebrities and tourists, the meeting place for the Kiwanis and Lions clubs, a first choice when the family went out to dinner.

Benjamin Levy carried his tray to one of the wobbly Formica-covered tables. By 1976, the families, the civic groups, and members of the hotel orchestras dressed in tuxedos no longer frequented the Concord. They had been replaced by people like Benjamin Levy, who was born in Turkey in 1899 and didn't own a tuxedo. They were European refugees like Sam Drucker, who had been eating alone since he moved to South Beach in 1959. Only five of the twelve thousand Jews from his Polish village survived World War II. His wife and children were not among them.[4] The conversation at the tables was no longer of the stars who were appearing in the glittering showrooms of the big hotels. Now elderly patrons discussed the 6.4 percent increase that would show up in their Social Security checks the next month. It probably would not reduce the loss of the restaurant's teaspoons, which disappeared out the door by the dozens each week.

Yiddish language newspapers such as the *Jewish Daily Forward* littered worn tabletops. Readers wanted to find out about what Israel Prime Minister Yitzhak Rabin was doing and whether Syria moving its troops from the Golan Heights suggested some agreement between the two countries. Others riffled through the pages of the *Miami Herald* and mused about Georgia Governor Jimmy Carter's surprising race for the Democratic nomination for president. The Concord's patrons were almost exclusively Democrats.

Benjamin Levy finished his breakfast and headed south. Slender palm trees fluttered their fronds slightly beside American flags that had been displayed liberally in anticipation of the nation's upcoming bicentennial celebration. It would be another couple of hours before shoppers would breathe life into Lincoln Road Mall. A clerk was preparing to open the post office window at Woolworth's. Jeanette Joya had arrived for another day of work at Moseley's and was sorting through the fine table and bed linens she would show to her well-heeled customers that day, as she had done for the past thirty years. Soon the mall tram would start making its round trips carrying elderly shoppers whose arthritic knees rebelled against walking the eight-block-long promenade.

The sun was heating the day, and the volume of traffic on the sidewalks was picking up. Women wearing wide-brimmed straw hats and trailing folding shopping carts made their way to do their marketing. People in roomy swimsuits and discreet cover-ups headed to the beach for a morning swim or to join their exercise group in the park. A few waited on benches for a city bus, one perhaps nervously waiting to ride north to be tested on the new CAT-scan unit at Mount Sinai Medical Center, the first in the county. Some simply sat.

Levy turned west toward Flamingo Park, once the site of polo fields and pale people in whites playing civilized games of tennis. He had lived on South Beach for six years, so he still was considered a newcomer, but he had become a regular at Friendship Corner No. 3 where he played cards with other men who talked about the old country and how the baseball season was going. Players already were lined up for their turns on the shuffleboard courts, ignoring the teenagers who were getting their time on the handball courts before the lawyers and stockbrokers showed up and invoked the seniority rule.

This was South Beach in 1976, home to more than fifty thousand residents, most of them senior citizens, and most of them Jewish. They were working people who had sent their sons to medical school and married their daughters to nice young men with good prospects. They had been frugal and saved their money. They had their Social Security, some had union pensions, and all wanted to spend a comfortable retirement in peace. The snowbirds came to the hotels for the season and retreated north to escape the humid summer months. The year-rounders settled into sunny rental apartments in the small buildings around Flamingo Park or south of Fifth Street. Some moved into cooperative apartments or one-bedroom condominiums bought by their children. The mouth-watering aroma of homemade chicken soup wafted through the halls.

It was the old neighborhood re-created in the tropics, with everything familiar and within walking distance. The kosher delis on Washington Avenue held cases of salamis and whitefish. Experienced shoppers dickered over prices at the open-front markets that carried plums and peaches that were extra ripe, easier for people with delicate digestive systems. People at the library, the thrift shop, and the drugstore knew them by face if not by name. Hibiscus bloomed outside their doors in January, and they could buy fresh orange juice at stands right on the sidewalk. There was a synagogue every few blocks. It was paradise, the promised land.

Their days were busy. There were appointments to be kept at the South Shore Medical Pavilion, where ninety-five out of a hundred patients paid with Medicare. The Jewish Senior Citizens Center offered a free hot lunch, art classes, and sing-a-longs. They took adult education classes in pottery, folk dancing, and bookkeeping. Card games, impromptu music performances, and meaningful conversation provided amusement in Lummus Park, a green, landscaped ribbon that served as the front yard for the Ocean Drive hotels between Fifth and Fifteenth streets. Couples and groups of single ladies went out to dinner, getting to their favorite restaurant in time for the Early Bird Special. There was entertainment or bingo or maybe an ice cream party in the lobby that evening, or they went to a Yiddish movie. They dressed up and gathered at the band shell or the oceanfront auditorium for the dances, featuring good music, big band music, not that disco stuff they heard from radios in passing cars.

By one o'clock each day, Levy was on the move again, strolling down Ocean Drive past Lummus Park, where women in flowered polyester sundresses and men wearing polo shirts and golf caps were sitting on the benches or under the seagrape trees in lawn chairs that they had carried with them. Their neighbors had retreated to the shade of the breezy hotel porches on the west side of the street. Men dozed while wives and widows critiqued the television shows they saw the night before and complained about their ungrateful children. They avoided talking about the threat looming over their homes and endangering the tight-knit community they had built on the oceanfront.

Levy always stopped in the park at Seventh Street to rest his seventy-seven-year-old legs and people-watch for a couple of hours.[5] The smoke from his cigarette blended with the pervasive aromas of Coppertone and Ben-Gay. Elderly women wearing ruffled bathing caps walked alongside suntanned mothers lugging towels, toys, and coolers while herding toddlers toward the beachside shower to wash the sand from their feet before climbing in their cars for the drive home. Across the street was the Beacon Hotel. Its main tower was five stories high, with faux columns slapped flat against the wall. Faded aqua paint highlighted slim horizontal stripes that worked their way across the front of the hotel and then hopped over to a three-story wing on the left. Air conditioners dangled from some windows; rusty water from their drains stained the white walls. Venetian blinds hung at varying heights behind the panes. A two-story sign with letters outlined in neon poked out from the tower. Five steps led to an arcaded terrace where a few retirees were resting in a row of aluminum chairs with vinyl-strap seats. To Levy and the others in the park, it looked pretty much like every hotel and apartment building on South Beach.

The hotels and apartments and the elderly residents drew Barbara Capitman, her son John, and their friend Leonard Horowitz to South Beach. John had enjoyed spending time in the area when his parents moved to Florida three years earlier and settled into a quiet apartment on the Venetian Islands between Miami and Miami Beach. His dad loved the old kosher restaurants and the pedestrian environment of South Beach. His parents reminisced about people they knew who had vacationed there when it was clean and sleek—so different from the gray buildings and gray winters up north.[6]

A lot had changed in those three years. Barbara's husband had died suddenly. She had moved to a condominium on Key Biscayne. John had graduated from Yale and was about to begin working on his master's degree in public policy at Florida International University. Her older son, Andrew, was traveling internationally, doing economic studies for exporters from Latin America. And South Beach was not clean and sleek anymore.

The Bicentennial had engaged Americans in a burst of patriotism. People were buying flags, planning parades, and trying to remember the second verse of "America the Beautiful." Television specials were reminding viewers of how, in two hundred years, America had grown into a powerful country that brought the world democracy and Coca Cola. All that reflection was prompting thoughtful designers to look at what the nation had built in those two centuries. The county's new monolithic fifty-story government center was being planned for downtown Miami. Tall, sharp-edged condominiums were replacing the graceful mansions of Millionaire's Row on the west side of Biscayne Bay. A dark, looming hotel and shopping mall complex was rising near the entrance to the Venetian Causeway, around the corner from the funky apartment where Horowitz lived. Barbara Capitman and Leonard Horowitz didn't like what they saw. It was a commonly held opinion, described by Christopher Alexander, who wrote in a 1965 issue of *Architectural Forum*, "The non-art-loving public at large regards the onset of modern buildings and modern cities everywhere as an inevitable, rather sad piece of the larger fact that the world is going to the dogs."[7]

That afternoon, the Capitmans and Horowitz decided to take a drive around South Beach. They started in the small triangle of land south of Fifth Street, the area originally known as South Beach until the town expanded northward. Ocean Drive and Collins Avenue were lined with unpretentious hotels built in the 1920s and 1930s. Some looked as though they hadn't been painted since. On the cross streets were old wood-frame apartment buildings that appeared to have developed a slight permanent tilt away from the constant breeze off the Atlantic. There were a few simple bungalows from the Beach's early days, some of them faced with native oolitic limestone (commonly called coral rock) and topped with steeply pitched roofs. Large windows shadowed by generous eaves kept them cool in the days before air conditioning. The city marina, which had seen better days, sat on the edge of the bay and across the street from a rusty water tower. Sprinkled among the jumble of old houses, hotels, and apartments were fruit stands, restaurants, auto repair shops, a meat-packing plant, warehouses, small manufacturers, several nondescript co-ops and condominiums built in the 1960s, some low-income housing, and the Beth Jacob Hall, home of the oldest Jewish congregation on Miami Beach.

They turned north of Fifth Street onto Ocean Drive. There was little traffic on the two-lane street, and few cars were parked at the meters on either side. Lummus Park, the broad sandy beach, and the Atlantic Ocean were to their right. This was the only stretch of Miami Beach where no buildings blocked the view of the ocean from the road. Block after block of small hotels were on their left. When they reached the Beacon Hotel, across the street from where Benjamin Levy spent each afternoon people-watching, Horowitz shouted, "Stop the car! Look at all these *fab*ulous buildings!"[8]

Leonard Horowitz was a designer by profession, flamboyant by nature, and an artist by providence. Under the hotels' layers of flaking paint, he saw something magical. To the left was the Avalon, blonde concrete eyebrows shading its windows. To the right was the Colony, where neon outlined the lettering on a spire and canopy worthy of a 1930s movie palace. A block south was the Park Central Hotel, its corners feathered by wraparound windows, giving it wings to float seven stories above a columned porch. A block north sat the Waldorf Towers, a cylindrical lighthouse tower looking out to sea from atop its rounded rooftop corner. Another block north was the Breakwater, three stories with a soaring tower and a roof deck surrounded by a railing that would be at home on any of the cruise ships that sailed along the horizon. Everywhere were walls of glass block, doorways trimmed with shiny black Vitrolite, brushed tin canopies overhanging porch steps, lines and curves of neon, porthole windows, arches and balconies, glass panes etched with flamingos and palm trees and tropical fish. And the names—Waves, Tides, Beach Paradise—shouted, "It's vacation time! Come play on the beach!"

America's Playground

People had been coming to play on the beach since the days when Dade County stretched from far south of Miami to Jupiter (the town north of Palm Beach, not the planet). From the 1830s when Richard Fitzpatrick slashed out the first plantation from the wilderness on the banks of the Miami River, settlers had rowed over to the beach to play in the relaxing waters of the ocean. Frosty New Englanders came to spend the warm winters with pioneers who had founded the little Coconut Grove settlement on the mainland. Women in high-necked silk dresses with leg-o'-mutton sleeves, petticoats, and extravagant hats joined men in celluloid collars, wool three-piece suits, and bowlers for tea under the palm trees one day, then packed a lunch basket and their scratchy woolen bathing suits for a day at the beach the next.

Early on a hot autumn morning in 1883, a ship neared the shore of the beach peninsula. The keeper for the Biscayne House of Refuge was on the lookout for the boat,[9] alerted to its imminent approach by the Key West customs house. In the cluster of people waiting on the beach was Henry Lum, a nurseryman from New Jersey.

The schooner anchored less than a thousand yards offshore, about four miles south of the lifesaving station. Muscular men hauled lifeboats into the surf and rowed out, tying up alongside the ship. The crew unloaded the cargo into the small boats, dropping some of the shipment into the water. The workers rowed to shore, emptied the load, rowed back out, and repeated the process. When they finished late that afternoon, thirty-eight thousand coconuts, including the ones they scooped out of the sea, were piled up at the edge of the beach.[10]

Over the next few months, laborers struggled to hew paths through the tangled vines and dense underbrush to plant the coconuts. Dark clouds of ravenous mosquitoes and sand flies made the work uncomfortable. The heat made it miserable. The snakes, crocodiles, and bobcats made it dangerous. At night, the workers retired to rough cabins that had been brought in sections by boat from New Jersey. The meager camp was set up above the high-water line, and dismantled and moved as new land was cleared for planting.[11]

The coconuts sprouted tiny seedlings, and Henry Lum and his investors eagerly looked forward to a lucrative annual coconut crop. That's when the peninsula's thriving population of rabbits discovered that they preferred coconut seedlings to their regular diet of sea oats. Lum battled the bunnies and other wildlife for seven years before abandoning his dream and the plantation.

Henry Flagler extended his Florida East Coast railroad to Miami in 1896 after he was lured south by a fragrant bouquet of citrus blossoms delivered to him in St. Augustine after a hard freeze devastated the central and north Florida groves. Well-appointed railway cars brought eager tourists, lots of them. The wife of William Jennings Bryan remembered her arrival: "One morning I stepped from the train at Miami, then a small village. The railroad station was covered with a huge bougainvillea and the whole place was a bower of flowers. As soon as I breathed the balmy air of Miami I knew this was the place."[12]

One visitor to the newly accessible frontier village was John Collins, an investor in Henry Lum's failed coconut plantation, who came to see where his $5,000 had gone. Collins, a wealthy Quaker, was nationally regarded as a pioneer in fruit cultivation. Although coconuts had proven troublesome, he saw potential in the waterfront land and assembled five miles of property along the coastline. Collins started planting in 1907, putting in avocado and mango trees brought over from Miami. He added tomatoes, potatoes, and bananas to generate cash flow while the trees matured. The harvest had to be hauled by wagon through the mangroves to the western shore, then loaded on a boat for a circuitous seven-mile journey across the bay to the train station in Miami. After four years of that onerous operation, Collins decided he needed a more direct route and made plans to dredge a canal directly from the farm to Biscayne Bay.[13]

John Collins's industrious farming operation was eating up his cash reserves. His children and their spouses had established successful businesses with his help. He urged them to come to Miami and look at his new enterprise with an eye toward investing in it. They spent a day at his "ranch" listening to their father's plans. They were impressed with the Red Bliss potatoes and Cavendish bananas, but while standing on the beach looking at the marvelous view of the Atlantic Ocean, they had another idea. At their downtown Miami hotel that evening, they made a proposal.[14]

The beach had become a popular destination for day trips from Miami. A two-story bathhouse pavilion, built in 1904, provided much-needed shelter for swimmers who didn't want to get too much sun. Ferryboats, including two pretentiously named *Mauretania* and *Lusitania*, made twice-daily trips from Miami's downtown docks. Pleasure seekers landed at a wooden pier and then carefully crossed an elevated boardwalk over the muck and undergrowth to reach the pavilion.

Collins's offspring saw a bright future on the eastern side of the bay, not in fresh veggies but as a seaside vacation resort. They offered the seventy-four-year-old Collins their financial support for dredging his canal if he also would build a bridge across Biscayne Bay connecting with the mainland. Opening the beach to motor traffic would let the family cash in on its extensive beachfront landholdings. The result was the formation of the Miami Beach Improvement Company.[15] The sandy peninsula had a name and its first real estate developer.

John Collins and his son-in-law, Thomas Pancoast, went to see local bankers J. N. and J. E. Lummus to seek financing for the bridge. The banker brothers knew a promising opportunity when they saw one.

Collins and Pancoast got the loan for the bridge, but, before work got under way, the Lummus brothers made an investment of their own to buy almost six hundred acres of land at the southern tip of the sandbar.[16]

The owner of the bathhouse was less enthusiastic. The bridge would be stiff competition for his ferry service. His attempt to legally halt construction of the span failed, so he started making improvements to turn the simple pavilion into an oceanside casino.[17] Before long, visitors to Smith's Casino could kick up their heels in a dance hall, have lunch at an open-air restaurant, frolic in a saltwater swimming pool, and relax in comfortable wicker chairs on a wide shady veranda overlooking the ocean while the children played on the swings and slides on a sandy playground. They had a choice of more than 150 changing rooms, each supplied with a clean bathing suit and towel for a quarter. Those rooms furnished with "better suits" cost fifty cents.[18]

The bridge slowly began to cross Biscayne Bay from north of downtown Miami. People on the mainland made daily visits to the bay front to check the progress as a million and a half feet of lumber was assembled into a two-and-a-half-mile-long structure, the longest wooden bridge in the world. Delays and construction problems quickly pushed the cost far beyond the original budget. With the bridge one-half mile short of its destination, Collins and Pancoast ran out of money.[19] Advertisements already were bringing interested buyers to Collins's Miami Beach Improvement Company. They were excited at the prospect of having their personal 50-x-130-foot piece of paradise for a reasonable sum—$400 to $1,200 per lot, including free bridge tolls for five years.[20] A work stoppage would be a disaster.

Collins and Pancoast went back to the Lummus brothers. They were erasing the footprint of the old coconut plantation cabins with their own Ocean Beach development. Land salesmen on the ferries peddled "high-class suburban property" on rock-paved roads with the promise of electric lights, telephones, and street cars to follow, all of which could be had for only 10 percent down and the balance in small monthly payments.[21] The bankers were not in a position to provide additional support for the bridge project. However, Indiana millionaire Carl Fisher had been watching the progress while staying at his winter home on Miami's fashionable Brickell Avenue. He approached Collins with a business proposition. Fisher, who had built a fortune by manufacturing automobile headlights and a legacy by creating the Indianapolis Speedway, agreed to back bonds for the bridge in exchange for two hundred acres of prime land stretching from the ocean to the bay.[22] He added another one-hundred-plus acres as part of a separate deal with the Lummus brothers.

Opening day for the new bridge was a major event in the city of Miami. Women in high-necked cotton dresses and broad-brimmed hats and men in long-sleeved white shirts stood in the sun on thick planks left from the construction as Thomas Pancoast became the first person to cross Biscayne Bay by automobile.[23] An invitation-only caravan of black Packards, Cadillacs, and Fords followed him across the two-lane span, creating the first bumper-to-bumper traffic jam in Miami Beach history.

Collins had planned to charge one dollar per car and twenty-five cents per passenger to use his bridge, but fare on the ferry was only a quarter. The Lummus brothers and Carl Fisher paid Collins $2,500 a year to reduce the toll to twenty-five cents per car.[24]

Fisher's idea for his three hundred acres was far grander than the humble seaside family retreat being built by the Lummuses. His hotels would be opulent, suitably luxurious for the elite and the prosperous who played croquet and were accustomed to having their afternoon tea served from sterling silver. His building lots would be generous in size to accommodate the most ostentatious winter residence. It would rival Newport and Jekyll Island.

The Lummus brothers had much less lofty goals. The first new house, built in 1913 by a Miami resident, was a simple two-story cottage with tall windows, a screened porch across the front with a sleeping porch above it, the entire structure raised a few feet aboveground on concrete piers for ventilation and surrounded by a patchy lawn. A chimney climbing up the side of the house was mute evidence that it did get cold in Miami on occasion.

Hungry dredges went to work gouging out soft bay bottom and depositing the spoil among the mangroves on the west side of Miami Beach to create solid land. Streets were laid out and named. Another casino was built. In 1915, Collins, Fisher, and the Lummuses joined forces and incorporated their land as the Town of Miami Beach.[25]

William J. Brown, a Miami plumber, bought two lots from the Lummus brothers, a nice property with a view of the ocean just north of Smith's Casino. His construction crew laid foundation beams on top of the one-hundred-foot-long hull of a shipwrecked vessel they found buried in the sand.[26] On that, they built a simple two-story building of Dade County pine, a wood that was soft and easy to work with when first cut but dried to a hardness that defied a strong man to drive a nail into it. Brown's new building had sleeping apartments on the second floor and kitchenettes and dressing rooms on the lower level. When the clapboard siding was painted white and four coconut palms were planted on either side of the roofed entrance, it opened as Miami Beach's first hotel.[27]

It was at William Brown's thirty-six-room Ocean Beach Hotel that Joe and Jennie Weiss of New York registered when they arrived in Miami Beach. Weiss secured a job running the sandwich bar at Smith's Casino. Three years later, in 1918, Joe Weiss bought a little house on Biscayne Street around the corner from the hotel. He hung a "Joe's Restaurant" sign from a palm tree in the front yard and nailed two hand-painted signs above the striped awning over the door to announce that they were serving "seafood and shore dinners."[28] The morning paperboy always opened the screen door quietly to set the paper softly inside the porch so he wouldn't wake Joe and Jennie and the sleeping children.

The Weiss family's arrival disclosed another major difference between the Lummus brothers' Ocean Beach development and those of Collins and Fisher, the long-term impact of which none of them envisioned.

Visitors to the south end of the beach were content with the activity of the beach and the casinos. Carl Fisher wanted his moneyed guests to be properly amused. Gar Wood, whose well-varnished speedboats were the envy of every knowledgeable sportsman with a yachting cap, was attracted by the calm blue waters of Biscayne Bay. Fisher laid out a race course south of the Collins bridge for Wood and his *Miss America* hydroplanes. A Cuban Army polo team was brought in to provide entertainment. Lake Pancoast, named after Collins's son-in-law, became safe anchor for conspicuous yachts where men in white pants and blue blazers sipped martinis while sitting on cushioned furniture on the teak aft decks. Long-legged beauties in bathing suits were photographed frolicking at Carl Fisher's Roman Pools with its trademark windmill. President Warren G. Harding accepted an invitation to play golf on Fisher's new eighteen-hole course. His caddy for the photo opportunity was one of Fisher's pet elephants, who also lent their bulk to the land-clearing operation. Miami Beach was advertised nationwide as "America's Winter Playground." A stream of well-bred socialites, well-connected politicians, and well-paid celebrities began to arrive by private train car.

The Roaring Twenties brought to South Florida a real estate boom that rendered hyperbole inadequate. Eager buyers jostled for space in packed streets, frantically trying to get the attention of land traders who hawked land options from wood plank platforms. Henry Flagler's trains pulled into the downtown Miami depot daily with as many as seventy-five coach and private Pullman cars in tow. Builders couldn't keep up with the demand for accommodations. Laborers and land salesmen took shifts renting beds in boarding houses or dozed on benches in the park.[29] Ambitious suburban towns were created overnight as developers sought to establish their legacies and enrich their bank accounts.

Another connection from the mainland was needed to handle the traffic to the south end of Miami Beach. The county began construction on an earthen causeway from downtown Miami to Fifth Street on South Beach. Fisher took his dredge and started threading artificial islands along the route of the causeway, creating Hibiscus, Palm, and Star islands, which would become some of the most exclusive private addresses in the new city.[30] The causeway's terminus on Fifth Street created a subconscious divide that further separated the houses, hotels, apartments, and businesses south of Fifth from their pricier neighbors to the north.

Fisher's first luxury hotel, the Flamingo, opened New Year's Eve 1921. It commanded the eastern side of Biscayne Bay as if by birthright. It was an instant landmark by land and sea because of the massive glass dome that crowned its eleven-story central tower, illuminated at night in a smoothly changing rainbow of colors. Private cottages were tucked in discreet locations for visitors who desired more privacy than could be found in a two-hundred-room hotel. Guernsey cows were brought in so that guests would have fresh cream for their coffee. Japanese gardeners kept the landscaped grounds manicured. Fisher spent $300,000 to surround his discriminating guests with furnishings of appropriate refinement and quality. A stockbroker's office was installed so that investors could track their bulging portfolios.

Carl Fisher's wealthy friends were lured by the beauty of the tropics and a 1924 amendment to the Florida constitution that prohibited income tax and inheritance tax. Magnificent homes along Indian Creek and the oceanfront were built by names that adorned American corporations: JCPenney, Maytag, Honeywell, Hearst, Reynolds, Kresge, Ford, Gannett, and people whose fortunes were too new for them to be welcome in Palm Beach. They could have their Rolls Royces repaired at Allen J. Smith's garage on Fifth Street, identifiable by the familiar interlinked RR logo over the doors.

One of the most imposing homes belonged to Harvey Firestone. A high hedge surrounded the oceanfront estate, originally built by oil tycoon James Snowden. Massive entrance gates opened to a drive alongside a reflecting pool bordered by Italian cypress and palm trees. The three-story mansion provided elegant surroundings for the Firestones' winter guests. His pals Thomas Edison and Henry Ford could relax after dinner in the billiard room. A morning game of tennis could be followed by a swim in the pool or off the private beach. Ladies could discuss the afternoon's activities during a quiet stroll in the paterre gardens before lunch.

The frenetic pace of construction continued throughout Dade County. Laborers unloading ships and trains could not keep up with the deluge of materials arriving daily. Docks and railroad yards overflowed, and new shipments backed up. A railroad embargo was imposed in 1925 to give workers time to clear the logjam. The situation worsened early the next year when a large sailing ship, the *Prins Valdemar*, capsized and barricaded the Miami harbor for several days.[31] Building began to outpace demand as city-bred buyers realized that they weren't well-suited for the tropical life and returned north, and the speculators ran out of gullible customers. Although prices began to plummet, native hammocks, pine woods, and mangroves continued to be ravaged and replaced by roads, plazas, and stuccoed houses.

Then came the hurricane.

Hurricanes didn't have names then. Anyone who was in Miami the night in 1926 when it hit would call it "the hurricane," and a decade later everyone else would know which one they meant (the way that men sitting in the lobby at the Nautilus Hotel knew that "the war" was the one fought in places named Verdun and The Somme). It was the off season, so many hotels and big homes were closed, the wealthy winter visitors still at their northern homes or their autumn retreats. A weak storm had hit in July, which lulled new South Florida residents into complacency.

The hurricane started battering Miami Beach at two o'clock on the morning of Saturday, September 18.

The wind set up a resonant wail in the window screens, and the gusts kept popping open the doors of the bungalows. The howl blended with the soulful bleat of the horn from a barge as it and its crew were carried out to sea. A father ordered his family to run to shelter at a hotel down the street. As soon as his son stepped outside, the wind spun and dragged him a half block before roughly depositing him against the side of a neighbor's house.

When the winds subsided at daybreak, residents thought it was over. But the eye of the hurricane was sitting right over Miami Beach. After it passed, the storm worsened. Sheets of salt spray were blasted against wood houses by wind gusts of 150 miles per hour. The storm surge pushed the ocean and the bay up to meet in the middle of the southern tip of the peninsula.

By the time the skies cleared, roofs were gone, furniture was scattered on the streets, and boats were smashed against their docks. The glass dome of the Flamingo Hotel was missing, and hotel lobbies had mounds of sand piled up to the top of the registration desks. Windows were broken, and homes were flooded. Portions of the casinos lay in ruins. The mainland was similarly ravaged. Another weaker storm, which struck a month later, disrupted desperate efforts to rebuild.

The real estate boom was over. Empty suburban streets bordered with sidewalks and street lamps stretched into the piney woods. Blueprints gathered dust in locked real estate offices. But Miami Beach was too alluring for the tourists to stay away. They returned to the tropical resort when snow began falling in the northeast—that is, until the end of October 1929. Spread too thin with his Miami Beach projects and another real estate development at Montauk Point, Long Island, Carl Fisher was financially wrecked by the real estate bust and the stock market crash. He mortgaged the green polo fields, floated bonds against his magnificent hotels, sold the golf course, but in the end he lost it all.[32]

Miami Beach weathered the depression better than most of the country. The vastly wealthy were now simply very rich and could still afford to vacation well at a warm winter resort. The luxury hotels continued to welcome the nouveau riche and those who inherited the family fortune, the opportunists and those who had married well. Restaurants were filled, and private clubs hosted elegant dinner dances. Posh shops on Lincoln Road catered to their discriminating clientele.

The still-employed middle class also wanted to escape the national gloom, even if it was only for a week. On South Beach, dozens of small hotels were built quickly and cheaply on the empty lots of Collins Avenue and Ocean Drive. The architects designed them to be easy to build, and decorated only the street side of the buildings, using a new streamlined look that was gaining popularity. An economy-minded couple could get a hotel room for $8 a day or opt for the "American plan," which included breakfast and dinner, for $11 a day. If they had a few extra dollars, they could hop on a plane for a quick visit to Havana for $36, round trip.[33] Modest apartment buildings sprang up along the streets that criss-crossed the interior of the island to provide housing for seasonal visitors and the thousands of people needed to supply services in stores, hotels, and restaurants. The result was a 1930s resort filled with hotels that had the sleek style of the SS *Normandie*, the romance of a Fred Astaire movie, and the exuberance of a Busby Berkeley musical to distract guests from noticing that their accommodations were small, spare, and inexpensive. The permanent population of Miami Beach soared from sixty-five hundred in 1930 to twenty-eight thousand by the end of the decade and ballooned to seventy-five thousand during the winter tourist season.[34]

The end of World War II meant new cars and the end of gas rationing. Miami Beach responded by introducing modern motels, which cost 50 percent less to build than a first-rate hotel. Vast parking lots appeared to accommodate the Buick and Mercury station wagons coming from New Jersey and Michigan. The motels didn't have ornate lobbies with fountains, uniformed doormen, or lavish public spaces decorated with antiques. The elegant dining rooms gave way to coffee shops. The cramped rooms and convivial lobbies of South Beach were left to the lower budget tourists.

Glitzy hotels rose in Middle Beach to cater to the booming professional and management classes. Harvey Firestone's fabulous estate, demolished in 1954, made way for construction of the Fontainebleau Hotel (which, in spite of its French spelling, always has been pronounced "fountain blue" in Miami Beach). The self-contained resorts came complete with their own gourmet restaurants, expensive shops, and flashy nightclubs. They turned their backs to the street, eliminated the inviting porches, and lifted the lobbies above ground level, requiring guests to drive up a ramp to reach the front doors of their temples of relaxation.

There was another difference between the new hotels and the older South Beach neighborhood that had been illustrated by Joe and Jennie Weiss's arrival in 1918. Like much of the United States in the first half of the twentieth century, Fisher's organization and Collins's company had practiced open anti-Semitism in their hotel and land sales businesses. Sixty-five percent of other Miami Beach hotels and apartments followed their lead. Owners of apartment buildings painted "Gentiles only" in black letters on the side of their buildings and hotels posted similar signs in the lobby. The restriction was mentioned openly in advertising. John LaGorce, associate editor of *National Geographic Magazine*, wrote in a promotional pamphlet that Miami Beach was a vacation wonderland for "a regular American of the approved type." Exceptions were made only for "the right kind" of Jews, such as department store magnate Bernard Gimbel and John Hertz, the founder of Yellow Cab.[35]

The Lummus brothers were more egalitarian than Collins and Fisher. Their Ocean Beach development opened its hotels and apartments to anyone, and lots were sold to those who were "white, law-abiding and could afford the down payment."[36] (Blacks could stay in the city overnight only if they were live-in domestic servants or the few farm workers who lived on the remaining part of the John Collins farm). Jewish visitors began to fill the hotels and apartments of South Beach. Kosher restaurants, groceries, bakeries, and delis opened to cater to the expanding market. Synagogues were founded. An invisible border south of Lincoln Road created two Miami Beaches. For Jews going on vacation, South Beach *was* Miami Beach.

Gentiles-only policies officially were outlawed in 1949. As Jewish workers in the northeast reached retirement age, they continued to gravitate to South Beach to spend their golden years in the warmth and safety of a familiar neighborhood where there were kosher markets and synagogues were abundant, Joe and Jennie Weiss's restaurant was familiar, and Yiddish was prevalent on the streets. More affluent Jewish tourists, however, began to move up the beach to the showy new hotels and motels. The city had put the garage for the garbage trucks south of Fifth, along with the city dump. South Beach became the "wrong" end of the island.

By the mid-1950s, South Beach hotels were looking for new ways to attract paying customers. Owners began putting illegal cooking facilities in their rooms, a practice that raised protests from seasonal apartment owners who lacked the advantage of an oceanfront location and feared a loss of business. The hot plate patrol found a violation in the room of one Mrs. Pepi Moskowitz, who tried to cover for the hotel owner by saying that she brought the offending appliance with her from New York and wasn't aware of the infraction.[37] But the trend had been established. By 1970, many hotel rooms had kitchenettes to attract long-term guests, and lobbies where tourists once frolicked became the sitting rooms for residential hotels for the elderly.

Behind the sun-wrinkled faces and arthritic hands of South Beach were memories of Tsarist Russia, the Great Depression, Nazi Germany. They were garment workers and deli owners and furniture makers who had spent their early days in the United States in places like the Lower East Side of New York, where seven people crowded into one dark apartment with windows that looked only into the next room. They remembered times when a crust of bread was worth more than gold, and were not careless with a bit of food even if they could spare it. They were people strong enough to survive the worst and not ask much from life in return. They managed to save enough money to get a little place where it was warm in the winter and they could be surrounded by people who shared a similar culture, traditions, and memories.

On South Beach they re-created the *shtetls* of Eastern Europe, a close-knit society where, if Sylvia wasn't in her regular spot on the park bench in the morning, someone would go check up on her in the afternoon. They were happy if the hotel was kosher and the room was clean. The streets were flat with no hills to climb to get to the market. They had everything they needed and only wanted to be left alone.

That was the neighborhood where Barbara and John Capitman and Leonard Horowitz drove around on that afternoon in 1976. They looked at it and saw an idea for the future. Anyone else would have seen a neighborhood that was doomed.

CHAPTER 2

Eyebrows and Racing Stripes

The heady years of Miami Beach's vigorous tourism industry had faded, lost to jet travel, the glittering casinos of Las Vegas, and the exotic ports of the Caribbean. Small hotels and homes with waterfront views began disappearing to make way for towering cookie-cutter condominium and rental apartments with off-white walls, shag carpeting, and frost-free refrigerators. Occupancy was restricted to senior citizens. They insisted on the peace and quiet of sitting by the pool without the squeals of children at play.

For young families, it was increasingly difficult to find housing on South Beach. Families moved farther up the beach or to the mainland suburbs. Senior citizens and seasonal visitors who could afford to buy condos moved out of the hotels and apartments. Seasonal rentals became monthly, then weekly, and prices fell, making them affordable for people on very limited budgets. The average age on South Beach soared, and the need for Little League fields and schools dwindled. It seemed that every comedian on television had a grandmother who lived in Miami Beach, providing material for an endless stream of "old people" jokes. Advertising that had lured new Jewish retirees to the condos and apartments shifted the city's demographics so dramatically that national publications labeled the city a "Jewish resort." Between 1880 and 1925, an estimated 2.5 million Jews had immigrated from Eastern Europe. The nation had the impression that they all had retired to Miami Beach. The reputation of Miami Beach as a seaside Hebrew home for the aged was turning away the jet set and the young, free-spending tourist. The city leaders desperately wanted a change of image to revitalize their only industry.

Miami Beach wasn't the first resort area to fall on hard times or have trouble deciding how to deal with changing demographics. Key West, which was almost a century older, had a colorful history that celebrated its notable literary heritage and its bawdy seafaring past. Like Miami Beach, a relatively small number of permanent Key West residents provided services for a seasonal tourism industry. In the 1960s, it, too, had been dangerously run-down and in danger of losing its unique identity. By the 1970s, it was being re-created into what people thought Key West should be.

Many years earlier, San Antonio had bolstered its image by developing its popular Riverwalk. During the early years of the twentieth century, the river had become an open sewer, afloat with garbage and trash. Two major floods that spread two feet of polluted water over the historic downtown area provoked serious discussion that the city pave over the river. Through the efforts of the San Antonio Conservation Society, a plan to enhance the river with stone pathways and bridges, shops, cafés, and old-fashioned street lamps became a reality as a Works Progress Administration (WPA) project that was completed in 1941,[1] and had inspired a dramatic urban revival.

Even earlier to appreciate the value of its historic architecture was New Orleans. The restoration of the Vieux Carre, commonly called the French Quarter, began in 1927 and made New Orleans one of the most popular tourism destinations in the South. Likewise, Savannah and Charleston had parlayed their antebellum charm into flourishing tourist attractions.

At the same time that people were investigating ideas for an Art Deco district on South Beach, San Diego had adopted a strategy targeted at reviving its Victorian-era Gaslamp Quarter, which had fallen into disrepair as a seedy neighborhood of porn theaters and "adult only" stores. The city was implementing guidelines to bring back the area as a shopping and entertainment district. Meanwhile, the Rouse Company was renovating rows of nineteenth-century warehouses and shops around the Fulton Fish Market into what would become New York's South Street Seaport. J. Jackson Walter, president of the National Trust for Historic Preservation, quoted the mayors of Chicago, Providence, Philadelphia, Savannah, and Dallas as having given credit to historic preservation as "a cornerstone for future prosperity."[2] Detroit, Pittsburgh, and Seattle had elected strong pro-preservation mayors in recent years.[3] Each city had recognized that the atmosphere, the life, and the architecture that its citizens had created over the years was appealing to tourists. They tapped into the emotion that architect/planner Christopher Alexander described as "a longing for some real thing."[4] City leaders were discovering both the real estate and tourism benefits of their distinctive neighborhoods. Developers were learning the economic advantages of renovation. Environmentalists applauded the recycling of existing buildings.

Miami Beach had a very different strategy in mind. The city leaders firmly believed in what *New York Times* architecture critic Ada Louise Huxtable labeled *the divine right of development.*[5]

The city commission shocked the residents of old South Beach in 1975 when it declared the area south of Sixth Street "blighted" and targeted it for complete redevelopment.[6] The first step in rebuilding the resort business would be to get rid of the embarrassing old buildings and the embarrassing old people on the south end of the city. It was time to get rid of the garages and the meat-packing plant and the unsightly warehouses, the public housing projects, and the rusty old water tower.

Mayor Harold Rosen later admitted, "It wasn't that blighted. That was just a word we had to use. Some parts of it were bad, but the majority was good. I think we just wanted to change the image. It was becoming a lot of small co-ops for the elderly and we didn't want a retirement community."[7]

In reality, 80 percent of the buildings south of Sixth were in good or excellent shape, according to a University of Miami study. Twenty new condominium apartment buildings had been built there since 1968. Only 6 percent of the buildings were considered to be in poor condition.[8] The city's housing authority had just opened Rebecca Towers North, a senior citizens' rent-subsidized building of bright apartments with central air conditioning and a spectacular view of the bay. But a typical city block in the area contained ten individual lots under separate ownership. Government condemnation was the only practical way to consolidate tracts of land large enough to attract major developers. State approval of a redevelopment area and authorization to condemn property required that the area be declared blighted.

It was a self-fulfilling prophecy.

The South Beach redevelopment scheme began modestly enough. In

1973, twenty of the city's power brokers, led by the president of the chamber of commerce, showed up for breakfast in the luxurious high-rise apartment of Stephen Muss, one of the Beach's biggest landowners and developers.[9]

Miami Beach was unlike traditional cities where neighborhoods were bound up by expressways and empty factories that triggered their deterioration. Nor was it suffering from staggering unemployment, because so many of South Beach's residents were retired. The area had only one industry: tourism. Tourists helped support the police and fire departments, helped buy new garbage trucks and flowers for the parks, helped keep the beaches and streets clean. One new hotel wasn't enough to revive an entire industry. Miami Beach couldn't compete with trendier resorts by offering only a nice beach and a warm winter. By the 1970s many tourists were seeing the city only from the deck of a cruise ship as they sailed out of Government Cut on their way to someplace more exciting.

Muss and his colleagues decided that resurrecting the city's flagging tourism industry would require tearing down part of the Beach and beginning from scratch. Old South Beach was the obvious location. A master planner was needed to design the project, someone who had the vision to build something that people from around the world would travel to visit. They anted up the money to hire a consultant and put together a compelling slide show that persuaded the city commission to create an independent and powerful redevelopment agency in 1973.[10] Stephen Muss was named its vice chairman.

The people who lived in the targeted area were terrified at the prospect of losing their homes. Residents north of Sixth feared that the development would dump dangerous amounts of traffic into their neighborhood. Worse, they worried that owners of buildings adjoining the redevelopment area would cash in by selling their properties for new development, and block by block, all of South Beach would vanish.

In anticipation of redevelopment, the city placed a building moratorium on everything in the South Shore area, as the district south of Sixth Street was being called. All new construction was banned, and building owners were prohibited from making major repairs, improvements, or additions. Hotel and apartment house owners saw no reason to put money into buildings that they were to lose in short order. Hotel guests had to endure leaky roofs. Apartment dwellers were stuck with outdated kitchens and bathrooms. Health and safety violations at the city's own subsidized housing projects went unattended. Barren lots became overgrown dumping grounds. Lack of maintenance took a quick toll on old buildings sitting on a barrier island that was constantly exposed to salty sea breezes. The occasional tropical storm or hurricane accelerated the decay. The area quickly began disintegrating into a slum with a spectacular ocean view.

In the summer of 1976, the redevelopment agency unveiled its blueprint for the 230-acre development. The $365 million project would be the most costly private construction urban renewal undertaking in America. In size, it was larger than New York's World Trade Center, which had just reshaped lower Manhattan by demolishing blocks of Civil-War-era buildings and thriving businesses. The New York City project also sought to stimulate redevelopment beyond the edges of the target area. And, like the World Trade Center, the Miami Beach proposal would erase the comfortable grid pattern of streets and separate itself from the rest of the neighborhood. Tax-supported bonds would provide the funding. A master developer would orchestrate the implementation. The agency ignored those who said the whole thing was a pipe dream. They were too smart, too experienced, and too busy to waste their time on a fantasy.

There would be nine luxury hotels, exclusive island residences, impressive offices, a convention center, a sea habitat attraction, a marina, and more than twenty-five hundred residential units, all of them expensive. Islands would be created and connected by a 2.7-mile network of canals, which prompted a much-too-frequent comparison with Venice. A costly model of the finished product displayed the concept in detail, with tiny hotels and condominiums, tiny office buildings, tiny canals crossed by tiny bridges, rows of tiny trees lining tiny streets, tiny yachts in the marinas, tiny tennis courts, even little bitty stop signs.

Old South Beach was not pretty by anyone's standards. It had been the "wrong side of the tracks" for decades. The redevelopment agency's designer, Steve Siskind, had done a masterful job of blending high- and low-rise buildings with plenty of open space. What staggered people was the scope. Fewer than ten existing buildings would be spared, including Joe's Stone Crab—the landmark Miami Beach restaurant that had started as Joe and Jennie Weiss's little seafood stand.

One thing was missing. There were no places for the six thousand residents, mostly elderly Jews, whose low-cost hotels and apartments and moderate-priced condominiums would fall to make room for the new tourists. No plans were included to house or relocate them.

Some South Beach residents remembered when Knickerbocker Village was built on the Lower East Side of Manhattan in the 1930s as a state-sponsored slum-clearance project. Monthly rental for the new units was almost four times what tenants had been paying in their old tenements.[11] Higher rents had pushed them out to other slums without the familiar corner grocery, the drugstore, the bakery, and the established connections that made the old neighborhood a home.

Opponents of the redevelopment were outraged that people of South Beach who had earned the right to grow old peacefully were being discarded to benefit private developers. As Barbara and John Capitman and Leonard Horowitz had looked around the neighborhood where Benjamin Levy made his daily rounds, they had seen the possibility for renovated housing for the thousands of senior citizens who called South Beach home, combined with restored hotels, entertainment, and restaurants to bring back the tourists. An active, vital historic neighborhood.

An awareness of the need for independent housing for the elderly was beginning to enter the consciousness of the industrial design world, partly because of the work of people such as Sandra Howell of the Massachusetts Institute of Technology, who was writing about how new solutions were needed to meet the demands of an aging population. Barbara Capitman had written for industrial designers, and her husband had written a book about corporate social responsibility. She was attuned to the needs and possibilities.

Barbara Capitman, a middle-aged widow, looked at the neighborhood and saw a different time—a time when she didn't have strands of gray in her short, dark hair, when her face was still unlined, when her waist encouraged belted dresses instead of the loose-fitting ones she now favored. Past the blocks of empty parking spaces and groaning air conditioners, she saw an era of Gershwin and Fitzgerald, of women wearing fashions by Mainbocher driving along palm-lined streets in Bentleys and Bugattis. She heard the music of Woody Herman and Benny Goodman playing in the hotels, and pictured sophisticated couples sipping champagne on breeze-swept terraces. South Beach, by re-creating the Art

Deco glamour of the 1930s, could become a national paradigm for the needy elderly, talented artists, young professionals, and moneyed visitors to live together respectfully and enjoy the kind of lives that each of them wanted.

If Barbara Capitman was going to convince anyone that a 1.7-square mile area of small, deteriorating buildings on prime oceanfront real estate was worth preserving, she needed more information and an organization. In 1976, the south end of Miami Beach wasn't appearing on anyone's historic architecture radar.

She organized a meeting with the pedagogical title, "An Inquiry into the Restoration of the Art Deco Miami Beach Hotels of the 20s and 30s." Two hundred architects and designers showed up in a cavernous room in Miami's Design District to hear twenty speakers talk about a neighborhood of Miami Beach most of them didn't know except as an area they drove through to get to someplace else. Capitman had chosen the designers for two reasons. First, they were the people she knew from meetings of the local chapter of the American Society of Interior Designers. And she felt they needed to be doing something for the community instead of "only working for the very wealthy, spending thousands of dollars on valences with matching headboards."[12] The meeting went on until one in the morning, the thinning audience fortified by refreshments served by John Capitman and Leonard Horowitz.

A second meeting was held a few weeks later. Dennis Wilhelm saw the newspaper announcement at his home in Coconut Grove. Wilhelm had grown up in Cincinnati where the design of the Union Terminal sparked his interest in the 1930s style. Once he had bought his first Art Deco lamp, he had to have more. He had the eye of a gifted collector and slowly began accumulating Art Deco treasures. It wasn't until he saw a book with a lamp on the cover similar to his first one that he learned that what he was collecting was called Art Deco. His house had become as much a gallery for his growing collection as it was a place to live. After the meeting, Wilhelm introduced himself to Barbara Capitman. Something about the tall, blond young man caught her eye. She showed up at his house the next day to look at his collection. From a voluminous bag she pulled a certificate, wrote "Best Deco Collection" on the line, and presented it to him on the spot, drawing him in as a staunch volunteer.[13]

Over the next few weeks, small groups of people like Wilhelm gathered in hotels, homes and design offices, discussing the kind of ambitious ideas generated by the synergy of like minds brainstorming over coffee and cake late into the night. They were a ragtag circle of artists, elderly women, art collectors, young gay men, architects, and designers. They considered themselves intellectual to the core. Their planning had the innocent enthusiasm of a Mickey Rooney–Judy Garland musical, but, instead of putting on a show, they were going to save a neighborhood.

There was plenty of experience on which to draw. The National Trust for Historic Preservation, created by Congress in 1949, was encouraging renovations across the country. Community movements gained some teeth in 1966 with adoption of the National Historic Preservation Act that followed the loss of New York's monumental Penn Station. In the following ten years, the number of cities with landmarks preservation commissions had quintupled to more than five hundred.[14] Just a few months earlier, Congress had provided tax incentives for rehabilitation of older buildings as part of the 1976 Tax Reform Act. The tools were in place.

South Florida was not new to the preservation movement. Miami was a relatively young city, incorporated in 1896, but many of its earliest buildings had been lost to hurricanes, fire, and new development. The Cape Florida Lighthouse, built in 1825, was the area's oldest surviving structure. A park on the Miami River was the site of the Fort Dallas Barracks, built in 1849 as slave quarters. Soon it was to be joined by the oldest known residence in the county, the small, wood-frame Wagner House from 1858 that was being moved out of the path of the new Metrorail system. The first Coconut Grove School, built in 1887, had been moved to the grounds of a church and restored. The oldest building in the county was an import. The Spanish Monastery was built in 1141 in Spain, brought to the United States by William Randolph Hearst in 1928, and reassembled in North Miami Beach as a tourist attraction twenty-six years later.[15] An organization had been formed in 1957 to encourage volunteer support for Villa Vizcaya, an opulent Italian 1914 Renaissance estate that had been acquired by the county as a historical house and art museum. The threatened demolition of the magnificent ten-acre Douglas Entrance in Coral Gables to make way for a supermarket sparked creation of the county's first citizens' preservation group, the

Villagers, which successfully thwarted the leveling. Dade Heritage Trust had been founded in 1972 as Dade County's first nonprofit organization to be charged with the mission of preserving historic architecture countywide. In 1973, thirty-eight years after the nation's first historic preservation ordinance was enacted in Charleston, South Carolina, the city of Coral Gables adopted the first historic preservation law in Dade County to protect its superb collection of Spanish Mediterranean buildings, plazas, entrances, and fountains. By 1977, twenty Dade County buildings were listed on the National Register of Historic Places, but none of them was in Miami Beach.

But the South Beach enthusiasts were not building on past achievements. Barbara Capitman had very definite ideas about what she wanted to do, and they didn't fit within the framework of the established preservation network. Dade Heritage Trust was considered too white glove, too polite, and too broadly focused to attract the attention she wanted for South Beach. Her group was made up of designers, not seasoned preservationists. Their focus was on the design and time period of the buildings and the people who lived there.

The mainland and Miami Beach were separated by the waters of Biscayne Bay, five thousand years of Jewish culture, and the determined independence of twenty-eight individual municipalities.[16] Although the new association was going to focus on South Beach, Barbara Capitman wanted a name that would be inclusive of those who lived on the mainland and that would reflect the emphasis on design. She decided to name it the Miami Design Preservation League, with herself, her sons, Leonard Horowitz, and two others as the founding members. Its purpose would be to preserve the neighborhood by creating a historic district called "Old Miami Beach."

First, they needed to make sure they were on the right track.

Art Deco had been a recognized design since its introduction at the *Exposition Internationale des Arts Decoratifs et Industriels Modernes* in Paris in 1925, although the term *Art Deco* didn't enter the lexicon until 1966, when it was devised by a writer doing a catalog for a retrospective of the Paris show. Its design elements were quickly adapted by architects looking for a new form of expression. The first Art Deco skyscrapers began appearing on New York's skyline in 1929.

Architects created a streamlined style that was inspired by the automobile, the train, the ocean liner, and the airplane. Out went the Corinthian columns and pedimented porticoes along with the cherubs and heavily carved chair backs. It didn't seem prudent to build ornamented palaces with cupolas, turrets, and gothic windows in a nation gripped by economic depression. New materials, such as Vitrolite, chrome, stainless steel, and glass block, allowed designers to marry the functional look of the Arts and Crafts movement with industrial technology. It was interpreted in polished granite and limestone on New York City's Chrysler Building, the Empire State Building, and the Chicago Board of Trade.

The entertainment industry splashed the new look across the nation's movie screens. *The Divorcée*, starring Oscar-winning actress Norma Shearer, introduced 1930 audiences to the glamour and sophistication of a New York Art Deco apartment. Glorious movie theaters sprang up around the world, none more spectacular than New York City's Radio City Music Hall or the sleeker Center Theater. The Art Deco style appeared in the literature of F. Scott Fitzgerald, the designs of Erté, Electrolux vacuum cleaners, and Zephyr trains. By 1932, Phillip Johnson had ushered in the international modern style to those on the cutting edge with an exhibition at the Museum of Modern Art in New York,[17] but Deco still was filtering down to the regional level. Art Deco created Union Station in Tulsa, Bloom High School in Illinois, the Cochise County Courthouse in Arizona, the Suislaw River Bridge in Oregon, the Bank of Ireland in Belfast, and a newspaper office in Napier, New Zealand.

Most people, if asked in 1976 about the chances that prodevelopment Miami Beach would designate the entire southern end of the island as a historic district that would focus on preserving its Art Deco buildings for the elderly, would have laughed off such an absurd idea with a sarcastic, "Sure, the day it snows in South Florida." On January 20, 1977, it snowed in South Florida.

It had been warmer a few days earlier when a small band of league volunteers assembled on the steps of the Amsterdam Palace, an ornate Spanish Colonial hulk of an apartment building on Ocean Drive. It seemed an unlikely meeting location since the Amsterdam was one of the few buildings on the street that was not Art Deco. Their quest was to explore South Beach to determine if there was a sufficient concentration of Art Deco buildings to qualify as a historic district.

They split into pairs: art collectors from Miami Beach, architects from

Miami, designers from Coconut Grove, some people from the design center audience. Each twosome was assigned a ten- to fifteen-block sector. By car, bicycle, and on foot they spread out, covering an area from Biscayne Street at the southernmost tip of the island to Lincoln Road eighteen streets north, and from the ocean to the bay, about a dozen blocks at the widest point.[18] Most of the area was the old Lummus brothers' development; a small part was within Carl Fisher's former domain.

They went from building to building, peeking in lobbies, slipping through pedestrian alleys to see rear facades, searching for distinctive features. On Alton Road they found the Firestone Tire store with its layered canopy daringly cantilevered over the drive. Reverently, they passed the site of Carl Fisher's Flamingo Hotel that had been erased by unremarkable condominium towers. Along Lincoln Road they counted block after block of retail buildings that once housed some of the most fashionable shops in the country. At the corner of Jefferson Avenue was the Lincoln Building where Carl Fisher's real estate salesmen escorted customers up to the seventh floor balcony to see the view for miles and pick out the lots for their new homes.[19] South on Collins Avenue they saw the St. Moritz, the New Yorker, the Sands, the Royal Palm—tall, slender Art Deco hotels with a restrained Streamline style.

One duo walked along quaint Espanola Way, a cozy Spanish village of hotels, apartments, and shops with red-clay barrel tile roofs. On Drexel and Jefferson avenues, gray-haired ladies watched suspiciously as strangers wandered past block after block of apartment buildings with names like the Palm Gardens, the Rosebloom, or the Claire (after an important lady in the original owner's life). They admired screen doors decorated with metal cutouts of palm trees, flamingos, and egrets and pointed at odd light fixtures, piston-shaped planters, stacks of concentric flat canopies, and racing stripes that were thin, wide, fluted, and incised. The paint was peeling in spots, metal railings were showing signs of rust, awnings were faded, but most of the buildings were tidy, and the shrubbery was trimmed. An effort had been made.

Those assigned to Washington Avenue saw the glass block wall of the Cameo Theater, the curves, circles, and towers of Hoffman's Cafeteria. They marveled at the Depression Moderne post office and noticed that the clock on the tower of the Blackstone Hotel showed the time six hours different on one side than the others, and none were correct. On Ocean

Drive, hotel residents were puzzled as people wandered through, chattering about intricate terrazzo floors,[20] hand-painted murals, ribbons of neon tubing, etched glass windows, stylized stair railings, and fireplaces faced with tinted scagliola. John Capitman drove from pair to pair collecting completed forms and keeping the surveyors on track.

South Beach's Art Deco was different from the era's icons like the Chrysler Building. It was pared down, ornamented with plaster and stucco instead of marble and granite. It reflected its tropical setting and its resort function. It was everyday Deco. But a lot of everyday items—from Superman lunch boxes to Fiestaware salt shakers to grandma's soup tureen—were becoming collectibles. Maybe it was time for twentieth-century middle-class architecture to take its place and be recognized as valuable and worthy of preservation.

At the end of a very long day, the tired volunteers reassembled back at the Amsterdam Palace. Carl Weinhardt Jr. and Fred Bland reviewed the results of the day's endeavors. Weinhardt was the highly respected silver-haired director of Miami's Villa Vizcaya and the only experienced Miami preservationist in the group. His Harvard degree would add credence to the conclusion. Bland, a New York architect in town working on the convention center expansion project, had photographed and researched many Beach buildings because of his interest in the Art Deco style. The patterns of Miami Beach's development emerged from the scrawled pages. The city had been designed for tourism with hotels along Ocean Drive and Collins, shopping strips along Washington Avenue and Alton Road, apartments and single-family homes in between. The development profile looked like a giant price bar code.

The survey teams anxiously awaited the decision from Weinhardt and Bland. Were there enough Art Deco buildings in the area for it to be considered a historic district? What should the boundaries be? Would it matter that there were so many buildings of other architectural styles?

South Beach did not have the only Art Deco buildings in Dade County. Downtown Miami boasted the imposing Alfred I. DuPont Building, a 1938 Depression Moderne office tower. Walgreen's occupied a three-story 1936 Streamline-style store at a prominent corner on Flagler Street. The oldest Art Deco building in the county was the Sears Roebuck store, built in 1929. Even Miami City Hall was in an Art Deco building, the former Pan American Seaplane Terminal in Coconut Grove, where people would gather on the observation deck in the afternoons in the 1930s to watch the "Flying Clippers" land in the bay. Homes, schools, and commercial buildings in older suburbs reflected the era's fascination with the Deco look.

Finally, Weinhardt made the announcement: the area definitely was Deco.[21]

The area was not only Deco but also Mediterranean Revival and Mission and Moorish and some old Florida vernacular. The styles had evolved over the span of two decades, from the 1920s to the early 1940s. There was Mediterranean vernacular, Mediterranean Deco, Moorish Deco, all blending fluidly from one to another. The area's architectural significance was that the sheer concentration of so many buildings of similar style and scale created a whole that vastly outweighed the sum of its parts.

This was the cause Capitman had been seeking. Her husband's sudden death from pancreatic cancer had traumatized her, causing a permanent tremor in her voice that some people mistakenly took as a sign of timidity. Her sons had been urging her to get involved in some socially relevant activity. What she saw on south Miami Beach energized her. It was an opportunity to meld the things she knew. She had a taste of being an activist from her days at New York University, where she had said farewell to idealistic friends who were following Ernest Hemingway to adventures like the Spanish Civil War.[22] She had honed her liberal ideas in conversations with her neighbor Betty Friedan when they were pushing baby strollers together.[23] She inherited a lifelong interest in art and design from her parents. Most of all, she was a gifted writer who knew how to use words to express other people's passions, to tell a story in a way that generated enthusiasm.

It didn't matter that the buildings weren't old enough to meet national standards as historic, or that the residents hadn't signed up to be part of some sociological experiment in providing housing for the elderly as part of a mixed-use neighborhood, or that the city had its own ideas about how to revive tourism. Those challenges could be overcome.

The Miami Design Preservation League had a name, a goal, and a corps of passionate volunteers. None of the founding members lived on South Beach. Its base of operations was Capitman's Key Biscayne apartment, a trip that was thirty minutes and a twenty-five-cent toll each way from South Beach. There was no hue and cry from the public to save South Beach's Art Deco buildings. The residents had children who were older than the buildings where they lived. To people who had strolled along Old Town Square in Warsaw or walked in the snow past St. Petersburg's Winter Palace, or shopped along the wide boulevards by the Dâmbovita in Bucharest, the hotels and apartments of South Beach didn't seem architecturally or historically important. South Beach wasn't an important architectural district; it was simply where they lived. City officials already had made it clear that maintaining the area's aging population or aging buildings wasn't in their plans. The league—a small society with neither money, influence, nor broad-based support—was planning to effect a heroic change in the future of a city that wasn't interested.

It wasn't the first time that such a David-and-Goliath contest was engaged to save an aging neighborhood. Ten years earlier, activist Jane Jacobs had rallied her neighbors against a plan by New York's powerful Robert Moses, who intended to slice a ten-lane expressway through Manhattan south of Houston Street, taking out more than four hundred historic buildings. No one had been able to stop Moses as he slashed and burned through established New York neighborhoods in his aggressive public works program. But Jacobs triumphed, the expressway was abandoned, and SoHo began its rejuvenation. Her success reverberated across the nation.[24]

The Miami Design Preservation League decided not to try to stop South Shore. Instead, they wanted to create a unique environment that would halt redevelopment in its tracks at Fifth Street. They set about marketing South Beach's Art Deco architecture with the intensity of a television network launching its fall season. They needed a big, splashy event to get the volunteers excited, attract the media, and put the public and city leaders on notice that they intended to make a difference. They chose the Cinema theater on Washington Avenue, built in 1938 as the French Casino, a dazzling setting for movies and live stage productions under a ceiling dotted by twinkling stars. Sagging business had reduced it to only sporadic seasonal operation.

The theater had deteriorated over the years. Volunteers went to work sprucing it up for a marquee evening in March. They polished the mirrored tiles that hid gold-leafed columns in the lounge. Carl Weinhardt climbed behind the abalone-shell-clad lounge bar and discovered an intricate mural behind a pile of rubbish.[25] They cleaned up the private box seats with curved rails that formed a waterfall cascading down both walls of the auditorium, where three hundred pink seats awaited an audience.

By the time guests arrived that March evening, the Cinema had been transported back to the thirties. They were greeted by slender women draped in soft dresses that settled effortlessly around the hips and dapper men in wide-lapeled suits that required confidence to wear successfully. Leonard Horowitz had raided closets and attics to collect the period fashions. Architects and designers, wealthy art collectors, and starving artists mingled under the dramatic Deco chandelier in the lobby and glided down the sweeping staircase, holding a cocktail in one hand and conducting animated conversation with the other. A jazz band from the University of Miami played on a stage that once had a revolving turntable decorated by showgirls. Important speakers took the microphone, but guests were having too much fun to pay a lot of attention.[26]

The party was a huge success. However, the enthusiasm was short-lived when the theater's owners announced the next day that the Cinema would be closing permanently. It didn't make economic sense to keep it open.

The league saw a chance to make its mark quickly. The Players Repertory Theater was Miami's only professional resident theater company and was looking for a permanent home. The Cinema would be perfect. The league could guide the renovation of the Cinema and show South Beach its potential. It announced that the Players could open its next season in the renovated Cinema. The league claimed its first success.[27]

Capitman pounded out one press release after another on her Olympia electric typewriter. She hounded newspaper reporters for stories about "Old Miami Beach" and the new Miami Design Preservation League, to the point that they started avoiding her. She used exaggeration and hyperbole so artfully that spellbound writers saw the dramatic spires, the glass block, and the porthole windows, and didn't notice that some of the buildings hadn't been painted in twenty years and that stucco was falling off the walls.

Articles about "Old Miami Beach" were published in *Saturday Review*, *Preservation News*, the *New York Times*, the *Wall Street Journal*, airline magazines, and European publications. Stories that appeared in local media were picked up by newspapers in Los Angeles, San Francisco,

New Orleans, Dallas, and New York. It was popular copy. Millions of readers had visited Miami Beach, and thousands of GIs had been stationed there during World War II. People who had not made the trip had fond memories of listening to Arthur Godfrey's radio and television shows broadcast live from Miami Beach in the 1950s, tuning in to *The Jackie Gleason Show* broadcast live from the Miami Beach Auditorium or *The Tonight Show* on location at the Fontainebleau, or watching the Beatles on *The Ed Sullivan Show* live from the Deauville Hotel. The world had seen the city and its famous hotels in movies.

In the media, Capitman talked about South Beach becoming a smart resort with sidewalk cafés, afternoon tea in the courtyards, and jazz under the stars, a setting that would recapture the romance of Bogart and Bacall while updating and upgrading the hotels to develop a new year-round tourism market. That kind of talk frightened hotel owners who were suspicious of ideas that would change a business they had spent their lives building. They didn't like the city's scorched-earth approach, but the league's ideas sounded like something that would cost them money and disrupt a comfortable routine.

It would take money to do the complete survey of the area that was essential to creating a historic district. Owing in large part to the efforts of Denis Russ, the youthful, copper-haired chairman of the city's grant advisory committee, the league received a ten-thousand-dollar grant for a survey. Two tiny rooms in the Twenty-first Street Community Center were furnished as an office for the league beginning in January 1978. The graceful one-story Mediterranean-style building with its arched windows was one of the oldest in Miami Beach, built in 1916 by Carl Fisher as a clubhouse for his new golf course. The golf course was long gone, replaced by a convention center, an auditorium, and a brand new city hall. Instead of men in knickers comparing scorecards, the place was busy with senior citizens taking art, dance, and sewing classes. Whether by design or fortuitous coincidence, it was the perfect setting for a campaign that planned to renovate old buildings to better house the elderly.

The league had enough funds to hire a small staff for the duration of the grant. Barbara Capitman was first on the list, as director of the project. For the position of assistant director, she selected Diane Camber.

Camber had been visiting her mother in Miami Beach when she saw an article in an architectural magazine about the Streamline Moderne buildings on South Beach. A year later her mother passed away, and she moved back to the house her father had built forty years earlier. Her interest was drawn to a newspaper item that the league was looking for volunteers, including art historians. Camber had graduated from Barnard with a degree in art history and studied at Juilliard and Columbia. She had lived in Boston and New Orleans, cities with vigorous historic preservation programs.[28] She was young, pretty, well-dressed, energetic, and, best of all, a Miami Beach native with an impressive pedigree, someone sorely needed to try to overcome the league's "outsiders" image. She could talk about Art Deco in a scholarly way. The league wasn't about to let Diane Camber out of its clutches.

The survey began. On Saturdays, Sundays, and evenings a battalion of architects, designers, historians, students, and enthusiastic volunteers set out on the streets of South Beach. Again, the elderly residents sitting in lawn chairs looked with retired curiosity at the young people staring at their buildings. This time, the volunteers went to each apartment house, hotel, and store collecting information. The survey teams took hundreds of slides, usually paid for out of their own pockets. Most of the elderly residents did not drive, so cars rarely were parked in front to obstruct the view. Other volunteers worked in the office typing, mapping, and collating the information.

Conditions were sad in some of the residential hotels, and, frankly, some of them didn't smell very good. Occasionally the volunteers would encounter a skeptical hotel owner, answer his questions about what they were doing, and, while they had his attention, caution him to take good care of the green Vitrolite wainscoting. While Carl Fisher had spent huge amounts of money to create festooned salons and elegant ballrooms in the 1920s, the simple 1930s hotels of South Beach had intimate lobbies decorated with geometric terrazzo floors, stylized fireplaces, and murals. Most had one small elevator about the size of a phone booth and a registration desk that wasn't much larger. The hotels consumed all of their building lots, leaving only narrow pedestrian walkways between them. Service alleys bisected each block from north to south to spare tourists the unsightly view of garbage Dumpsters and delivery trucks. A handful of hotels had swimming pools, and the really lucky ones had a few parking spaces at the rear of the building.

Although the area south of Sixth was politically off limits because of the South Shore redevelopment, the volunteers filled out forms for the hotel built by plumber William Brown in 1915 and for homes from the early days, like the little prefab house shipped from Chicago in 1913 and assembled in one day at Third Street and Collins Avenue for Mrs. Philip Clarkson.[29]

Conditions were as varied inside the buildings as outside. Most were clean and well-maintained. Some residential hotels had deteriorated along with their occupants. Scattered among the older structures were small, modern condominiums, some lifted above their ground-level parking lots, leaving a vacuum that jarred the visual pattern along the sidewalks. The texture of different layers of health, wealth, and taste blended into a single image.

Meanwhile, another historic architecture investigation was being conducted on Miami Beach. Metro-Dade County had started a comprehensive survey to create a database of all historic buildings in the county. Ernie Martin, a San Francisco transplant, headed the county's Office of Community and Economic Development. Martin had the enviable job of parceling out the fourteen million dollars in federal grant funds the county received that year. He wanted to fund a historic sites survey, an interest he had from his studies in regional planning and a year in the Model Cities program. Martin sought a mechanism for the survey. He tried the planning department, but they didn't want to do it. Parks and Recreation was equally uninterested. So Martin set up a division of historic preservation in his own office.[30]

He hired Ivan Rodriguez to head the project. Rodriguez had a master's degree in architectural history and historic preservation from the University of Florida. He also had an edge for doing the Miami Beach portion of the survey.

Rodriguez's family had come to Florida from Cuba when he was fourteen. In Cuba, his father had been an accountant for an American exporting company and owned a small furniture factory. He was defiantly anti-Castro. The exporting company had been confiscated by the government, the furniture company was going to be seized, and young Ivan was nearing the age for mandatory military service. It was time to get out of Cuba. Like most Cubans who fled during that period, they assumed they would return within a year or two. All they were permitted to take from their home were three changes of clothing—no cash, no jewelry, no photo albums, no treasured family heirlooms. They didn't have much with them when they joined the small but growing colony of Cuban exiles who settled into the inexpensive apartments of old South Beach, despite the "No Cubans" signs in the windows next to the "For Rent" placards. Rodriguez went through his teen years at Beach High. His parents still lived in Miami Beach, although they had moved a little farther north, near the Convention Center.[31]

With Ivan Rodriguez, everything was by the book. He and his trained staff used the standards of the Historic American Building Survey and completed official Florida Master Site File forms for each property. They were looking for outstanding examples of Dade County's history, architecture, and culture. It was impossible to eliminate all subjectivity, but the training of the team, the professional supervision, and the use of nationally accepted standards gave the county's results immediate validity.

The league had its own ideas about how to do a survey. They recorded everything built before 1950, a decision that would later come to haunt them. They complied a list of more than twelve hundred buildings on South Beach that they deemed significant. Rodriguez documented fewer than half that number for the entire city of Miami Beach.

Volunteers worked hundreds of hours to get the league survey finished before the grant deadline. The final forty-page report concluded, to no one's surprise, that the city should work toward establishing an "Old Miami Beach" historic district.[32] The next step was making it a reality. For that, they needed help.

Once they learned about the resources available to assist historic preservation programs, they took full advantage of them. Federal weight and expertise were needed to try to educate local leaders about the advantages of a historic district. Barbara Capitman didn't hesitate to appear unexpectedly in the offices of Florida congressional representatives or to make landfall with her entourage in the office of some hapless federal bureaucrat and start pleading her case for funding or technical assistance. She persuaded the chief of planning for the National Register of Historic Places and representatives of the National Trust for Historic Preservation to come to Miami Beach.

She presented the area to them with the zeal of an evangelist. Chris Delaporte, director of the Heritage Conservation and Recreation Service

(HCRS),[33] arrived at the Miami airport late one night. Usually he was met by a delegation including some city officials, taken to lunch or dinner, and given the VIP tour. In Miami he was met by Capitman. She packed him into in her two-seat car and hustled him off for a street-by-street inspection of the district.[34]

Federal support was positive but cautious. Randy Roark, an Atlanta architect, was sent by HCRS to evaluate the area's prospects as a historic district. A newspaper reporter caught up with Roark on the porch of the New Yorker Hotel on Collins Avenue. "All over the country, historic districts have been great tourist attractions," he told her. Those were precisely the words the league wanted the city officials to hear. He also warned that historic buildings had been lost because of the pressing demand for new construction.[35] That was a very real threat on Miami Beach.

Roark was the man who would make the decision that could disqualify the area as a historic district before they even got started. There was an accepted national criterion that buildings be at least fifty years old to be considered for the National Register of Historic Places. It was set aside only in cases of extraordinary buildings, such as New York's Chrysler Building, which was listed on the National Register at the youthful age of forty-six. For South Beach's 1930s and 1940s Art Deco buildings to be the basis for a National Register district, an exception would have to be made. South Beach's qualifying merit, by national standards, was its architecture, not the history of events and people who had passed along its streets. Roark decided to recommend a waiver of the age rule.

A federal job-training grant provided the league with a staff of fifteen to work on plans for the proposed district. Expert assistance in preparing the National Register nomination would come from two interns sent by the HCRS. Elan Zingman and Everett Scott, graduate students at Columbia University, were working on their master's degrees in historic preservation. One of the curriculum requirements was to do a one-semester internship.

Neither Zingman nor Scott had any particular interest in or knowledge of Miami Beach. Earlier in his studies, Zingman had taken a class trip to Savannah, where he met Leopold Adler.[36] Adler had offered to help Zingman when he needed to find a job and put him in touch with Chris

Delaporte from HCRS. By May 1978, Zingman was driving to Florida. He had to learn who the architects were, what interested them, where they went to school, what their influences were. The men (and they all were men) who had designed the small hotels and apartments and stores didn't pretend that they were creating architectural masterpieces. Known only regionally, they lacked the stature of trendsetters of the day such as Frank Lloyd Wright, Walter Gropius, Eero Saarinen, and Mies van der Rohe. The names L. Murray Dixon, Henry Hohauser, Albert Anis, and Roy France weren't listed in the anthologies of great American architecture.

Scott's assignment was to photograph the buildings so he could compare them to historical photos to determine what changes had been made over the years. Volunteers, armed with multiple-choice forms, retraced their steps from the earlier survey and marked off the appropriate boxes to indicate the style, type of construction, kind of roof and windows, number of stories, exterior finish, location of main entrance, and number of porches, verandas, and balconies.

In his room at the Governor Hotel, near the league's temporary offices, Zingman filled yellow legal pads with the narrative that would make their case. Capitman gave him very specific instructions about how she wanted it written. She wanted it to be moving, inspirational, so she could use it for other purposes and say that the adulatory language had the imprimatur of the National Register nomination. Zingman knew it wasn't standard procedure, but he followed her instructions.[37]

The league may have set a record for the shortest time taken to prepare a district nomination to the National Register of Historic Places. The boundaries extended from the ocean to an irregular line near the bay on the west, and from Sixth Street north to Dade Boulevard, the road leading to the route of the old Collins bridge. A strip on the western side of the island that was newer construction was excluded, as was everything west of Washington Avenue north of Lincoln Road and all of old South Beach south of Sixth Street. They knew the city would find a way to kill the nomination immediately if the South Shore redevelopment area was included.

The required statement of significance barely mentioned the history of Miami Beach except as it related to its architectural development. There was no notice paid to Henry Lum's coconut plantation, John Collins's canal, the city's tawdry gambling days, or any of the thousands of people who had made their mark on the city in its sixty-three years of incorporation.[38] It did not claim that the district was rich in history or individual landmarks. Its stated significance was as an architectural time capsule that reflected a particular time, climate, and attitude.

Capitman was anxious to get the nomination submitted so it could be used as leverage against demolition of any more buildings. Once it had been sent to Tallahassee, she could say, "Don't destroy the buildings. They are a part of the soon-to-be-designated Art Deco Historic District."[39] However, even designated historic areas had been unable to use their status to prevent unwanted intrusion. New Orleans's Vieux Carre was almost severed by a riverfront expressway that was proposed in 1946 and lived under the threat of its devastating construction until the proposal finally was rescinded in 1969.[40] The planned extension of Interstate 710 into South Pasadena, California, would bisect five historic districts and demolish 1,050 historic homes, including splendid Arts and Crafts homes by architects Greene and Greene. Properties already acquired by the California Department of Transportation in anticipation of the long-delayed construction were being destroyed by sheer neglect.[41]

The completed paperwork for more than twelve hundred buildings spread over a one-square-mile area of southern Miami Beach was submitted to the state historic preservation office in August 1978.

CHAPTER 3

Tchotchke Paradise

One result of Miami Beach's linear development pattern was that it had no defined center. There was no "downtown" Miami Beach from which the city radiated. Lincoln Road had been built as the upscale shopping area. The larger hotels had their own shops selling resort wear, jewelry, perfume, men's clothing, and other goods appealing to free-spending tourists. A commercial strip had developed along Alton Road on the west side of the island. Stores were scattered around the area south of Fifth Street.

Washington Avenue served as the main retail corridor of South Beach. It hosted a steady cavalcade of slow-moving women carrying capacious purses and shopping bags, some followed a few steps back by slower-moving husbands. The street was lined with small shops that sold everything cheap and everything kosher from matzos to chow mein noodles. An hour could be spent going through the racks of clothing at the Cancer League Thrift Shop, where a sale sign advertised blouses at three for $4.95. Stores offered a clutter of shell-encrusted toothpick holders and manual can openers and tapes of Yiddish songs. By the end of their route, the ladies' shopping bags carried challah from the Butterflake Bakery, a piece of whitefish from the Odessa Food Center, and maybe a storybook from Torah Treasures for the youngest granddaughter. Business was not good, however. Ziggy Shwartz was pessimistic. There were no tourists to buy the *tchotchkes* at his American-Israeli Religious Store, and his elderly Jewish customers were dying off.[1]

One of the most prominent features of Washington Avenue was the post office. Even people who didn't like Art Deco—and they were legion—found a certain federal grandeur and elegance in the 1939 building. It was Depression Moderne in origin, built as part of President Franklin Roosevelt's WPA. A cylindrical lighthouse cupola on the rotunda roof paid homage to its coastal location. Inside the three-story-high rotunda, the cupola's decorative skylight was surrounded by a brilliant sunburst painted against a Miami blue sky. Elderly residents and harried secretaries stood together in the long line, occasionally striking up a conversation with a secretary from a Miami Beach law firm or the photographer in town on assignment. Post office workers stuffed letters, bills, magazines, and yellow delivery notices into long boxes behind a curved bank of small brass-plated doors. Shop clerks and tourists, passing each other at the marble-topped stamp tables, ignored the three-panel mural of barely clothed Native Americans cowering, consecutively left to right, at the arrival of the Spanish conquistadors, from Spanish soldiers on horseback, and from American soldiers at the end of the Seminole wars.

Local support from the league, city hall, and the Miami Beach postmaster resulted in the old building getting a four-hundred-thousand-dollar facelift that included cleaning the keystone and brass, replacing the roof with identical blue barrel tiles, and sensitively placing a ramp so the building was accessible to all.[2] It was a restoration victory that pleased all.

The Players Repertory Theater had been unable to reach an agreement with the owners of the Cinema theater. Since its closing following the league event in 1977, the owners had not been able to find another practical use for a building with a three-hundred-seat auditorium. One late summer day in 1978, Dennis Wilhelm was walking past the theater. It was noon, and the theater door was open. He walked into the lobby and was stunned when he saw that part of the upward sloping floor had been jackhammered away. Beautiful glass mirrors, elaborately etched with revealingly draped nymphs, intricate floral motifs, and leafy borders, had been removed and were carelessly tipped against a wall. The dramatic Deco chandeliers were gone.[3]

The demolition work at the Cinema spurred Michael Kinerk into becoming seriously involved in the league's activities. It had been only a matter of time. Kinerk and Wilhelm shared so many interests that some people referred to them in a way that sounded as if they were one person—MichaelandDennis. They were young, idealistic, and engaged in challenges with a zeal that exhausted other volunteers. Kinerk had a big interest in movie theaters, the old ornate ones. A native of Bloomington,

Indiana, his knowledge of Art Deco was limited to a 1972 visit to Radio City Music Hall and the collection that Wilhelm had installed in their house. A threat to one of his beloved movie houses energized him. Kinerk, the newsroom technology director at the *Miami Herald*, started making calls to the owner's New York offices and pleaded with them to leave the theater intact.[4] He didn't realize that the Brandt family that owned the Cinema was the Trans-Lux corporation, the oldest listed company on the American Stock Exchange, innovators in movie theaters and projection technology.

Like many South Beach property owners, the Brandts didn't want to wait for some promised historic district or intended redevelopment to revitalize the neighborhood. They wanted the Cinema to pay its own way, and retail stores seemed the best option. The alterations Wilhelm saw were intended to level the lobby floor and remove some walls, columns, and a section of the dramatic sweeping staircase to make space for two storefronts. The highly stylized chandeliers already had been sold to a wrecker for one hundred dollars each.[5]

Capitman wanted a public demonstration. The only person she could find available on short notice was Diane Camber. The two women stood in the landscaped median of Washington Avenue across from the theater and staged their protest by waving hastily made signs and shouting. The workers shouted back. As soon as the television and news reporters interviewed Capitman, she left.[6] Kinerk's phone calls were more effective. The Brandts agreed to wait for a couple of months to give the league time to try to find another use for the building.

While at city hall to confirm the Cinema theater situation, the league discovered, to its horror, that demolition permits were pending for several other buildings within the proposed district.

Barbara Capitman went on the attack. She believed they had to save every building, to win every battle, or they would lose the war. The league feared a domino effect. They needed them all: the hotels and restaurants to attract the tourists, the apartments to house the young and the elderly, the stores to cater to visitors and residents. She told a reporter, "People love historic Williamsburg. Williamsburg is always thronged with people and it doesn't have Florida's beaches and weather. I believe the Art Deco District will thrive on cultural tourism."[7] She neglected to mention that John D. Rockefeller Jr. started the restoration of Colonial Williamsburg with the family fortune and that only eighty-eight of its five hundred buildings are original. The rest are reconstructions. Colonial Williamsburg, less than half the size of the proposed South Beach historic district, didn't have fifty thousand people living within its boundaries on some of the most valuable oceanfront real estate in the country.

In a push to prove that Art Deco could be the tourism draw that Miami Beach leaders coveted, a major event was planned for October 1978 to publicize the area, lure visitors to the neighborhood, and generate local support. It would be the same week that three thousand members of the National Parks and Recreation Association would be in town for a convention. "Art Deco Week" would feature an opening night ball, kite flying and sand castle building on the beach, big band entertainment, a fashion show, art exhibits, 1930s bathing beauties, and tram and walking tours of the neighborhood.

The two women who chaired the festival spent weeks walking up and down Ocean Drive and Collins Avenue, evaluating hotels and talking with the owners. They looked for spaces that would be suitable for social gatherings and exhibits, which hotels had the porches with the best views, which were in the best condition.[8] As hotels were selected and the owners were coaxed into participating, volunteers went to work to spruce up the areas to be used for the events. Gallons of fresh paint were applied to tired walls. Long-hidden Art Deco fireplaces were revealed. The goal was to create the glamour and style of Broadway musicals, Greta Garbo, and Artie Shaw.

Kinerk and Wilhelm were put to work on their first love, the cinema. Capitman wanted a major film festival at the Lincoln Theater. Kinerk and Wilhelm rented the theater and ordered the films. Camber was put in charge of the tours. She knew the history of the Victor Hotel, the Ritz Plaza, and others because her grandfather had built them. She could recall days in high school when students would go off campus at noon to the crowded hamburger and ice cream shop on Espanola Way. She could point out where her father bought an oceanfront lot on Collins Avenue that was their private beach. She had dozens of stories about incidents that happened on South Beach and people whose names visitors recognized.[9]

The league moved its headquarters into room 104 of the Cardozo Hotel on Ocean Drive. The Cardozo's owner wasn't sure that this Art

Deco idea had a lot of merit, but he was willing to try something new. The buzz of activity increased as Art Deco Week neared. No one had time to talk about the National Register nomination or grant applications or renovating housing for the elderly. Tour guides were being hustled through a dry run. Board members were pressing the newspapers and television stations for coverage. Souvenir tee-shirts had to be sorted and brochures and posters distributed. Entertainers had to be confirmed. The tram route had to be double-checked. The week would be the Miami Design Preservation League's coming-out party.

It rained.

The Moon Over Miami dance drew a good crowd at the Edward Hotel on Collins Avenue. Guests were dressed in rhinestone headbands, feather boas, and tuxedos that hadn't been seen since they started making movies in color. A moongate allowed passersby to view the pool and patio area, where honored guests sat on metal folding chairs to watch a water ballet by a team of teenage girls.

The few vendors they had signed up for the weekend street festival moved under cover in the Cardozo, setting up tables in the lobby and in a couple of unoccupied rooms on the first floor. Dennis Wilhelm was there with his Deco collectibles, antiques, and books. Woody Vondracek, who had become the league's unofficial artist-in-residence, sold prints and Christmas cards. Only a handful of visitors viewed the Radio City Music Hall photo exhibition, the film festival, and the rest of the week's events. Most were league members and local curiosity seekers, not the hordes of tourists Capitman had promised.

One of the curiosity seekers was Lynn Bernstein. She came to Miami Beach in 1974 from Philadelphia for a quick vacation with friends. She loved the area so much she decided to stay and live a carefree life, working at a variety of hotel jobs that she didn't consider particularly rewarding. She saw an item in the paper about Art Deco Week and was attracted by the league's spirit of purpose. She drove to Ocean Drive with a friend, who chose to stay in the car while Bernstein ran through the rain into the Cardozo. She explored the lobby where Vondracek was selling his Christmas cards and prints, then down the hall where Wilhelm had his books and collectibles displayed.

When she wandered into the office in room 104, someone asked her if she could make a copy of something. The next thing she knew, she was at the Xerox machine. Two hours later she was still in room 104, talking to Barbara Capitman, Leonard Horowitz, Dennis Wilhelm, and the others. Her friend was still sitting in the car outside.[10]

Lynn Bernstein signed up as a league volunteer, helping sort through the piles of leftover posters, shirts, newspaper clippings, and unpaid bills that critics pointed to as proof that the Art Deco district as a tourist attraction was a harebrained idea. The event fell far short of its promise, but it was a success for Bernstein. Three weeks later, she was hired as part of the office staff.

Return Our Hoodlums

Miami Beach city officials already were struggling with how to resurrect their tourism industry when they learned in 1977 that Ben Novak was having financial problems at the city's largest and most famous hotel, the Fontainebleau. He was scrambling to come up with a five-million-dollar mortgage payment to avoid the forced sale of his hotel. And it was *his* hotel.

The Fontainebleau originally was as unwanted by the city as an Art Deco district. The pressure to revive the building industry after World War II was intense. The heirs of Harvey Firestone took the city to court in 1950 to rezone the lavish estate to allow construction of a hotel or apartment building. The city had refused and offered to buy the property for one million dollars. The heirs wanted $1.4 million. The city made a second offer to buy a smaller portion of the property. It also was refused.[11] Eventually, the matter ended up in court, where the city lost and was forced to rezone all the big oceanfront estates to allow development. Ben Novak, whose family owned a resort in the Catskills, bought the Firestone estate for $2.3 million in 1952.[12]

Two years later Novak began construction of the Fontainebleau, designed by Morris Lapidus, who didn't know the meaning of the word *overdone*. Novak used the Firestone mansion as his headquarters. When the hotel was finished, he moved into his new owner's suite, and a wrecking ball demolished the Firestone mansion's porte cochere, the graceful arched windows, the red tile roof, and the six chimneys to erase all but the memories of the magnificent home.

The curved facade of the Fontainebleau became an instant landmark. It was the epitome of the "building as sign" as described by architect Robert Venturi in his book *Learning from Las Vegas*. It didn't even have its name out front. Lapidus's design was labeled tacky and vulgar and roundly panned by the establishment design press from New York. The tourists loved it.

By 1977, the Fontainebleau complex had grown to 1,250 rooms, twelve acres of carpeting, 265 cabanas, two swimming pools, seven tennis courts, two gyms, five bowling lanes, and an ice skating rink.[13] The kitchens easily could serve a luncheon for a convention of two thousand while handling smaller groups in private rooms and the regular noontime crowd in the restaurants. But the Fontainebleau was showing its age. It hadn't been updated, and the service was surly. The local joke was that if you dropped a quarter on the floor of the lobby and a bellman picked it up to return it to you, it would cost you a dollar tip to get it back. It still served as the city's premiere convention hotel, but it had lost much of its luster as a tourist destination.

Novak—wavy silver hair, a neatly trimmed mustache, and usually adorned with expensive jewelry—had lived in the hotel for its twenty-three years. He had mortgaged it heavily to finance other projects that were not returning profits as hoped. The court already had forced the sale of 440 acres of his land in West Dade where he had been building an apartment development.[14]

Novak would have to sell his flagship property. One prospective buyer, who was staying at the hotel, had the bathroom ceiling fall on his head, followed by the plumber. Redevelopment agency vice chairman Stephen Muss became the new owner of the Fontainebleau and signed a management agreement with the Hilton Hotel chain. He immediately started making changes. He demolished the cabanas, one pool, the ice skating rink, and the bowling alley. He built a gigantic swimming pool with waterfalls and grottos and planted lots of palm trees. He put a sign out front.

There was plenty of space left for a casino.

Gambling had been part of Miami Beach from the 1920s. The business in those days was run by the S&G Syndicate, six publicly known Jewish "hoodlums" who raked in an estimated $50 million a year in their heyday. The big hotels were partners in the enterprise and rented out prime spaces in their pool cabana areas to bookies for $15,000 to

$30,000 a year.[15] Officials were paid handsomely to turn a blind eye to the activities. For many years, the S&G had its offices in a building owned by a former mayor. The bookies and the syndicate were alerted to occasional police raids that were conducted for show. The bookies were back in business within twenty-four hours, and full of apologies to their best customers.

All this activity was watched with great interest by a seasonal Miami Beach resident who lived on Palm Island, one of the exclusive enclaves of the rich. Al Capone enjoyed retreating from the pressures of his full-time job in Chicago to his two-story island mansion with its gatehouse, swimming pool, and boat dock. But all the money being generated by the S&G was too much to resist. Capone's Chicago mob controlled the racing wire that distributed racing news nationwide, and he figured he should get a piece of the Miami Beach action. Frank Costello's New York gang had similar thoughts and set up a syndicate to compete against the S&G. Miami Beach had tolerated the locally run gambling industry, but the arrival of out-of-town gangsters did not sit well with the city fathers. One councilman complained, "More notorious national criminals live in Miami Beach than in any other city of this size in the United States."[16]

By 1949, the amount of money involved in Miami Beach gambling was staggering. A conservative estimate was that the bookies were shelling out one million dollars a year for immunity from arrest.[17] Local officials asked the Congressional Crime Committee, headed by Senator Estes Kefauver, to come to Dade County to investigate allegations of criminal activity. The resulting crackdown was not well received in all quarters. The lackeys who surrounded the S&G were good customers at Miami Beach retailers. The reaction of merchants at 21st and Collins resulted in what must be one of the strangest headlines in newspaper history: "Return our hoodlums, merchants ask."[18] In the aftermath of the hearings most gambling operations closed up shop for good.

The "Let's Help Florida Committee" was formed to put casino gambling on the November 1978 ballot. The subject surfaced from time to time as a solution to resurrecting the tourism industry, particularly in Miami Beach, to give it another weapon in its competition with Las Vegas and the Caribbean. However, it required a voter-approved amendment to the state constitution. The pro-casino campaign was financed primarily by the major hotel interests, including Stephen Muss. If approved by voters, the amendment would permit casinos on a sixteen-mile strip from Hollywood, in Broward County, to the southern tip of Miami Beach, including the redevelopment area.

The committee, in a $2 million campaign, promised that Beach tourism revenue would increase from $3.5 million to $10.5 million a year.[19] They pledged that there would be new hotels, new jobs, and property taxes for the city coffers. They pointed to the success of Las Vegas, which had doubled its annual tourist visits in the previous decade. Opponents warned that casinos would hurt Miami's emerging international banking business, deter family tourism, and attract organized crime. There were those who said organized crime had never left, as witnessed by the presence of reputed mob associate Meyer Lansky, who was under daily FBI surveillance even as he browsed through the magazines at the Miami Beach library.[20]

Casinos were as big a threat to the South Beach neighborhood as the South Shore redevelopment. When casinos were approved in Atlantic City in 1976, land speculation ran rampant and housing for low-income residents grew scarce as rents soared and speculators bought and closed buildings in anticipation of turning a quick profit. Older buildings were demolished, including grand hotels on the Boardwalk that were listed on the National Register. Social services were cut. Street crime increased. While the strip of the Jersey shore became congested with tourists and gamblers, inland blocks deteriorated even faster and threatened to turn a depressed city into a slum. Opponents of the amendment foresaw a similar bleak fate for all of South Beach.

Dade County voters rejected the initiative by 53 percent, and the referendum failed three-to-one statewide.[21] But everyone knew the idea would return.

With the casino threat out of the way, attention returned to the National Register nomination. The state historic preservation office had some problems with the nomination, especially the flowery language of the narrative. A revised draft, more in keeping with accepted standards, was delivered to Tallahassee in September. The state office said it still was not complete or correct. The third submission passed muster.[22] It was expected to be at least a year before the office took final action on the nomination. But Capitman pestered the state staff by phone almost daily to hurry it up. Momentum was important.

Antidistrict sentiment was growing and becoming more organized. Business organizations closely tied to the construction industry saw the district as a threat to future development. A major new hotel desperately was needed. To attract a hotel developer, oceanfront property was essential, and many of the most desirable sites fell within the proposed district's boundaries. The city commission, loaded with prodevelopment commissioners elected in 1977 with the financial support of the South Shore proponents, was firmly against any action that potentially could restrict new construction.

The hotel and apartment and store owners simply weren't interested in their buildings being designated as historic. They had lived with the buildings as the paint faded and the plumbing became fussy and the floors warped. They didn't see why other people would find them beautiful or interesting. Elderly residents liked things the way they were and saw no need for government intervention. They weren't nostalgic for the 1930s, a decade they remembered for the punishing poverty of the depression and the personal terror of the beginning of a world war. City officials and developers were appalled at the prospect of having almost 15 percent of the city frozen in time. If every old building was saved, where could anyone build?

What many thought, but only some were saying in public, was that the whole idea was patently ridiculous. Middle-aged residents scoffed at the idea that buildings built during their lifetime could be deemed historic or meaningful. People came to South Florida to get away from the old, to start anew in a clean modern sunny place, leaving the black walnut armoire and carved mahogany buffet behind. They questioned how an area that was built as a tourist destination could be compared to real neighborhoods in real cities. A quaint historic village might work elsewhere, they said, but Miami Beach was different—which, of course, was the whole point of trying to preserve it.

To most people, history was events and people, not architecture. Historic buildings were where big things happened. Most people overlooked the importance and charm of their own town while they raved about ones that required a ten-hour drive and two nights at a Holiday Inn. Few people in Oakland thought about their Paramount Theater as being architecturally significant. Legislators in St. Paul considered legislation rather than the influence of the Minnesota capitol's architect, who also designed the landmark Woolworth Building in New York City. Washington, D.C., travelers were more concerned about finding a parking space at Dulles International than admiring Eero Saarinen's design. But they would travel hundreds or thousands of miles to look at buildings with lesser pedigrees. The resort architecture of South Beach was its contribution to the national story.

A surprise came in late November when the state preservation office decided to break with procedure and hold a hearing in Miami Beach for public comment on the nomination. The number of property owners affected because of the size of the district was so vast that normal channels for commenting on the nomination seemed inadequate.

More than 130 people on both sides of the issue filled the commission chambers for the hearing. Most of the speakers supporting the district came from the cultural community. Their argument echoed that of Thomas Bever, writing in the HCRS publication *Economic Benefits of Historic Preservation* (May 1978):

> There is a movement growing in this country, a movement that offers a solution to problems of unemployment, inflation, poor housing, dying inner cities, and depressed small towns. It provides an alternative to urban renewal. The movement goes by the various names of historic preservation, heritage conservation, neighborhood revitalization. This movement of rehabilitating old neighborhood houses or adapting old commercial buildings for new use is not limited to any particular region of this nation. . . . In addition to giving people a sense of time, place and meaning in terms of where they live, historic preservation has been successful for purely business reasons. It costs less to rehabilitate a building than to construct a new one, and these preserved buildings can compete successfully in the marketplace.

The league had mustered enough local and national support for the opponents to see the handwriting on the wall. There was going to be a historic district whether they wanted one or not. The businessmen's tactics were redirected toward containment. They said they were reluctantly willing to accept the concept of an Art Deco district, but only a small one, maybe a few blocks of Ocean Drive.

Letters were mailed on December 28 to twenty-five hundred property owners in the district, notifying them of a meeting by the state review board for final action on the National Register nomination. The board meeting was set for February 8, 1979, on the campus of the University of Florida in Gainesville.

City leaders rallied their forces. Members of the chamber of commerce, the Board of Realtors, and the Resort Hotel Association met over tuna salad and outlined their strategy.[23] They realized it was pointless to argue against a style of architecture, even if they didn't like it. They focused their protests on the size of the district and the chilling effect it would have on development throughout the south end of the city. They expressed a robust skepticism about the potential of an Art Deco district. The director of the Resort Hotel Association, who apparently never had been to Savannah or Charleston, said, "No one in their right mind just walks around and looks at old buildings. They want to see glassblowers and cobblers."[24]

On the morning of February 8, a handful of league members checked in at the airport for the flight to Gainesville. When they lined up to board the plane, they were unhappy to see that their opponents were on the same flight. They settled into their seats, preservationists on the left, city officials and business leaders on the right.

Michael Kinerk sat next to league president Andres Fabregas. Fabregas was a Deco-inspired architect who had been selected to design the new Miami Beach City Hall. He and Kinerk shared a love of the cinema. Fabregas recalled his mother taking him to Ginger Rogers and Fred Astaire movies when he was growing up in Havana. It gave them something to talk about to keep their minds off the task before them.

Apprehensive league members and a determined city contingent crowded into a conference room at the Florida State Museum in the new Dickinson Hall for the 2:00 p.m. meeting. Before their item came up for discussion, they sat patiently while the review board approved a nomination for a site in the town of Jupiter Inlet.[25]

It was their turn. Each of the six review committee members had received a copy of the nomination, including the rewritten version of intern Elan Zingman's statement of significance calling the district the "largest concentration of 1920s and 1930s era resort architecture in the United States." A specialist from the state historic preservation office presented a slide show about the "Old Miami Beach" district. The chairman, a University of Florida professor of architecture, cautioned those who wanted to speak that they each would be limited to five minutes.

Fabregas spoke on behalf of the league, as did Diane Camber and Barbara Capitman's eldest son, Andrew, who had come to Miami Beach to help his mother with the campaign. Four of the city and business representatives spoke in opposition. After a brief discussion, the chairman called for a vote. Everyone held their breath as the vote was taken. The historian voted yes. The archaeologist voted yes. The anthropologist voted yes. Two hours and ten minutes after the meeting began, the Miami Beach Architectural District received a unanimous recommendation from the committee to be listed in the National Register of Historic Places.[26] Barbara Capitman called the victory "a triumph of rationality and academic worth over bigotry and greed."[27]

Three months later, on May 14, 1979, word came that the Department of Interior's Heritage Conservation and Recreation Service had officially declared one square mile of South Beach as the Miami Beach Architectural District and added it to the other fifteen hundred historic districts listed on the National Register, including those in Key West, Tampa, Pensacola, and Tallahassee. It was one of the largest in the country and the first twentieth-century district to go on the National Register, a mere upstart compared with proven tourist draws such as Natchez and St. Augustine. The league planned a party for the following night. The chamber of commerce vice president was disappointed with the outcome but planned to go to the league's party anyway.

The residents of the area, whose well-being was supposed to be the impetus for the undertaking and whose assumed support had been the basis for many grant requests, were baffled. They didn't understand what all the fuss was about. One elderly man was prophetic: "It will force out elderly residents. You know they want to get rid of them. They'll spend money on the hotels to bring in the young people. That's the way it is."[28]

CHAPTER 4

Do It Yourself

One common salvo fired at preservationists nationwide was, "If you want it saved, buy the buildings and do it yourself." Barbara Capitman decided that's exactly what she would do. She relied heavily on her sons in different ways. John was her emotional rock. He had left Miami to pursue his doctorate at Duke University. In their phone calls, she told him about people who were stabbing her in the back and how tough things were. Andrew was the go-to business guy. He was twenty-nine years old, with a prep school and Ivy League education. He was living in New York and putting together limited partnerships for projects all over the world. He didn't know anything about running a hotel. That didn't stop his mother from convincing him to move to Miami Beach and buy one.

The three Capitmans together had about $50,000, most of it from the sale of their family's summer house in Martha's Vineyard.[1] They put a deposit on the Cardozo Hotel on Ocean Drive at the corner of Thirteenth Street, and Andrew Capitman set out to put together a limited partnership to buy it. Before he could line up enough money, the option expired and he had to come up with another deposit. It took five months and the help of Miami-Dade County economic development boss Ernie Martin to find financing. Miami banks had redlined South Beach as a bad investment and were not interested in lending money on a dreary old hotel.

On June 19, 1979, Andrew Capitman and a group of investors became the owners of the Cardozo Hotel for a purchase price of $800,000.[2] He spent the morning of the closing racing around to collect checks from people who were willing to come in on the deal. Michael Kinerk and Dennis Wilhelm had wanted to invest, but Andrew Capitman turned them down. It was a high-risk adventure for people in the top tax brackets, who could recoup their investment through a tax write-off.[3]

The Cardozo had been painted dull beige with faded brown trim. A brown-and-beige striped awning bent awkwardly over the entrance steps between mauve-tinted keystone columns that surrounded the porch. Air conditioning units protruded from several windows. Metal chairs with orange vinyl strapping were lined up on either side of the front door. It was classic Miami Beach Deco, occupied by the regulation coterie of elderly residents.

This was where the Capitmans and Leonard Horowitz and the league would show the world what could be done. They were going to prove the truth of the statement by Dr. John Brademas, president emeritus of New York University, in *Remaking America*: "Wise preservation can renew the integrity and utility of a structure and reestablish a place for it in the life of a community."[4] Their vision was to create a living study of blending elderly and young, residents and tourists, all enjoying a period atmosphere created by the buildings, entertainment, and glamour of the best of the 1930s. Most critics were betting that the Capitmans would lose their shirts. Andrew wouldn't have bet against them.

Obviously, one hotel wouldn't turn the tide. Andrew Capitman knew that the strength of the district was in numbers. The location was incomparable. Although modest, the South Beach hotels had all the basics for success. But each was too small to compete with the hotels farther north. With a collection of hotels, one owner could have enough rooms to market them competitively. He saw an opportunity for the Art Deco hotels to cater to the niche market of sophisticated travelers who were turned off by the big hotels with their unsophisticated, impersonal service. What he had was a crumbling hotel with faulty plumbing and a leaky roof. He came back from the closing and sat down on the porch in one of the aluminum chairs. In front of him was an empty street and an ocean. Inside were twenty elderly year-round residents, some of whom had the same ailments as the hotel. He had about $700 left in his bank account.[5]

But timing is everything. As he sat there, a pretty, slender woman came up the steps. The league had requested technical help from the Heritage Conservation and Recreation Service. Help had arrived in the form of Margaret Doyle, a young professional historic preservationist from the Technical Services Division. Doyle checked in as the Cardozo's first nonelderly guest. John Capitman and his fiancée came down for the Fourth of July weekend. Mother and younger brother decided that the lovely Miss Doyle would be perfect for Andrew.[6] The couple was married six months later.

People scoffed at the notion that the purchase of one building could spur the renovation of an entire district. But it had been done before. Dana Crawford started buying buildings in the Larimer Square area of Denver in 1964. She bought one building, renovated it, and then bought another and another. The area began to catch on. An urban renewal project to demolish both sides of Larimer Square was approved in 1967. Crawford fought building by building to keep the bulldozer at bay. Although dozens of downtown blocks and irreplaceable Victorian storefronts were lost, Dana Crawford's tenacity proved the catalyst for the revitalization of Denver's Lower Downtown area.[7]

Soon Barbara Capitman was holding court on the front porch of the Cardozo. She usually was found sitting in a chair with a commodious bag beside her filled with photo slides, press releases, sheaves of memos and notes covered with geometric doodles, magazine and newspaper clippings, fabric swatches. Even her own sons joked that she looked like a bag lady.

One of the first young people to move into the Cardozo was Woody Vondracek, the artist who was creating a career and an image for the district with his distinctive Art Deco posters. He could hear the sounds of the surf from his room. He could open the windows and let the louvered doors pull the sea breeze through. He got a kick from being able to turn on the same light fixture that had been there since the hotel was built. And he could get decent meals at the nearby cafeterias for four bucks.[8]

Margaret Doyle, though, launched the Cardozo. She designed and supervised the renovations that gave the hotel a sheen of 1930s glamour. A broom closet was emptied out to make room for a tiny kitchen with a microwave oven to heat up sandwiches and pastries. Mattresses and old refrigerators were moved out of another small room to make space for a café. Young people drawn to this emerging South Beach stopped in after work to have a glass of wine and nibble on crudités, relishing the carefree days that come between college and buying life insurance. Everyone could find a parking space right in front of the hotel.

The Cardozo was missing only the hotel guests. Barbara Capitman's publicity machine generated a small article in the *New York Times*. A friend of Dona Zemo's spotted it and called Dona at her home on an organic farm in Connecticut. She knew Zemo was interested in Art Deco and had helped design a health food store in the Art Deco style, including a poster by Woody Vondracek.

The moment Dona Zemo stepped out of the taxi in front of the Cardozo, she felt as though she had found paradise. She had experienced the era of beatniks in Greenwich Village and the transition of SoHo and could see the possibilities beyond the beige paint and lawn chairs. She and her friend checked into an oceanfront room for forty dollars a night.[9] It was her's friend's birthday so they decided to celebrate. Before the night was over, the whole Cardozo gang was in their room for a party.

The next morning the phone rang in Zemo's room. It was a woman with a creaky voice that Zemo didn't recognize. The woman asked if they could meet in the lobby. Zemo went downstairs and encountered Barbara Capitman. Capitman swept up Zemo with the force of a tornado and looked much as if she had been in one. She reminded Zemo of the New England intellectuals she knew at home, people who were passionate about their thoughts and unconcerned about their appearance.

Zemo and her friend hung around South Beach for a few days, met some people, shopped at a Deco second-hand store on Washington Avenue. On her flight home, Zemo made a decision. The enthusiasm that drew others into the gravitational pull of South Beach had captured her. When she got back to Connecticut, she called Andrew Capitman and asked for a job. Two weeks later she went back to South Beach, intending to stay for three months. A week later, Andrew Capitman made Zemo the manager of the Café Cardozo.

The real estate agent who handled the Cardozo deal for Andrew Capitman was a twenty-three-year old real estate agent from Key Biscayne. After hearing Barbara Capitman's patter about the Art Deco district one day, Linda Polansky drove over to South Beach and was awestruck by its beauty and potential. A native of Westchester, New York, she was comfortable with the small-scale atmosphere of South Beach. It took her about thirty seconds to decide to get involved. Polansky knew she had made the right decision when she found Espanola Way.[10]

Espanola Way was built in 1922 as a commercial accompaniment to the Roney Plaza Hotel, an elegant, oceanfront Spanish-style resort, where live flamingos wandered in the landscaped gardens. The narrow street was unlike any other in South Beach—an intimate thoroughfare with the feel of old Madrid. On this street Diane Camber's father had introduced eighteen-year-old Desi Arnaz to the American audience in his restaurant.[11] When Linda Polansky first saw the narrow street, she found forgotten storefronts built right up to the sidewalk, without the front porches that characterized the hotels of Collins Avenue and Ocean Drive. Alleys and courtyards were tucked behind the rough stucco walls of repair shops and second-hand stores. Arches, red barrel-tile roofs, and balconies with wrought-iron railings added to the Latin spirit. The westernmost block was closed off at Jefferson Avenue, creating a cul-de-sac that helped protect a unique block of single-family homes that were holding on for dear life.

Espanola Way's warm Mediterranean style appealed to Polansky more than the streamlined Deco buildings. Polansky earned her broker's license and opened a real estate office on Espanola Way. She wanted to move to South Beach from Coconut Grove but couldn't find an apartment. The building managers all said she was too young.[12]

The Clay Hotel stood at the entrance to Espanola Way at the corner of Washington Avenue. During prohibition, it was a gambling and bootlegging den. One day, Polansky went in and met the owner. He was an elderly Jewish man with ill-fitting dentures. He also was a bit hard of hearing. He asked Polansky, "You a broker? I don't talk to brokers. You a buyer, I'll talk to you." She told him she was a buyer.[13]

The Clay was a flophouse, but Polansky fell in love with it. She found investors who were willing to put up the money. She had analyzed hotels and hotel operations during her days working for a New York bank, but had no experience in running or renovating a hotel. She jumped in and hoped for the best.

Barbara Capitman also moved to South Beach and rented a Pennsylvania Avenue apartment in a three-story building with sunny corner balconies reached by doors with porthole windows. Towering Royal palm trees flanked the sidewalk and shaded the front of the building from the afternoon sun. She filled the apartment with art by family and friends, including a sculpture of her as a lovely young woman, done by her mother. The white-walled living room had a simple fireplace, where she displayed two Picasso pitchers that she bought on a trip taking her son

John to school in Switzerland when he was in tenth grade. Bookshelves overflowed with well-used architecture books and design magazines. Her mother's Deco-era desk sat by a window in a corner of the living room.[14]

It appeared that the league was on the road to success. But storm warnings were being raised. Hard-working volunteers were abandoning the organization because of what they saw as Barbara Capitman's demand for total fidelity. The planning department refused to work on another project with the group because it considered the league difficult to work with. A fifty-two-thousand-dollar state grant hung in the balance for six months because the city was reluctant to provide the matching funds.

Problems mounted within the redevelopment agency, too. Controversy had dogged the agency for the three years since it unveiled its scheme. The Department of Environmental Regulation objected to the canal system. The bond validation hearings were stalled as State Attorney Janet Reno argued against the legitimacy of the city declaring the area "blighted." The regional planning council questioned the agency's financial projections as "highly optimistic." The plan did not provide public access to the beach. The price of the project had soared to $850 million. Master designer Steve Siskind was lauded by some as a brilliant visionary who had molded the redevelopment agency's idea into a spectacular concept, but often he came across as disingenuous and brash. He and the city manager butted heads on numerous occasions. The city manager wanted Siskind fired. Instead, the city manager found himself looking for a new job. Siskind won a raise that made him the highest paid public official in the state.

Stephen Muss and the others who had initiated the project were hard-driving businessmen to whom time was money and they didn't waste either of them. Everyone had thought the moratorium on South Shore would be in place for about a year or two while all the pieces were being brought into place so the project could get started. As time dragged on, the condition of buildings south of Fifth Street continued to deteriorate.

The uncertainty wore on the patience of the residents. They were angry that they were being forced out of their homes with no place to go. People who had Nazi concentration camp numbers tattooed on their arms did not want to hear the word *relocation*. At one city commission meeting to discuss the need for subsidized housing for the elderly who were being displaced, tempers became so enraged that Miami Beach K-9 officers were called in to restore order.[15]

The residents finally won a promise for seven hundred fifty new housing units, all on Sixth Street, outside of the South Shore redevelopment area but within the Art Deco district. The redevelopment agency put together a package of relocation and rent subsidies and a grievance procedure to help with the move. Supporters of the project encouraged residents to get on board. They warned that the real estate south of Fifth Street was too valuable to linger undeveloped. If the city's master plan with its new relocation benefits didn't succeed, then they would be displaced by individual developers who would be under no obligation to help them. Morris Katowitz didn't think he would find another place for the twenty-four dollars a month he paid in maintenance fees for the co-op apartment he shared with his wife.[16]

Rita Blum wasn't worried. Neither was her sister Shirley, who lived next door to Rita and her dog Sam. They had lived in the tidy green and white cottages across the street from Joe's Stone Crab restaurant since 1943. Their mother had told them about plans to redevelop the area, and she died in 1962.[17] The sisters figured nothing would happen any time soon.

One of the more outspoken opponents of the project was Mel Mendelson, whose wholesale meat-packing operation had been in the family and in old South Beach for three decades. Mendelson knew how Miami Beach politics worked. For years, city nabobs huddled in the back room of the family's butcher shop to eat steaks, drink beer, and make deals. Mendelson vowed to spend his last dollar to stop the redevelopment project.[18]

South Beach residents fought back with their votes in 1979. Two years earlier, a slate of candidates backed by proponents of the South Shore redevelopment project had swept into office. The tide had turned against the stalled project, and the Stephen Muss-backed coalition was tossed out in favor of candidates who were not as enthusiastic about demolishing South Shore, including new City Commissioner Mel Mendelson.

The redevelopment area was nearing its sixth year of the moratorium on construction and repairs to its aging apartments and hotels. Steve Siskind quit. Depending on whose story you believed, either he had promised too much too soon, or he left over a salary dispute. He had won every battle along the way, but he lost the war. Negotiations between the redevelopment agency and the partnership of three developers wore on without progress.

Those residents who could afford to leave and those whose property had been condemned by the city moved away from South Shore, although many of them stayed on South Beach. Many of those left behind were old, poor, sick, and couldn't afford the rent elsewhere. Owners of condos and homes couldn't sell their property. Some hunkered down, determined not to leave until someone forced them out. When the redevelopment agency announced that it was going to do a survey of the residents about relocation, the dark joke on the park benches was that the only question should be, "Would you like to be pushed (a) into the bay, (b) into the ocean, or (c) into Government Cut?"

The Art Deco district was being dragged down, too. The population was getting older, dying off, and new retirees were not moving into the area because of the increased crime. Property owners were hanging on in the hope that a real estate turnaround would come soon. Landlords and hotel owners were becoming desperate.

Paradise Lost

Easter week 1980 in Havana was much like any other April week. People went about doing their regular jobs in government offices and the sugarcane fields and the state-owned factories. There were no Easter baskets, no new spring dresses for Easter Sunday. Under Fidel Castro's Communist dictatorship such religious activities were forbidden. But for a half dozen men riding in a bus through the deteriorating streets of Havana that Tuesday in April, it was a week that they hoped would change their lives.

The bus rattled along streets lined with aging buildings and derelict cars. It turned toward the beach and into the once-beautiful neighborhood of Miramar, leafy streets lined with gracious Spanish Colonial homes built by Havana's elite in the early twentieth century. As it neared the Peruvian Embassy on Avienda Quinta, the bus picked up speed. The faces of the men were determined, their jaws set. They had made their decision.

The driver, Hector Sanyustiz, did not slow. Shots were fired. A bullet ricocheted. A guard fell dead. The bus crashed into the embassy grounds and the six Cuban citizens asked for political asylum.[19]

In 1979, Fidel Castro's government relaxed its policy and allowed Cuban exiles in the United States to return to the island to visit family and friends they left behind. More than 250,000 Cubans, most of them upper and middle class, had fled their homeland in the four chaotic years following the 1959 revolution. Another 125,000 Cubans left during the "freedom flights" from 1965 to 1973. Then Castro bolted the emigration doors.

Through the small crack in the door in 1979 came tens of thousands of Americanized Cubans to visit *abuelos* and others whom they hadn't seen for too many years. They came with stories and pictures of nice stucco homes in orderly neighborhoods, supermarkets brimming with fresh fruits and vegetables and meats, of department stores filled with the latest fashions, of new cars and gas stations on every corner, of color TVs and dishwashers, of good jobs and owning their own businesses, of McDonald's hamburgers and *quinces* held at fancy hotels, of piles of presents under Christmas trees and candlelight services at the Catholic church.

The image of such a paradise in America was seductive to Cubans living under the spartan demands of the Castro regime. They had either grown up in or grown used to the Marxist system. They attended the rallies, worked at their assigned jobs, did their one hundred fifty hours of volunteer work every year.[20] Many only wore the mask of a contented revolutionary. Frustrated men began talking about ways to escape, careful to discuss such things only with those they knew they could trust absolutely and in places where no one could overhear. The daring ones hijacked boats and built rafts to attempt crossing the Straits of Florida, praying they would be spotted by a friendly ship or plane or the U.S. Coast Guard. Others sought asylum at foreign embassies where they would have a chance to leave Cuba for a friendly nation and, from there, emigrate to the United States.

Castro was becoming increasingly irritated, not only at his disloyal comrades but at the embassies for protecting, housing, and feeding them. He was angry with the U.S. government for enabling his people to enter its country so easily. He decided it was time to stop it. He would punish the Peruvians, overwhelm them, make an example of them. He vowed that the Cubans who took asylum there would never leave the island.[21]

On Good Friday, three diesel bulldozers rumbled past the trees that divided the two lanes of Avienda Quinta and ground to a halt in front of the gates. Men and women on their way to work paused in curiosity. The drivers reduced the cement guard posts in front of Peru's embassy to rubble. When the work was completed, they rumbled back down Avienda Quinta, and the guards left.[22] Castro's intention was to allow hundreds of people to take advantage of the apparent lapse in security and overwhelm the embassy. Unable to house and feed so many, he reasoned, the diplomats eventually would have to turn them over to the Cuban government.

Soon a cluster of young men arrived. They checked the street for soldiers, then climbed over the embassy fence. More young men joined them, as did families with small children and young married couples. By midnight, three hundred people had entered. By 3:00 a.m. there were five hundred.[23] People dozed on benches and the lawn or talked quietly in small clusters.

On Saturday, most residents of Havana heard rumors that the embassy was open. The Voice of America confirmed the reports. People from Havana, from Lawto, from Cojimar, rushed to the embassy carrying what possessions they could. Their desire for freedom outweighed the fear of reprisal, overcame the loss of leaving home, gave them the courage to withstand the shouts and insults of the government-organized mobs who chased them, threw stones at them, and called them traitors. A constant parade of tow trucks struggled to clear the clot of cars and taxis and buses that were abandoned in the street.[24] By Easter Sunday the number of people inside the embassy swelled to more than ten thousand. Leaders of Miami's Cuban exile community, Cuban embassy officials in Switzerland, and other diplomats tried to find a resolution to the situation. Tens of thousands of passionate Cuban exiles staged rallies in Miami demonstrating support for those at the embassy.

As Miami officials were contending with Cuban protestors clogging streets and engulfing parks, a steady flow of Haitian refugees was arriving in South Florida. There already were twenty-five thousand Haitians in South Florida by the end of 1979, and another three to four thousand had arrived since. The *Miami News* reported that on April 13, 692 more Haitians arrived on leaky boats and rafts. At 1:25 a.m., 115 men and women landed on the beach in Fort Lauderdale. At 10:00 a.m., another 37 beached in Marathon. At 12:40 p.m., 45 men and 13 women landed in Pompano Beach. The last group was found after midnight at Mile Marker 89 in the Florida Keys.[25] Unlike Cuban refugees, Haitians did not qualify for political asylum and were not entitled to legal status and public assistance.

A small flotilla of boats from Miami converged on Key West, hoping to launch a mercy mission to carry food and medicine to the refugees in the embassy in Havana. When the weather cleared, the boats left for Cuba in defiance of warnings from the U.S. State Department. On April 21, 1980, the *Dos Hermanos* and the *Blanche* returned to Key West with forty-eight refugees from the Peruvian Embassy who had passports and safe conduct passes in hand.[26]

International pressure against Castro intensified. He formulated a new scheme to regain control of the situation. He opened the Port of Mariel, about forty kilometers west of Havana. Those who wanted to leave the embassy could go, but they had to go by boat. No more planes. In fact, anyone who wanted to leave the country could go. The doors were open.

Cuban-Americans rushed to the marinas of South Florida and launched a makeshift navy to rescue their families and friends. Restaurant owners and jewelers and machinists and insurance salesmen shoved fistfuls of cash into the hands of boat owners in Miami, Fort Lauderdale, every dock in the Florida Keys. In fishing boats and lobster boats, sport cruisers and Chris Craft yachts, in forty-foot Sea Rays and twenty-five-foot Boston Whalers, they set out for Cuba with ebullient spirits and, too often, very little knowledge of navigation.

When they arrived at the port of Mariel, the boats each were given a number and told to wait at anchor. When their number was called, they pulled alongside the dock. Soldiers loaded each boat with strangers and ordered them to go. Their relatives were nowhere to be seen. Three miles out from Key West, the boats anchored and waited for the Coast Guard to direct them in.[27] Their occupants were dirty, hungry, sunburned, and seasick, but they were free. Some were free from more than communism.

It didn't take long for U.S. officials to realize Castro's ploy. In addition to allowing the embassy refugees and general population the freedom to leave the country, he opened the doors of the prisons and jails. He emptied mental health institutions. He rounded up the homeless, gays, drug addicts, prostitutes. They all were taken to Mariel. When the boats arrived, Castro's operatives forced "undesirables" on each vessel along with those who were leaving voluntarily. Castro intended to embarrass the United States and punish Miami by overloading them with people he was confident would cause trouble.

One month after the Mariel refugees began arriving, Miami's African-American community, minority in size to both the white and Hispanic populations, erupted in violence. Four white police officers were charged in the fatal 1979 beating of black insurance executive Arthur McDuffie. The trial had been moved to Tampa, but word of the officers' acquittal reached Miami on Friday evening, May 16. A demonstration was scheduled at the courthouse for the following day. Outraged residents weren't interested in waiting for a peaceful protest. The historic black neighborhood of Liberty City, northwest of Miami's downtown, exploded in violence that swiftly spread to other black neighborhoods. White drivers were yanked brutally out of their cars and beaten with bottles, bricks, guns, clubs. A black clenched fist from a car window was the only ticket to a safe ride through the streets. Light-skinned blacks were told to stay home.[28]

Trucks and cars and buildings were set ablaze. Half of the fires were allowed to burn out of control after fire trucks were attacked. Police had to provide protection for firefighters battling an enormous blaze in a lumberyard. The smell of burning rubber, businesses, and vehicles was carried by the wind to distant neighborhoods. Tire companies, packing-houses, a post office, service stations, an elementary school, drugstores, and markets were burned to the ground. Most of them were looted first. A doctor stood outside the office where he had treated residents for five dollars a visit for thirty years, where babies he delivered were taken care of for free until they were two years old. He pleaded with people he had known all their lives to leave his office alone. They burned it to the ground.[29]

People on South Beach could see columns of smoke from hundreds of fires blotting the western skyline across the bay. The news coverage terrified the elderly residents of South Beach. They cowered behind locked doors.

The weekend of violence left fifteen dead, three hundred injured, one thousand arrested, and $100 million in property damage, most of it in the Miami inner-city neighborhoods of Liberty City, Overtown, and northwest Coconut Grove. Hospitals overflowed with the dying and injured. An area seventeen miles long and seven miles wide was locked down under an 8:00 p.m. to 6:00 a.m. curfew. Within the curfew area, schools were closed, and bus service and garbage pickup were canceled. Police received almost 23,000 calls for help. More than a thousand National Guard troops were called in, and Miami was proclaimed a federal disaster area.[30]

The flow of refugees from Mariel continued. Castro abruptly ended the boatlift on September 25 and demanded that all boats in the harbor leave. The last boat docked in Key West four days later. In five months, more than 125,000 Cuban citizens had reached the shores of South Florida in more than two thousand vessels. Their ancestors came to Cuba from Spain in the sixteenth century, were brought from Africa as slaves in the seventeenth and eighteenth centuries, and were lured from China as laborers in the nineteenth century. Their grandfathers fought beside Jose Martí in the war for independence in 1893. Now they had fled scarce supplies of food and clothing, rationed gasoline, deteriorating housing, and mandatory attendance at President Castro's marathon speeches.

Dade County was reeling from the tumultuous events of the summer. Tent cities hastily were erected underneath expressways in downtown Miami and in the parking lots at the Orange Bowl stadium as local officials scrambled to handle the staggering numbers of people. Many were taken in by family or friends, given a place to live and a job, and absorbed into the established, successful Miami Cuban community. Those who could be identified as serious criminals were sent to American prisons. But that still left tens of thousands with no resources, nowhere to go. They needed housing and food, clothing and health care, every type of social service. Thousands of children needed to attend school when it opened in September.

Officials thought of South Beach, with its old apartments and hotels, many empty after the exodus of those fleeing the South Shore redevelopment and the steady attrition of the elderly population. There had been a growing Latin American colony in the area since the 1960s. A refugee family could rent one of the dingy, cramped rooms with their $119 a month government checks. Three or four people could pool resources and move into one of the tiny, musty apartments. It had to be better than living in the hot squalor of the tent cities. It was estimated that by the first of June, eight thousand Cuban refugees filled the empty apartments and hotels of South Beach.[31]

The South Shore area looked remarkably like Havana. There were palm trees and soft sand beaches. There were Cuban markets, and people in many stores and restaurants spoke Spanish. Buildings that echoed Spanish Colonialism and the Roaring Twenties stood lifeless with paint peeling from rough stucco walls and broken red clay barrel tile roofs. The plumbing didn't work. There were no air conditioners to subdue the summer heat. There were no jobs. Everyone around them seemed to be poor. Just like Havana—this was not the American paradise about which they had heard. They had risked a lot to reach the shores of freedom, and they expected more than what they saw.

Many of the refugees who came to South Beach were the "undesirables." Some saw their forced relocation as an unexpected chance for a second opportunity. Some were angry at being torn away from their homeland. Some saw it as an opportunity to revert to old habits. Some of them moved into Rosine Smith's cozy Ocean Breeze Hotel. Smith had dreamed of retiring on South Beach when she bought the hotel on First Street in the early 1960s. She worked hard to make it nice. When the city targeted her neighborhood for demolition, she lost heart and wanted to sell, but no one would buy. The little hotel had started to show signs of wear. The only people who would rent were those who had no other choice, including Mariel refugees. One beat her repeatedly with a hammer, punched and kicked her, and tied her up. He took all her cash. She almost died.[32]

Linda Polansky received a call from city administrators and was asked if they could put fifty refugees at her Clay Hotel on Espanola Way. The government would pay for them. She thought that they would be relatives of Miami families. The people who were living in the Clay when she bought it had sunk to the lowest levels of society. They barely managed to scrape together fifty bucks a week for a room as a respite from living on the street. The refugees who were delivered to her hotel were worse. There were robberies and armed assaults every day. If she left a vacuum cleaner in the hall for a few minutes, it would be gone when she returned. She had fifty fires in the first six months. When she heard sirens during her morning tennis game, she knew they probably were heading for her hotel. More than once on her way to work, she had to step over the chalk outline where someone had been gunned down or stabbed during the night.[33] She was trying to put together a deal with a lawyer and a developer from Tennessee to buy another building. The developer arrived by taxi to meet Polansky at the Clay. When he stepped out of the car, the first thing he saw was the bleeding body of a man who had been killed in the street. He backed out of the deal.

Dade County was becoming numb with the stress of dealing with overwhelming numbers of refugees, dismayed at the violence in the black community and the rising crime rates. It was a county under siege. The vicious Colombian drug cartels had chosen Miami as their favorite port of entry for the booming international cocaine trade. Local dealers discovered the addictiveness of crack cocaine. Drug gang violence was turning the streets red with the blood of shooting victims. Easy access to a seemingly unlimited supply of narcotics swelled the incidence of robberies, burglaries, and muggings as desperate users sought to pay for their habits. By August, the Miami Beach police chief told the commission that nearly three hundred former prisoners from Cuban jails were living in the city, plus an untold number who turned to crime after their arrival. Two children, aged four and seven, were sexually molested by a man who served time in a Cuban jail for murder. Thirty-four rapes were reported in the month of July 1980, compared to twenty-two in all of the previous year. There was a similar sharp increase in assaults.[34] The danger on the streets was keeping the South Beach elderly prisoners in their own apartments. *Time* magazine featured Miami on its cover with the doomsday headline "Paradise Lost."

The bad situation on South Beach was becoming much, much worse.

The Developer

The year that Miami Beach millionaire developer Carl Fisher built his luxurious Nautilus Hotel overlooking Biscayne Bay, Abraham Resnickowitz was born in Rokiškis, a small city in northeastern Lithuania near the Latvian border.

Resnickowitz grew up in a life of privilege with his parents and two sisters as part of the large Jewish community in their town. The Rokiškis telephone directory listed his father's name and number, evidence of his prestige as a government bureaucrat and owner of a roofing paper company.[1] As with most wealthy Jewish families in the community, when the boy completed yeshiva, he was sent to Kovno, the provincial capital in central Lithuania, to continue his education.

The country emerged from World War I as a fragile and politically chaotic independent republic. Like the rest of the citizens of Lithuania, the Resnickowitzes were unaware that the 1939 nonaggression pact between Adolph Hitler's Third Reich and Joseph Stalin contained a secret provision that "assigned" their country to the Soviet Union. In June 1940, the Soviets decided to exercise their annexation rights under the pact. The Red Army invaded and installed a communist government. One year later, Hitler reneged on his agreement, and the German army attacked the USSR, prompting violent anti-Soviet uprisings among the Lithuanian people.

The Soviets were unable to cope with both the popular revolt and the Germans at the same time. The Soviet army withdrew, leaving the Resnickowitzes and their neighbors to face the consequences.[2] More than 165,000 Lithuanian Jews died at the hands of the Nazis, including Mr. and Mrs. Chaimas Resnickowitz and both of their daughters. Stranded in the provincial capital, young Resnickowitz was captured and confined to the Kovno ghetto. He saw his neighbors taken away by Nazi officers and realized they were never to return.[3]

On a chilly night in 1944, Resnickowitz and four other men snipped through the barbed wire that kept them prisoners and ducked through the darkened streets of Kovno.[4] The German soldiers spotted them, raised their guns, and fired. Resnickowitz ran through a field, his eyes fixed on the safety of the woods beyond.[5] He wandered through the forest, watchful for Nazi soldiers searching for him, listening for sounds of the Soviet Army as it struggled to retake the territory. He found Russians, not the army but a small band of ragtag soldiers who had escaped a German prisoner of war camp. They joined forces with some resistance fighters who were operating from the woods using Soviet weapons that were being airdropped to secret locations. At the age of seventeen, Abraham Resnickowitz became a saboteur.[6]

Resnickowitz was fluent in German, Russian, and Lithuanian, as well as Hebrew and Yiddish. As the Soviets advanced westward, he was recruited into official service as an interpreter. When the Red Army took Berlin in May 1945, Lieutenant Abraham Resnickowitz marched with them. As soon as he saw a chance, he slipped over to the western sector where the Americans awaited.[7]

Some of those American forces had done their training in Miami Beach.

The war visited Miami Beach early. In 1939, people on the beach watched in dismay as the lights of the SS *St. Louis* passed only a mile offshore on its way back to Europe with more than nine hundred Jewish refugees still on board. A young boy named Herbert standing on the deck of the *St. Louis* with his family saw the skyline of hotels and palm trees and promised himself that one day he would return.[8]

On May 14, 1942, the Mexican tanker *Portrero del Llano* was struck by German torpedoes just south of Miami Beach. It drifted the length of the peninsula with its cargo of oil burning out of control, creating a floating torch against the black of the night sea and sky. The city was ordered to have partial and full blackouts after the *Pan Massachusetts*, another tanker, was struck off Cape Canaveral.[9]

Miami Beach was tailor-made as a training center for the military, and the Army Air Corps took full advantage of it. Raw recruits looked around at the palm trees, the beach, the sparkling white hotels, and lots of girls in swimsuits and decided it was a pretty good assignment. Private First Class E. H. Boyles of Monticello, Mississippi, couldn't believe his luck to be at the head of the check-in line at the Boulevard Hotel across from the Collins Canal, the first hotel to be taken over as barracks.[10] An Atlanta native sprawled out in an upholstered chair in one of the Boulevard's bright rooms and wrote, "Dear Mum. The army has gone swell all of a sudden. This is the grandest place you ever saw. Looks like I'm gonna enjoy this war."[11]

Almost two hundred Beach hotels and more than a hundred apartment buildings were being used as barracks by the end of 1942. Hotel owners who had charged tourists twelve dollars a day for a room were getting twenty cents a day from the government. Soldiers checked in, were processed, immunized, given uniforms and haircuts. Clark Gable had his mustache shaved off while fellow recruits grimaced.[12] Men who had honeymooned in Miami Beach eighteen months earlier found themselves back at the same hotel, sharing a room with someone who had worked there as a busboy.

The officer in charge of quarters ran through the halls blowing his whistle to roust the enlisted men from their beds at 5:30 a.m. They marched to the Colony Theater on Lincoln Road to either get assignments or watch training films at the French Casino (later to become the Cinema theater). The Miami Beach Golf Course became a drill ground, and the beach soon was filled with soldiers doing calisthenics, marching, and taking artillery practice beside the ocean. Carl Fisher's luxurious Nautilus Hotel was converted to a military hospital. The Helen Mar Apartments overlooking Lake Pancoast became the USO headquarters. The Army Air Corps moved its headquarters into the National Hotel on Collins Avenue, where sentinels kept a watch for submarines from its tower. First Lady Eleanor Roosevelt paid a visit to Serviceman's Pier, formerly the Municipal Pier, that was staffed by local volunteers who provided a library, dance hall, movie theater, swimming, and live entertainment. At about 4:00 p.m., troops marched back to their hotels to clean up and change into their Class A uniforms for dinner. The warm evenings drew them onto the streets to USO shows, dances, and the dozens of bars selling Cuba Libres and ten-cent beers.[13]

Eighteen private homes, taken over for officers, were frequently visited by generals who enjoyed mixing business with pleasure at the tropical base. As a result, the barracks were open to inspection at any time. Soldiers never sat on their beds during the day for fear of leaving wrinkles.[14]

They weren't the only soldiers spending part of World War II in South Florida. A prisoner of war camp was built north of Miami Beach near Baker's Haulover Inlet. Jewish children walking to school saw German and Italian POWs in distinctive prison garb trimming trees and tending the gardens of their hometown.[15]

Between 1942 and 1945, more than a half million Army Air Corps soldiers, one-quarter of all officers and one-fifth of the enlisted men, trained in Miami Beach.[16] Some of them, no doubt, were in Berlin on that day when Abraham Resnickowitz slipped away from the Russian army. His family and most of the people he knew all his life were dead. An uncle arranged for Resnickowitz to join him in Cuba, a country controlled by a corrupt government and organized crime but with plenty of opportunity for success. A slender, handsome young man with a charmingly crooked smile and warm friendly eyes, he was a popular bachelor in Havana's Jewish society. His single days were over the moment he met the lovely Sarah Litwak, who escaped from Europe to Cuba before the war began. They were married in 1949.[17]

Resnickowitz was intrigued by his father-in-law's Havana real estate holdings. He began using some of his earnings from working for his uncle's textile business to buy a piece of property here, another there until he amassed substantial wealth. Before long, Abraham Resnickowitz had two young sons, a nanny to care for them, and a beautiful new home on Avienda A in the beachfront section of Miramar.[18] But the political winds were changing in Cuba.

The dictatorship of Fulgencio Batista led to unrest among the working classes and the underprivileged. Fidel Castro assembled a small troop of guerillas in Mexico and invaded his homeland in 1956. A handful survived the ambush that awaited them and escaped to the Sierra Maestra mountains. New recruits joined them, and they grew in strength and popular support. After fighting to a standoff against Batista's federal army and gaining further influence by organizing a general strike in 1958, the eventual outcome was clear.

Batista fled Cuba on New Year's Eve 1958. On New Year's Day, Resnickowitz woke his nine-year-old son Jimmy and told him that Fidel Castro was the new president of Cuba. Resnickowitz had lived under a Marxist government before. A year later, the Resnickowitz family left their beautiful new home and their fortune to seek freedom in the United States.

Like most Cubans who fled to the United States during the early years of Castro, the Resnickowitzes thought the move was temporary. Resnickowitz was disheartened after he returned to Cuba a few months later to appraise the situation. He started liquidating his properties for a fraction of their worth to have a little money to start over again. He left Jimmy in Miami Beach with his grandparents at the Majestic Hotel on Ocean Drive, and the rest of the family went to North Carolina, where his uncle had established a new textile business. Two years later, on a buying trip he and his uncle were involved in a serious car accident. His uncle was killed, and Resnickowitz was in a coma for several days. When he recovered, he returned to Florida to stay and moved Sarah and the boys into a small apartment on 11th Street on South Beach.[19] His story of escape and survival was shared by many of his neighbors.

Again he started dabbling in real estate. He built a small apartment building, then another. He bought hotels and apartments. He built condominiums, some of the units bought by veterans who had trained in Miami Beach and fallen in love with the place. He became a U.S. citizen and shortened the family name to Resnick. And he built another fortune.

Abe Resnick supervised his real estate business from a cluttered second-floor office over a hardware store on Alton Road, one street west of the historic district. He brought his older son, Jimmy, in as a partner in 1970. His younger son became a doctor. He built another beautiful house for Sarah. By 1980, he had built seventy condominiums and owned thirty-three other properties, including the New Yorker Hotel on Collins Avenue, one of the district's outstanding examples of Art Deco architecture. Its architect, Henry Hohauser, designed more than eighty buildings in South Beach during the building boom of the late 1930s and early 1940s. The New Yorker's oceanfront terrace was the setting for a festive cocktail party for delegates to the 1978 meeting of the Florida Trust for Historic Preservation. It was the new organization's second statewide meeting, and its choice of Miami Beach as the conference site gave the league a sense of validation.

Inviting the Florida Trust to use the New Yorker did not, however, indicate Resnick's support for their ideas and goals. "There's nothing historic there," he said of the district.[20] Not a surprising observation from someone who grew up around buildings from the sixteenth century.

The city's building department was in full agreement that, National Register aside, there was no special reason why deteriorating buildings should be preserved. In January 1980, the Waldorf Towers Hotel on Ocean Drive underwent its mandatory forty-year inspection. The lighthouse cupola on the corner failed, and the city engineer ordered it removed.[21] Two months later, the Wellington Hotel, built in 1925, was pronounced *in extremis*. The owner made plans to restore the deteriorating three-story Mediterranean-style building and received preliminary approval for a federal grant to subsidize the project. The city declared the hotel unsafe and threatened to tear it down unless the owners did.[22]

The Pantheon had survived in Rome since A.D. 128, people still could worship in the Hagia Sophia built in the sixth century and the Amida Byodoini temple built in Japan in the eleventh century, visitors could still explore Angor Wat built in the twelfth century or buy an apartment in the building where Galileo lived in Florence. But New York's magnificent Penn Station was razed after only fifty-six years. In Miami Beach, forty-five-year-old buildings routinely were judged to be in danger of imminent collapse and ordered by the city to be demolished. It was a judgment that had some merit.

During the 1920s when the supply chain of building materials was bogged down and the 1930s when cost control was paramount, builders took a few shortcuts. Waiting for a costly shipment of sand seemed ridiculous when there was an entire beach of it sitting right there in front of them. Rather than paying for fresh water piped in from the mainland, they could use the brackish water from the mangrove areas along the bay. Both the sand and water contained high amounts of salt. If the building was kept watertight with a good coat of paint and well-sealed roofs, doors, and windows, then there was no problem. But once moisture seeped inside the building, the damp salt interacted with the steel reinforcing bars and beams, and the concrete would begin to crumble. Even buildings that used clean sand and water suffered similar contamination from salt spray if they weren't maintained properly. It sentenced a building to extinction at a tender age in Miami Beach.

Which is why Abe Resnick didn't give a second thought to tearing down the unassuming El Chico nightclub near the convention center in 1980.

The league's ever-efficient grapevine spread the word when a bulldozer began heading for the vacant nightclub near the convention center on the northern edge of the district. They were able to halt the bulldozer for several hours while demanding that the city stop the demolition.[23]

In the small crowd that gathered was Paul Silverthorne, who had hitchhiked to Miami Beach after painting scenery and sets for the 1939 World's Fair. In those days there was so much work in Miami Beach for mural painters that they were busy day and night, even during nightclub performances. He came to the El Chico for a last time to see how the ten panels of Mexican scenes that he painted had survived over the years. The mural was covered with wallpaper that had fused to the surface in a fire. When he tried to pull the paper off for a last look at his work, the plaster crumbled in his hands.[24]

No reprieve came. The onlookers watched in agony as the round mahogany bar and striped banquettes and Silverthorne's murals were smashed to bits.

Resnick angered preservationists again a few months later when he demolished the Boulevard Hotel, which was across the street from the northern boundary of the new National Register district. It was a stately Mediterranean Revival building surrounding a courtyard, with shops filling a portion of one side of the triangular shaped lot. The wrecking ball tore through the rooms where PFC Boyles checked in on that November day in 1942. It ripped off the rooftop promenade where guests could view the skylines of Miami Beach and Miami. Chunks of concrete crashed to the ground from the airy dining room. A dump truck drove through the middle of the building. At the end of the day, the American flag still flew on the flagpole beside the debris.[25]

Preservationists called the demolition an act of defiance and charged Abe Resnick with committing architectural violence. The Miami Design Preservation League and the preservation movement on Miami Beach needed a villain, and Resnick filled the part. The Resnicks didn't understand the commotion. The building wasn't Art Deco. It wasn't in the historic district. It was falling apart and expensive to maintain. They only bought it to build something new on the lot.[26]

Resnick's viewpoint was shared by developers along coastal Florida. It was time to tear down the old, small buildings and replace them with bigger, newer, fancier ones. High-rise condominiums were sprouting up along the Atlantic coastline as fast as speculators could buy them. Prodevelopment candidates were being elected to city commissions throughout Dade and Broward counties by overburdened taxpayers mesmerized by the new tax dollars produced by increasing permitted heights and densities. Spectacular views of the ocean that were appreciated by Native American tribes, by early pioneers, by Civil War soldiers, by the barefoot mailman who walked the East Coast trail in the late 1800s, and by the tourists who arrived on Henry Flagler's railroad became hidden behind a wall of concrete with only fleeting glimpses of blue water flashing between buildings like a strobe light as motorists drove along A1A.

Even the Dade County School Board was threatening demolition of historic buildings on South Beach by 1980. Bordering Espanola Way was the campus of the old Miami Beach Senior High. A new high school was built in 1960, and a long line of students paraded up Washington Avenue carrying the textbooks to the new building. The old school became Ida M. Fisher Middle School, named after Carl Fisher's mother. To its east was Leroy Fienberg Elementary, a low-slung Mission style building constructed in 1920 as Central Beach Elementary before the geographic middle of the Beach moved north with the city's growth. The aging of the South Beach population left both schools underutilized and the school board was seeking new uses for the buildings. First, they turned the old high school into an adult education center. Then they proposed tearing down the 1920 elementary school and moving its students to other Beach schools.

That's when Nancy Liebman and her fellow PTA veterans mobilized their forces.

The area had changed a lot since Liebman moved to Dade County in 1959. Her husband, a newly minted physician, brought her there from New Jersey with the promise that they would stay only one year while he did an internship at Jackson Memorial Hospital in Miami. Nine years later they were still in Florida, and they moved to Miami Beach. They wanted to live in a waterfront home in a neighborhood with parks, a library, where the kids could walk to school. They bought a home on a canal in Middle Beach, a convenient drive to the office for the doctor. Nancy Liebman, a former teacher, became active in the community and her children's schools, where she eventually became president of the PTA.[27] Liebman's youngest child was scheduled to be bused to the mainland in the reorganization. Liebman was going to do everything she could to prevent that from happening.

So was Matti Bower. Matti Herrera Bower came to Miami from Cuba in the 1950s. She and her husband had settled into the house at the end of Espanola Way where his family had lived since 1933. Her daughter was in second grade two blocks from her house, but she would be moved to an elementary school in North Beach if the school board proceeded as planned.[28] Bower also joined the fight.

Liebman and Bower and their PTA coalition combined their knowledge and resources with the Miami Design Preservation League to oppose both the redistricting and the demolition of the older school. When they all showed up at the school board meeting, the reaction was incredulous. The board expected parents to object to the closing, but board members were unprepared for the attack from a second front based on the intrinsic value of the buildings. The two-pronged argument worked. Not only was the PTA/preservationist alliance able to save both buildings, but it also persuaded the school board to keep all alterations to the buildings architecturally compatible. They also convinced the city to close a side street that separated the two schools, which effectively blended them into one campus along Espanola Way. The joint effort also gave the league a new crop of seasoned volunteers.

More than six hundred buildings in Miami Beach were quickly reaching the age when structural inspection would be required. All the early 1930s Art Deco buildings had hit the magic number. Within a few years, 40 percent of the city's buildings would need to be inspected. Many of them would be found wanting. Despite the endorsement of the National Register listing, convincing people such as Abe Resnick that the buildings were valuable and that money should be spent to restore them was proving to be a very tough sell.

The contest between Resnick and the league was about to take an even more dramatic turn.

Leonard Horowitz liked to sit in Lummus Park early in the morning and watch the pink-orange light of the dawn sun play against the hotels on Ocean Drive. He would stare at them until he could pick out every detail and shadow from underneath the thick coats of paint.

Horowitz had a reading disability, but he learned early that he could express himself eloquently with art. His father was a practical man. He wanted Horowitz to join him in the car business. Horowitz hated the car business. Every time he visited his father at work, all he thought was, "God, if only I could redo the showroom!"[29]

Irving Horowitz already had his hopes for a family automobile dynasty dashed when his older son announced he was gay and showed up at the car dealership dressed like a woman. He was counting on Leonard to carry on the family name. At his father's insistence, young Leonard Horowitz gave college a try, majoring in business. He left after a couple of years to attend the New York Institute of Technology to study design. In 1975 he moved to Miami Beach, where his mother lived, opened a furniture showroom in the design district, and began to pursue his hobby of painting.[30]

He became a familiar figure on his bicycle, sharing his disarming smile with everyone he passed in the neighborhood. He began looking more closely at the buildings. The little hotels, apartment buildings, and stores historically were white with only touches of jade green, ochre, or coral. That wouldn't create the excitement the buildings needed to fulfill their destiny as part of an architectural district and tourist destination. Horowitz visualized streets of pastel hues, echoing the primary color from one building in the trim of the next, using paint to accentuate their embellishments and draw the eye to their subtle details. He created a palette of colors from what he saw around him: golden sand, shell pink, seafoam green, Caribbean blue, sunrise orange. South Beach property owners couldn't imagine paying someone to choose paint colors. Their idea of developing a paint scheme was deciding which color to use as trim for beige.

Unexpected color combinations were familiar in Miami Beach. A man wearing lime green pants, a yellow polo shirt, a burgundy jacket, and white shoes fit in without notice. Nobel laureate and Miami Beach resident Isaac Bashevis Singer wrote, "They are so eager to appear young. Perhaps they try to convince themselves that here is the Fountain of Youth, that death will be confused by their clothes."[31] But when Horowitz painted the Carlyle Hotel on Ocean Drive buff, moss green, and mauve, the neighbors circulated a petition demanding it be re-painted.

Horowitz could hardly wait to get his paint brushes on some of the large Collins Avenue hotels. He wanted to try his palette on a building like Abe Resnick's New Yorker, a soaring hotel with rounded Streamline corners and strong Art Deco lines that cried out for special treatment. It wore its original colors, white with pale aqua trim on its detailing. It offered air-conditioned kitchenette apartments, a swimming pool, and a private beach, all in varying stages of decay.

Horowitz was a lousy businessman. He was always broke. His clothes often smelled of mineral spirits after he spent a day painting at his apart-ment. In contrast, Mitchell Wolfson Jr. was rich. Micky, as he was known to his friends, grew up on Miami Beach. He was from an authentic South Florida pioneer family. His grandfather was the man credited with per-suading Henry Flagler to extend his railroad from Miami to Key West. His father was the first Jewish mayor of Miami Beach. Mitchell Wolfson Sr. also owned Wometco Enterprises, a South Florida media conglomer-ate that included movie theaters and a television station. The junior Wolfson became friends with Michael Kinerk and Dennis Wilhelm and often was in the clique that finished evening league meetings and parties at their house, talking about Art Deco and possibilities and how excited they were to be part of it all.

Wolfson was quietly amassing an impressive collection of the detritus of society from the late nineteenth and first half of the twentieth century. He accumulated advertising, political propaganda, postcards, appli-ances, everyday objects that were executed with extraordinary design and reflected the life and times of those who used them. Much of his collec-tion was from the same period of design as the hotels, storefronts, and apartments of the Art Deco district. His interest in and knowledge of the era earned him a position on the league's board of directors. Wolfson looked at the New Yorker and saw something remarkable.

On a Wednesday morning in January 1981, Wolfson was sharing both his knowledge and his opinions with a reluctant audience in the parking lot of the New Yorker. His hands followed the curves and angles as he spoke of the building having a "special vocabulary." He gushed about its spirit and beauty, as if he were describing a gracefully aging movie star.[32]

The man to whom Wolfson was speaking was preparing to heave a ponderous wrecking ball into the object of Wolfson's adoration. His demolition company's banner fluttered from between the fifth and sixth floor windows. A hand-lettered sign in front of the hotel advertised "All Content [sic] for Sale." He saw warped molding, warped windows, a building that had stayed too long at the party.

A dozen picketers wearing jackets against an unusual winter chill were marching along the sidewalk in front of the hotel, carrying signs that shouted "Save Art Deco! Stop This Greed!" as workers hauled air conditioners, chairs, toilets, mattresses, and doors to a Dumpster sitting in a parking lot already littered with debris. Opponents of Deco were there, too, most of them Resnick employees and tenants, waving signs that said "Deco Schmeco," "Scrap Junk," and "Down With Deco."

The New Yorker had been unoccupied for only a week. The residents had been moved next door to the Sands Hotel, also owned by Abe Resnick. Resnick already had demolished another hotel to erect the 149-unit Georgian apartment tower on the lot to the north. It had been the site of the Georgian Hotel, where the Resnick family stayed on a vacation to Miami Beach during their years in Havana. When he was questioned about the New Yorker in 1979, he reassured league members that they should not be concerned. Although he hadn't yet decided what to do with the building, he did not plan to tear it down. Preservationists had their first warning that something was up at the end of December 1980 when the city's planning board voted to rezone both the New Yorker and the Sands to its south to allow both commercial and residential use on the property. Resnick was a member of the planning board, but did not vote.[33]

A week after the planning board vote, Resnick filed an application for a demolition permit for the New Yorker and made calls to have the utility companies turn off their services and to hire a demolition contractor. Preservation advocates exploded in outrage. Ivan Rodriguez felt helpless.

Now the county's director of historic preservation, he wondered if there was more he could have done to protect what he considered a major landmark, in spite of the contrarian position of the city commission. Horowitz threatened to throw himself in front of the bulldozer.[34]

Abe Resnick saw a rat-infested old building that was costing too much to maintain sitting on a prime oceanfront building lot where he could build a nice apartment building or hotel and shops. The Resnicks bought old hotels specifically for development purposes. He could see that the preservation movement was gaining speed. If he didn't tear it down, then it might be too late.

For Resnick, it was a matter of principle. He lost his home and his family in Lithuania to communism. He lost his home and his business in Havana to communism. Someone trying to tell him what he could do with his Miami Beach property sounded very much like the same thing to him.

Leveling a landmark building to make way for new construction was an old tradition on an island with a finite amount of usable land. A flurry of demolitions in 1950 included an apartment building from 1914 along with the 1921 mansion of early Beach resident William Taradesh. A store building at Fourteenth Street and Washington Avenue, built in 1914, was razed for a new retail building.[35] The Lummus Building, site of the city's founding, was demolished in 1941, with J. N. Lummus himself landing the first blow with a sledgehammer. Smith's Casino was torn down in 1964. The Roney Plaza, which many thought was the city's most beautiful hotel, was lost in 1968, replaced by a modern apartment building. Carl Fisher's own magnificent home on the ocean at Lincoln Road was taken down in 1961 to make room for a parking lot.[36] The building boom endangered many of the area's oldest buildings. They were worth more dead than alive. The demand for luxury condominiums with water views doomed Miami's Brickell Avenue mansions and old oceanfront hotels alike.

One week after the application for the demolition permit, a bulldozer crawled over the seawall, smashing the poolside cabanas beside the terrace where the league hosted its 1978 cocktail party for the Florida Trust. Wrecking trucks and Dumpsters arrived. The green-and-white striped awning over the front steps fell to the pavement. The only thing that remained of the neon letters that spelled out the hotel's name on the concrete canopy was a one-foot high W and a matching R resting on a pile of rubble.

The protests were loud enough to get Resnick to agree to halt the demolition long enough to let the league salvage whatever pieces of the building they felt had architecturally historic value.

A few weeks later, there was a breakthrough. The city commissioners endorsed the planning board's recommendation and voted to rezone the property from residential to commercial. The decision guaranteed Resnick permission to add retail shops on the property. It seemed that Resnick had what he wanted. To the surprise and delight of the league, he announced he would try to save at least the facade of the New Yorker and join it to the neighboring Sands and Georgian to create a complex of shops, condos, and hotel rooms. Resnick promised something spectacular that would set a new direction for Miami Beach. Barbara Capitman was thrilled. "This is the first time in recent history that a demolition has been stopped and the whole process reversed. This is really going to be the turning point of the city."[37] The victory was hailed by the National Trust for Historic Preservation in its April newsletter. The architecture firm of league cochairman Andres Fabregas was selected to come up with a design that would incorporate the New Yorker and the Sands in a restoration and new construction project. They came up with a bold concept that blended the hotels with two new towers, one of them fifty stories high.

Guests at the Sands Hotel were startled when the windows began rattling on the morning of April 24. Norman and Barbara Rosenfeld saw huge chunks of concrete plummeting past their fourth floor bathroom window. They grabbed their six-month-old daughter and raced outside. Next door, the Juelle Brothers Demolition Company was swinging an enormous ball at the upper floors of the neighboring New Yorker, smashing eyebrows and windows, punching holes in the stuccoed walls.[38] The chief of the demolition crew wasn't taking any chances this time. "I'm going to make enough damage so they can't stop me tomorrow."[39]

Diane Camber grabbed the phone to alert other members to join for a final protest. They raced to Collins Avenue. Capitman's voice quivered even more than usual. "All my worst fears have been confirmed. It's barbaric. You simply don't have a treasure and treat it like this." The

Resnicks' spokesman said only that the Fabregas plan was economically unfeasible.[40] By the end of the day, the New Yorker Hotel, by anyone's definition, was history.

The city commission was unresponsive to pleas to impose a moratorium on demolitions while guidelines were developed for the district. The city had no choice, though, in adopting a historic preservation ordinance. Ivan Rodriguez and his team had completed the three-year countywide survey, identifying almost six thousand buildings of historic significance. In July 1981, the Metro-Dade County Commission enacted a sweeping countywide historic preservation ordinance. It set up a powerful county board that would be able to designate individual historic landmarks and historic districts, regulate alterations to designated properties, and delay or prevent demolition of historic buildings. It gave the county's municipalities one year to adopt their own preservation ordinances or fall under the county's strict regulations.[41]

Miami Beach had no intention of letting the county meddle in its land-use decisions. The stringent requirements of the county ordinance were anathema to prodevelopment Miami Beach. The county law was the preservationists' best hope to ram through the kind of protection needed to protect the buildings in the fledgling district.

The nation's first foray into historic preservation was the Antiquities Act of 1906, which authorized the president to set aside historic landmarks and structures located on lands controlled by the federal government. It was followed by the Historic Sites Act of 1935, which established a national policy to preserve historic sites and buildings for public use and directed the secretary of interior to conduct various programs with respect to historic preservation. The big gun was the National Historic Preservation Act of 1966, which authorized the federal government to "accelerate its historic preservation programs and activities, and to give maximum encouragement to agencies and individuals undertaking preservation by private means, and to assist state and local government and the National Trust for Historic Preservation in the United States to expand and accelerate their historic preservation programs and activities."[42]

Local preservation law was born in Charleston, South Carolina, when the Standard Oil Company announced plans in 1929 to build a gas station at the corner of Chalmers and Meeting streets. It was a very pretty gas station with columns and old brick from a demolished mansion and balusters across the roof, but the idea of a gas station among Charleston's refined historic homes was not acceptable to the Saint Cecelia set. Susan Pringle Frost founded the Preservation Society of Charleston to fight its construction, unsuccessfully, but the struggle resulted in the city adopting the first preservation ordinance in the nation in 1931. When Standard Oil discarded the building many years later, it was acquired by the Historic Charleston Foundation for use as an information center. The irony was not lost on the preservationists.[43]

The city of Coral Gables already had a historic preservation ordinance that was more restrictive than Metro-Dade County's regulations. A handful of inner-ring suburbs enacted their own laws based on longstanding policies of reinforcing their independence from the county at every opportunity. Many of the county's municipalities, including all other beachfront communities, opted to let the county's regulations prevail because they had few, if any, historic buildings.

In an attempt to work out a compromise between preservationists and developers and to satisfy the county, the mayor appointed a committee to help in drafting the Miami Beach ordinance. Its membership represented both extremes with few in the center. Capitman was named to the panel. Also on the panel were Abe Resnick's business partner and a hotel owner who thought most Art Deco buildings should be torn down.[44]

Capitman called a press conference and accused the city commission of being "in collusion" with developers who opposed the district. The mayor was incensed. "This woman is doing more harm for her cause instead of working for a solution. I'm not going to succumb to her blackmail press-conference demands. Her tactics are deplorable."[45]

Capitman didn't see herself as being difficult. She saw herself as being right.

She certainly was not the first opinionated female in the area. Marjorie Stoneman Douglas, who single-handedly started the movement to save the Everglades with her *River of Grass*, said in 1947, "In [Miami], we have the sorriest, most spineless, narrow-minded, nearsighted, pusillanimous lot of so-called civic-minded people on earth."[46] Stoneman Douglas was never one to mince words, and neither was Capitman.

The big sticking point in the proposed ordinance gave property owners the power to veto historic designation. Objections to such restrictions were hardly new. When Boston first considered designating Beacon Hill a historic district in the 1950s, one-third of the property owners objected. Following the designation, property values went up 2,000 percent in the next twenty years.[47]

Miami Beach's ordinance would be the only actual protection of buildings within the National Register district, which came with no legal regulations, although the new Economic Recovery Tax Act promised hefty tax credits for remodeling older structures. After spending the summer of 1982 in hearings, meetings, and rewriting, the city commission agreed on an ordinance in the final week they could act before the county ordinance took over. A leading preservation lawyer in Washington, D.C., said it probably was the weakest of the nation's nine hundred existing preservation ordinances. A state historic preservation officer predicted it would not pass federal certification. To everyone's surprise, and partly as a result of the overwhelming workload in the state preservation office because of so many new municipal programs around the state, the law received federal approval.

The first requirement of the ordinance was for the city to appoint a historic preservation board made up of willing citizens who, it was presumed, were interested in historic preservation. As soon as the city commission unanimously selected fifteen of the eighty-five people who applied or were nominated for the advisory board, the protest flags were raised. Even one city commissioner agreed that the board was tilted against preservation. Three propreservation members were named, including Margaret Doyle. Barbara Capitman and Leonard Horowitz were not. Nancy Liebman was selected as an ex-officio member, to become a voting member within a few months. One member was the chairman of the Miami Beach Apartment Association, who called the idea of an Art Deco district "ridiculous."[48]

CHAPTER 6

Blinding Obsession

Dona Zemo brought one trunk with her when she arrived to spend three months working at the Cardozo. Andrew Capitman put her up at the Victor, the second hotel he purchased. After ninety days, she called her roommate, Jane, in Connecticut to say she was staying another three months. Jane decided to fly to South Beach to see what was going on. When Jane returned to Connecticut, she, too, decided that she wanted to give South Beach a try. She was going to stay three months.

Two years later, Zemo still was living in the Victor. Jane hadn't gone back to Connecticut, either. The Capitmans' hotels were hanging on, but money was tight. Zemo moved from running the café to the sales and marketing department. Instead of raises, she was given more and better rooms in the Victor.[1]

Andrew Capitman, his partner Mark Shantzis, and their investors had bought six hotels and an apartment building by 1982, including the Carlyle, Senator, Leslie, and Cavalier hotels on Ocean Drive. But after going from bank to bank and lender to lender, they weren't able to raise enough money to restore them.

For years lenders throughout the country had practiced redlining, a system that identified neighborhoods they considered bad risks because of demographic or social conditions. Redlining was outlawed by banking regulations, and banks claimed innocence, but applicants within the red lines on the maps routinely were rejected for loans, regardless of the value of the property or their ability to repay the loan. The Community Reinvestment Act of 1977 and the Home Mortgage Disclosure Act of 1975 attempted to pressure lenders to comply with the law by forcing banks to reveal their geographic lending practices before new branches and mergers were approved.[2] It didn't stop the practice. South Beach was seen as a bad risk, and local lenders did not want to put their depositors' money in a neighborhood with an unpredictable future.

Renovations on the little group of Ocean Drive hotels became do-it-yourself projects. Andrew Capitman called on Michael Kinerk and Dennis Wilhelm to help rehab the Victor under Margaret Doyle's expert guidance. Neither of them had any experience, but Kinerk had persistence and Wilhelm was resourceful. They were always up for a challenge. The Victor needed work, maybe getting rid of the smell of gas that lingered in the hallways. The lobby needed attention first. The patterned terrazzo floors were riddled with holes where area rugs were nailed down. The walls were shrouded in red flocked and silver mylar wallpaper. The stylized railings on the mezzanine and the dramatic chandeliers were defaced by brass spray paint.[3] The only thing in its original condition was the sweeping mural by Earl LaPan, a primitive Everglades scene popular with South Beach artists of the day.

The ceiling was given a coat of cocoa-pink and seafoam green. The marble wainscoting was polished, and the two fireplaces cleaned. The neon lighting in the cove ceiling of the dining room was repaired.[4] Wilhelm found someone who worked with spun aluminum to restore the chandeliers and wall sconces. A friend who was the maintenance engineer at Vizcaya showed them how to hire contractors, rent scaffolding, and schedule the work. Friends from the South Florida Theatre Organ Society pitched in to help.[5]

They were putting the finishing touches on the lobby the night before the 1980 Moon Over Miami Ball, the league's biggest annual social event. Wilhelm had the three monumental Deco chandeliers ready to hang. They cautiously hoisted the fixtures on to the scaffolding. That's when they discovered that the three pieces were not identical. There were subtle differences in the hanging hardware. Each of the three had to go back to the exact spot it originally occupied. They didn't finish until the next morning. They cleaned up the mess, grabbed a few hours sleep, changed into their tuxes, and joined the crowd partying under the restored chandeliers while Eartha Kitt entertained.[6]

Andrew Capitman had plans to turn the Victor into an entertainment hotel, maybe find someone to open a comedy club or cabaret. The Senator had a swimming pool, so it could be marketed to an active clientele. They had a lot of plans—what they didn't have was cash.

Finally Capitman was able to put together a limited partnership of investors to put $11 million into the operation.[7] They were excited at being able to completely shut down one or two hotels to do the restoration work instead of having to work around the guests. Their vision of rehabilitating the area for the elderly was changing, supplanted by the prospect of cafés and restaurants appealing to the young, the cosmopolitan, the wealthy—the same customers the city was hoping to lure to South Shore with its new development. One new investor dared to say aloud that gentrification was in the future of South Beach.

Gentrification was the elephant in the room that no one talked about. It was happening in cities across the country as people grew tired of the suburban commute and began reclaiming urban neighborhoods that their parents had abandoned a generation earlier. South Beach's population was, to a great extent, the same as always, although there was a growing Hispanic minority. City hall saw that as the problem. The same buildings, old and tired, were occupied by the same people who were there thirty and forty years ago. The tourism industry wanted fresh and young. South Beach's real estate was too valuable to languish. Every lot was only a few blocks from the ocean or the bay. Change was coming. The fixed-income elderly would be displaced, along with the hotel and bakery workers and the deliverymen and the Cuban families trying to cobble together a new life. The questions lingered: How long would it take? What would replace them?

The fully renovated Cardozo and Carlyle were ready to open their 145 rooms in mid-December 1982. At the Carlyle, guests would be greeted by a white-gloved concierge and escorted into the lobby where big band music set the mood.[8] Mark Shantzis and the Capitmans were counting on elegance, style, and service to overcome the shortcomings of small rooms, smaller bathrooms, and the lack of contemporary hotel amenities.

Before the opening, city officials and civic VIPs were invited on a tour. An elderly lady shuffled past, wearing a sleeveless sundress, sandals, and a floppy hat. She was carrying an umbrella to protect her against the sun and pulling a shopping cart. How could they get the Perrier and Möet crowd to come here? One prominent Miami Beach developer, who had built some of the Ocean Drive hotels, was even more skeptical: "The lots are too small, the area looks bad. I just don't see how they can operate and be economical. We threw them up overnight. Somebody's going to be burned in the end with this."[9]

The Carlyle's rooms were redone, the furniture was new, the walls were smooth and fresh with hand-colored framed prints in each room. There was an upscale restaurant in the lobby featuring seafood, steaks, salads, and an impressive wine list. Doyle installed long full-length green curtains to match the black and green Vitrolite bar. There was constant argument about the green: it was an inappropriate color for a bar, it wasn't a flattering color for the ladies, it wasn't a Deco color. The argument ended when renowned architect Michael Graves attended a luncheon at the Carlyle and gave them his endorsement.[10]

The walls of the Cardozo returned to their original hue of muted pink. The elevator doors were polished, and the telephone booth, its door perforated by a porthole window, was returned to service. Its tiny café offered light meals like broccoli and mushroom quiche, brie and fruit, and desserts including something called a Deco Delight, made of a chocolate fudge square, vanilla ice cream, and whipped cream. The name was taken from a dessert that Andrew Capitman remembered from summers in his youth at a yacht club in Martha's Vineyard.[11] The Cardozo became the place where South Beach regulars mixed with couples from the suburbs and residents of Middle Beach entertaining out-of-town guests, all feeling somehow virtuous about going to the Art Deco district for lunch or dessert after a movie. Sitting on the porch with the lights from ships twinkling in the distance, the moon rising over the ocean, someone softly playing a piano in the lobby—it was almost the glamorous Miami Beach of the league's public relations image.

The restored Art Deco hotels entered the scene after the worst summer in Miami area tourism in recent history. More than half of the county's hotel rooms remained empty. Hotels that had enjoyed 95 percent occupancy the previous year were down to 80 percent. Beach resort tax revenue had declined for the fourth year in a row. Seasonal connections of electric meters were down 50 percent. Unemployment was the highest in five years. Condominium construction had come to a screeching halt. The city's income from building fees was a half million dollars less than expected for 1982. The city laid off dozens of employees and demoted others.[12]

Many reasons were given for the downturn: The nation's economy was in a recession. Latin American tourism was down. The county's image still was suffering from the race riots, the Mariel boatlift, and the drug wars. Walt Disney World had opened Epcot, strengthening the "Mouse Curtain" across central Florida.

Three years earlier, experts had forecast that 1982 would be the crest of the construction boom. One marketing man predicted that the elderly Jewish residents would be priced out of Miami Beach and the city would be "only for the wealthy." Instead, the sites of planned luxury condominiums stood deserted, thirty-foot high steel pilings rusting in the salt air. "By Appointment Only" signs faded in the sun. The Collins Avenue property where Abe Resnick demolished the New Yorker remained unused. The sales trailer for his Le Boulevard project was closed, and weeds were growing around it. Not a single major new condominium project had started since the beginning of 1981.[13]

Developers who purchased Beach property in the hopes of demolishing an aging hotel and erecting a moneymaking condominium were stuck with paying mortgages, insurance, and taxes on boarded-up buildings. The fire department complained that owners weren't doing enough to secure their properties against the frequent fires started by vandals and vagrants. Money for security didn't fit into the owners' balance sheets.

Other hotel owners were taking a different approach to make ends meet. In the Grace Hotel on Espanola Way, an eighty-year-old man—painfully thin—was lying on his bed, an ulcer on his arm spoiling the air. He was found by five city and state officials led by the chairman of the Governor's Ombudsman Committee for Long-term Care.[14] Down the hall they found a ninety-one-year-old woman pleading to get out of her locked room. The unmistakable smell of a gas leak came from the kitchen. A bolt barred exit through an emergency door. Naked wires dangled from ceilings. The entire building reeked of smells that no amount of disinfectant or air freshener could conceal. There were portable toilets in three rooms. At the Blackstone hotel, the officials found frail residents who could neither bathe themselves nor eat and walk without assistance. A ninety-six-year-old man had not been out of his room for three months.[15]

These were the living conditions in some South Beach hotels that became unprofitable as seasonal rentals. They were the end of the line for sick elderly who had little money and no family to care for them. They had heart problems, Alzheimer's, crippling arthritis, and ailments that were the result of too many years of fourteen-hour workdays in poorly ventilated rooms fouled with the fumes of manufacturing. The hotel owners provided them with a room and meals in exchange for their Social Security and pension checks. They didn't have sunny sitting rooms or organized outings or physical therapy sessions, and there were no registered nurses on staff or medical facilities on site. These residents had nowhere else to go.

The crackdown netted twenty such hotels housing more than two thousand senior citizens.[16] Those who needed comprehensive care were moved to appropriate facilities. A few hotels were able to continue operating after the residents who needed full-time care were relocated. Others were closed by building inspectors for dozens of code violations. A few owners shut down and put the buildings up for sale. Some cleaned up their operations until the heat was off, then went back to business as usual. Each hotel that closed meant there were fewer places for South Beach's poor and ailing elderly to live.

Before the moratorium for the redevelopment project, the South Shore area had a lively community center, a busy fishing pier, a band shell where there were dances and concerts almost every night, and athletic courts. All were now closed. Years of neglect left the Rebecca Towers housing project for the elderly with $500,000 worth of needed repairs. The roof on the police station leaked. Streets were given only superficial maintenance. The city even stopped planting flowers in the parks. The city manager said it would be wasteful to spend money on an area slated for demolition.[17]

The city was still nursing along its plan for a rebirth of South Shore. The price soared to $1.2 billion. The latest version abandoned the Venetian resort idea and substituted a mini-city of corporate offices. Any enterprising, gutsy developer would get an incredible bargain. Property values on South Shore had increased by only 37 percent of the countywide average during the moratorium years. Identical condominiums built in 1960 now were worth twice as much on North Beach as South Beach.[18]

Another three-month extension was given to the moratorium in the summer of 1982. It had been nine years since the city first put a halt to building in the area. Two sets of master developers had come and gone, and the city was negotiating with a third. One resident challenged the city commission to "show the courage to stop this foolishness."[19]

A September 1982 city commission meeting was the final hour. Either the city and the developer would reach an agreement, or the project would die. That was fine with about five hundred angry residents who overflowed the commission chambers. They wanted to let the commission know exactly how they felt about what was happening to their neighborhood. An elderly woman pleaded with them in a trembling voice. She didn't understand how someone could come to this country, be a good American, and then have the government take away their home.[20]

They didn't have the power of groups like the tenants' unions who fought gentrification in New York through the Housing and Community Development Act of 1978.[21] The redevelopment agency openly admitted it was displacing the residents, so legal action was useless. As the number of permanent residents dwindled, their power at the voting booth also ebbed. They were living evidence of Douglas W. Rae's observation in *City: Urbanism and Its End*: "The transformation of place says little about the transformation of lives."[22] So far, Miami Beach had transformed the lives, but not the place.

A sparkling new development covering the southern end of the beach had become a blinding obsession that the commission was not willing to let go. So much land already had been assembled, and so many buildings demolished that some form of redevelopment was necessary. A master developer would have to guarantee relocation money for the residents who still were there. If it was done piecemeal by different developers, then the people who lived in old South Beach would have no compensation when they were forced to move and no help in paying for higher-priced apartments. After four-and-a-half hours of anger, argument, discussion, and some tears, the developers agreed to deliver a new, final contract by mid-September.

Before the next meeting, the mayor announced a major change that dumbfounded everyone. In a reported secret late-night meeting with the developers, a new plan was hatched to save as many existing buildings as possible. Gone were the canals, the squares, the plazas, and the wholesale demolition. Gone were the relocation funds. Developers would buy only the properties they wanted, as the market allowed, including all the land that the city had acquired.

Years of political infighting, governmental indecision, and high interest rates had taken their toll. The city, which now owned 54 percent of the land in the South Shore area, including streets and parks, finally put the project out of its misery and lifted the moratorium.[23] It was too late. Public policy had created a slum.

After nine years, South Shore was more downtrodden than ever. Most people who could afford to move had gone away, at least to north of Fifth Street. Retirement communities with recreation buildings, golf courses, and busy activity schedules were luring new retirees to Broward and Palm Beach counties. The elderly who used to spend their days chatting about Israel and baseball now talked about who was mugged, whose apartment was broken into, the murder down the street. Inflation was eroding their savings. They remembered when the area south of Fifth Street had beautiful streets with neatly kept apartments, parks, grocery stores, fruit stands, barbershops, and neighbors who said good morning and good evening and asked each other about their latest checkup at the doctor. Now the grocery store and fruit stands were deserted. They remembered when they walked in the parks at night and looked at the stars. Now the people on the street were prostitutes and dope dealers, and pink sodium vapor lights obscured the view of the night sky. The owners of the condominiums couldn't leave. No one would buy their apartments. Entrances of the remaining "nice" hotels were locked, security guards roamed the halls, and doors were chained.

Rosine Smith recovered physically from the beating she had endured at the hands of the Mariel refugee who had moved into her little Ocean Breeze Hotel, but she couldn't take any more. She posted a "No Rooms" sign on the front door, bought a mobile home in Central Florida, and vowed never to return to South Beach.[24]

Benjamin Levy still was spending his mornings at Friendship Corner No. 3 at Flamingo Park, but his legs were hurting. Soon he wouldn't be able to go to the park anymore. He would become one of those who stayed inside their small rooms.[25] Couples looked across the beach to the water's edge where they used to stroll at sunset. After a billion or so cubic feet of sand had been added, at a cost of $72 million, to widen the beach, the ocean now was too far away. Even the robust could not plow through that much heavy sand. As they walked down to the kosher markets on Washington Avenue, they watched over their shoulders for muggers. They knew the pickpockets would be waiting for them when they went to the bank to cash the $8 million worth of Social Security checks that arrived on South Beach each month. At the Ambassador Hotel, where families huddled trembling in the hallway during the 1926 hurricane, the seventy-eight- year-old caretaker was shot and killed trying to aid a woman tenant who was being harassed by her former boyfriend.[26]

Many of the elderly who remained in South Shore lived alone. They never married, never had children, or, like Sam Drucker, had lost their families to the Nazis. They were part of a larger tribe, though. They had spent a lifetime of doing without, of barely getting by, so their living conditions did not seem shocking to them. They remembered the days before Social Security and before pensions. They kept their savings safe, just in case. The man who searched through garbage cans for discarded bagels to feed the pigeons in the park remembered people in the camps who would give up their gold fillings to have something so delicious to eat. They were too proud to take food stamps, housing subsidies, or any other public assistance.

Outsiders did not see the deplorable conditions of people living in $100-a-month apartments with no bathroom or phone, and only a bare lightbulb hanging from the ceiling. Soup or beans, warmed on a hotplate, was called dinner. Clothes were stuffed in small cabinets or hung from hooks in the wall. Laundry was done in a stained plastic tub. A faded picture of a loved one was taped to the mirror or displayed in a plastic frame. A treasured piece of lace covered a dresser.

Bennie Mazor left Russia in 1919 and spent his life in New York City. He paid only $475 a year for his ten-by-seven foot room. Newspapers lined the floor, and tar paper was tacked over a hole in the ceiling. A broken chair rested upside down in a corner. Mazor had $30,000 in the bank and his monthly Social Security check, but he wasn't moving. He told a reporter, "The Tsar took everything from us, and then came the revolution. I never had money, never had a nice place to live. You understand? You understand? So I save my money, and I save my money. I want to live in a nice place before I die. You understand?"[27]

Mazor didn't go out to synagogue anymore. Neither did many of his neighbors. Temple Beth-Jacob, the only building on Miami Beach that had been individually listed on the National Register of Historic Places, was home to the oldest Jewish congregation on Miami Beach. Its eighty magnificent stained glass windows were beautiful evidence of its former days as a thriving congregation. Now it was in danger of losing its minyan.

Down the street from Mazor's building was the Nemo Hotel. It was a graceful Spanish-style hotel with an airy courtyard. The Nemo was built in 1921 as the first kosher hotel on Miami Beach. One of its first guests was Chicago Mayor Anton Cermak, who was shot to death in 1933 in an attempted assassination of President Franklin Roosevelt in Miami's Bayfront Park. The owner's daughter descended the Nemo's staircase in her wedding gown to be married in the courtyard in 1936.[28] In 1982, the trees in the courtyard were dead or dying. Men who spoke only Spanish sat at a plain table beside open windows and drank beer. The paint was cracking and the staircase was stained with blood from stabbings and shootings. An eight-by-ten room cost $50 a week. The Nemo produced more police calls each month than any other hotel in the city. Each call would bring six police cruisers to the scene. The code enforcement department cited it for hundreds of building violations. Its owner was vice chairman of the Minimum Housing Standards Board.[29]

Emanuel Reiss, age seventy, had his chair precisely aligned on the front porch of the Art Deco Leonard hotel on First Street. Years of minor adjustments gave him a perfect view of the wide beach and the ocean. His family had owned the Leonard since 1930. Back then, he could stand at the door and see Smith's Casino, a busy fishing pier, people having a wonderful time. Now he sat behind iron gates that were locked at night. Anywhere else on the East Coast, property with that view would fetch top dollar. Not on South Beach. Reiss hadn't lost hope, though. In fact, he was remarkably prescient. "This area has had its ups and it's had its downs. I think right now it's at the bottom, and it couldn't go much lower. But this area will bounce back. You come back here in ten years and you won't recognize it."[30]

Things weren't much better north of Fifth on Espanola Way, where Linda Polansky was fighting to make a go of the Clay Hotel. She fixed up the place—scraping seventeen layers of paint off the registration desk, painting the ninety rooms and sixteen apartments. One day Polansky was standing behind the front desk when two silhouettes appeared in the open door. They were carrying huge backpacks that would have toppled most of her guests. When they came closer, she realized they were young. It was the first time she had seen what she thought of as "normal" people in months, educated people with all their teeth and without tattoos.[31]

They told her they were hosteling, going around the world staying in spartan inns that were low cost and where they could live together, meet new traveling companions, and share stories of their travels. No hotels in the Southeast were licensed as part of the American Youth Hostels network. Polansky went to work and soon was marketing the Clay as a youth hostel. While Capitman was trying to draw the sophisticated and wealthy to Ocean Drive, she began attracting the young and adventurous to Espanola Way.

Young backpackers from around the world were drawn to the old hotel with its name in German lettering flanked by flamingos. They came from France, Luxembourg, South Africa, Oklahoma. A hand-lettered sign by the front desk displayed the rates, $8 a night ($9 in winter) for a room and bath. Each of the friendly young people behind the desk spoke at least three languages. Often they were hostelers themselves, working in exchange for lodging. Experienced hostelers knew they had to supply their own towels and bed linens. They also expected to share their room with up to three other people.[32] The kids didn't seem to mind the bunkbeds and mismatched furniture. They didn't seem bothered by the lack of air conditioning. They preferred to save their money for extra days on the road instead of luxury and enjoyed the chance to mingle with people of different backgrounds. They worked together to cook meals in the communal kitchen and organized parties in the lobby.

It wasn't the first time a youth hostel sparked interest in a lost neighborhood. The Association Home on Manhattan's Upper West Side turned an elegant 1881 red brick building, designed by Richard Morris Hunt, into a hostel that was generating a renaissance in the area. The same happened in Buffalo, New York, when a long-vacant clothing store was turned into a forty-bed hostel.[33]

There often was something dangerous happening at or near the Clay. Criminals mugged elderly women on Washington Avenue, ran down the few blocks to where Espanola Way was closed off, and escaped through the backyards of Matti Bower and her neighbors, where a police patrol car couldn't follow. Bower's house was broken into three times. She and her husband finally relented and put burglar bars over the windows.

The city decided that the Clay and a couple of other hotels were the cause of many problems, especially the Mariel refugees and near-homeless who still filled some of the rooms. They overlooked the fact that the city had placed the refugees there. City inspectors slapped Polansky with 344 code violations in 1981 and threatened to close down the hotel.[34] She fought back by going to court to allege that city commissioners made derogatory comments that encouraged city inspectors to target her hotel and two others. One had called the hotel a "haven for criminals." The city claimed legislative immunity from legal action, using a long-standing precedent that protected public officials for comments made during open debate. The case eventually made it to the U.S. Supreme Court. The high court sided with Polansky that the commission's negative comments unfairly spurred city inspectors to cite the hotel for violations. A lower court would rule later on the validity of the lawsuit.[35]

Polansky's tenacity was greater than that of some of her neighbors. Down the street from the Clay was the little restaurant that Osvaldo Bayona bought for $60,000 in 1981. Bayona was a Cuban exile who moved to Miami from New Jersey. He found himself catering to a clientele that carried weapons, and he made almost daily calls to the police to stop fights. He put the restaurant on the market at a loss, but he still wasn't getting any takers.[36]

The Jewish Community Center down the street also was nervous about the crime on the street, especially at night. The center had moved to Espanola Way from its old South Shore location. Life was too dangerous there, and the center had been told it was to be closed by redevelopment. The Espanola Way center started a "safe walk" program, which provided pairs of escorts to accompany members to bingo night and other activities.[37] They also had a bus that brought people from the old neighborhood. Almost 150 people regularly frequented the center. They listened to Israeli disco music, took exercise, folk dancing, and Spanish classes, and planned parties for every possible occasion including birthdays.

The residents of South Beach still ventured out after dark for the dances at the Tenth Street Auditorium. They dressed up in their best shoes, prettiest frocks, freshly pressed shirts and pants. They lined up at the door about 6:30, ready to pay the twenty-five cents admission charge, the same price they had paid for thirty years. Cushioned metal chairs were set up around the plain hall, much like a dance in a junior high school gym. A mirrored ball revolved over the dance floor. Bandleader Max Sutton started the evening with a lively number, just as he had for thirty years. The couples, many of them both women, wouldn't step onto the floor until Clyde sprinkled dance wax on the floor. The wax helped them glide more gracefully when they did the tango, the cha cha, the samba. Everyone knew that he used fifteen pounds of the powder each month. In fact, the can was empty, and he pitched a fist full of air at the floor. If he really used wax, then the polished terrazzo would be too slippery for the elderly dancers.[38]

After the dancers went home, the streets and the parks were taken over by the night people. Bag ladies bathed in the outdoor shower where sunbathers had washed off sunscreen and sand that afternoon. They searched the trash bins for food. Some of them never had money. Others had lived lives of affluence that ended when their husbands died and left them in debt. Most of the night people slept in alleys, doorways, and abandoned buildings. After midnight, a different crew took over the streets. Contestants going to the midnight drag queen contest at the Tijuana Cat shared the sidewalk with drug dealers and prostitutes, both male and female.[39]

The Mariel refugees and the elderly Jews had much in common. Both escaped a dictatorial homeland, came to the United States with not much more than the clothes on their backs, didn't speak the language, had to live in substandard housing and work at menial jobs as they tried to begin a new life in a culture that was totally foreign to them. They were terrified of each other. The climate on South Beach frightened even tough-talkers. A tattooed young Puerto Rican who bragged that he was a leader in a New York City gang decided to leave after two weeks because South Beach was "too weird, too dangerous."[40]

There was one business in the redevelopment area that continued to flourish. Joe and Jennie Weiss's simple seafood restaurant had become famous as Joe's Stone Crab at the southern foot of Washington Avenue. Joe's didn't take reservations. Everyone—doctors, celebrities, political bigwigs—stood in line for a table. The owner of Joe's Stone Crab was Joe and Jenni's son-in-law, Irwin Sawitz, the chairman of the redevelopment agency. He denied that the moratorium had hurt the area and still believed the project would propel Miami Beach back into the number-one tourism destination. But Sawitz bought a bargain piece of property next door to his restaurant just in case.

With the moratorium lifted and the redevelopment plan on life support, none of them knew what to expect next.

CHAPTER 7

Pastel Revolution

Conditions in Miami Beach were so bad by 1983 that the city's most powerful political consultant—the man who usually knew what the city commission would do before the vote was taken because he often told them how to vote, the man who was responsible for having elected most of the Miami Beach city commissioners since the early 1950s—said that he was moving his business to Miami because of the Beach's bad image.[1] Mayor Norman Ciment was so determined to rid his city of its "nursing home" image that he said board-and-care homes should be built with interior courtyards so the elderly residents wouldn't be visible to passing tourists.[2]

The Concord Cafeteria, where Benjamin Levy had breakfast every morning, was closing. People loved the cafeterias. They smelled of homemade borscht, sweet and sour cabbage, brisket, and beef stew. Customers knew there always would be rice pudding, fresh rolls, and an ample supply of horseradish at each table. Isaac Bashevis Singer was a familiar face at Beach cafeterias, even after winning the 1978 Nobel Prize for Literature. He particularly liked the rice pudding. The cafeterias reminded him of the Yiddish writers' clubs in Warsaw where the same menu was offered, the same conversations were heard.[3] The Concord was the eighth cafeteria to close on the Beach in fifteen years.

Ironically the city's economic depression was saving South Beach. Across the bay in downtown Miami, small hotels and stores and office buildings were being demolished because more money could be made from a parking lot than a small hotel or store. Not that many people wanted to park on South Beach, and for those who did there were plenty of available spaces on the streets and in the vast, empty parking lots.

One bright hope was a new organization, the Miami Beach Development Corporation. After the 1980 riots that tore apart Miami's black neighborhoods and the turmoil caused by the Mariel boatlift, the county government, and especially economic development director Ernie Martin, came under pressure to find an economic answer to the city's troubles. Martin went to Tallahassee and persuaded the legislature to allocate monies for eleven publicly funded community development districts in Dade County.

With its low-income status and substantial Hispanic population, South Beach was perfectly positioned for the program, especially since a main sponsor of the bill was a state senator from Miami Beach. The bill required that each district be governed by a neighborhood organization, with that board elected at an open meeting that any resident could attend. Denis Russ, who had helped the league with its early grants and had become a friend of the organization, worked with Barbara Capitman to put together the articles of incorporation and bylaws for the new Miami Beach Development Corporation.[4]

Business and civic leaders and residents were invited to a classroom at the Fienberg-Fisher School and were introduced to the concept of corrective capitalism. Andrew Capitman and Margaret Doyle were elected to the board. Barbara Capitman was not. She was a lightning rod, and the new group wanted to have a clean slate with the folks at city hall.

As its first executive director, the new development corporation chose Richard Hoberman, a league volunteer who had taken over responsibility for the tour guide program. Hoberman had grown up in his grandparents' house down the street from Diane Camber's parents' home. He graduated from the University of Miami, and then, like many of his Beach High classmates, he left to seek his fortune elsewhere. His search took him to New York, where he worked for the Department of Housing and Urban Development. Like mothers everywhere, though, Richard Hoberman's mom kept him current on what was happening in Miami Beach by sending him newspaper clippings on a regular basis, including stories about the Art Deco district. When he returned to the Beach in 1980, he became involved with the league as a tour guide. He had worked on preservation projects with HUD in the Hudson Valley, Brooklyn, and Newport. This new development concept was right up his alley. Lynn Bernstein, also moving from the league to the new organization, became the assistant director. Hoberman and Bernstein set up shop in an office on Lincoln Road and started to work.

The purpose of the development corporation was to act as a catalyst to spur business activity and investment on South Beach. They wanted to do something fast and visible to launch their enterprise. The prestigious national design firm of Venturi-Rauch had prepared a master plan for the renovation of the Washington Avenue mercantile corridor in 1978. It recommended facade improvements, new signage, landscaping, street furniture, and other, more subtle changes to make the street more hospitable to the elderly and Hispanic population. The development corporation came up with a much more limited project, applying makeup when cosmetic surgery was needed, but it was a start. Part of Lynn Bernstein's job became to persuade owners of retail stores to freshen up their buildings with a new coat of paint. The corporation would pay half the cost.

Leonard Horowitz's color palette of pastel tones like peach, cream, mauve, and aqua, which had been endorsed with the imprimatur of prominent Miami architect Charles Harrison Pawley, was embraced as the design standard for the project. It would be a tough sell: some owners were apathetic; others didn't want to listen to new ideas presented by some young lady from Philadelphia. Some didn't like the color scheme, and a lot of the absentee landlords simply didn't care. Bernstein scored her first success with the owner of sixteen storefronts in the 600 block of Washington. The first building to be painted was a Jewish bakery. Horowitz decorated it like a fancy birthday cake in shades of cotton candy pink, periwinkle blue, buttercream, and mint green. The design was so complex that it required a variance from Horowitz's own meticulously planned standards. A member of the planning board said it looked like a whorehouse.[5]

Bernstein's next task was to convince merchants to pay $25 to paint their awnings to match the new color scheme. That turned out to be as difficult as getting the buildings painted. A lot of them were barely staying in business, and $25 was a lot of money. They had done business the same way for decades and never worried about such things. Consumed six days a week trying to make a living, they didn't have time to fuss about awning colors or window displays. Once the first buildings were done, though, people began to get interested in the project. Within eighteen months the paint and awning project expanded to cover the commercial strip from Fifth Street to Lincoln Road, although Hoberman had moved on to a job with the county.

Horowitz stopped painting pictures. A six-foot canvas didn't seem adequate now that he had entire buildings to work on. Metal awnings and fake facades were ripped off, revealing Deco designs that had not been seen for years, and Horowitz was determined to highlight each one of them in a different color. The fastidious nature of the work drove the painting contractors nuts. Horowitz was there every day giving them detailed instructions for painting each bas relief form, each flute on each column.

Christo Javacheff had only one color in mind: pink. Specifically, pink polypropylene plastic, which he intended to float around eleven spoil islands in Biscayne Bay to create his $3-million *Surrounded Islands* artwork. Christo had gained international notoriety outside the art world with his *Valley Curtain* project in Colorado in 1972 and *Running Fence* in California in 1976.

Christo went from meeting to meeting with local, state, and federal agencies, collecting a mountain of permits and approvals. The project required the help of hundreds of people, including attorneys, a marine biologist, an ornithologist, a mammal expert, a marine engineer, consulting engineers, and contractors. It took six months for helpers to sew 6.5 million square feet of the woven polypropylene fabric into seventy-nine precisely engineered shapes to follow the contours of the eleven islands. Workers huddled in a former blimp hangar in Hialeah to fold the sections to ease the installation. Crews collected debris from the islands, carting away an estimated forty tons of junk—tires, refrigerators, mattresses, a castaway boat, and, yes, even a kitchen sink. More than six hundred specially made anchors were tapped into the limestone of the bay floor, and earth anchors were secured on the islands to hold the inland edge of the fabric.[6]

Andrew Capitman's Art Deco hotels were Christo's headquarters. The mellow atmosphere of the neighborhood was perfect for the artists. Christo and his wife, Jeanne-Claude, rented Dona Zemo's penthouse apartment at the Victor for the duration. The street was alive with the young, the artsy, the hip. During the final week of the preparations, more than four hundred workers, art critics, journalists, and art dealers descended on Ocean Drive for the event.

The troops were up early on the morning of May 4, 1983. A fleet of ten motorboats and an eighty-five-foot yacht shoved off from Pelican Harbor Island at 4:00 a.m. The outer edges of the floating fabric were attached to pink octagonal booms and ready to be unrolled for the "blossoming."[7] After three days of backbreaking work, eleven giant pink lily pads floated on Biscayne Bay. They could be seen from the bridges, from bayfront parks, from boats, from high-rise condominiums, and, best of all, from the air. Miami Beach sorely needed this bright diversion. Fourteen days later, the fabric was removed, without noticeable environmental impact. The workers and art critics and art dealers packed their bags, Zemo got her apartment back, and Ocean Drive returned to normal.

Normal was beginning to change, though. Guests at Capitman's hotels often were treated to late-night impromptu performances by the entertainers from the showrooms at the Fontainebleau who came to relax and clown around for their friends. Suburbanites, lounging on the porches in the evening and on Sunday mornings, reveled in the serene tropical urban atmosphere that reminded them of that carefree trip to the Riviera before they had children and mortgages. Dona Zemo seduced the companies of touring Broadway shows to house their casts in the hotels. The night that the press agent for *Sugar Babies* came to inspect The Carlyle Hotel, she filled the lobby with attractive, energetic young people. The show rented thirty-seven rooms. Andrew Capitman used the money to pay the maids and the handyman.[8]

Zemo made calls on the offices of cargo ships and small cruise lines. One evening a bus pulled up in front of the Carlyle and unloaded a complete ship's crew. They were housed on South Beach while their freighter went into dry dock for repairs. The captains and officers were housed in one hotel, chefs and managers in another, and seamen in still others. A new restaurant in the Carlyle's lobby was doing brisk business.

The Capitmans' limited success, however, was not changing any minds at city hall. The county was losing patience with the city's obstinate attitude toward historic preservation. There had been no movement to give buildings in the district the protection of local regulation. The entire neighborhood was still open to demolition. The historic preservation board had no real authority. The hotel and commercial areas of South Beach looked nicer, but, for all the buzz, nothing had really changed. Behind the sherbet colors were the same elderly Jews and struggling Cubans, mom and pop stores and kosher markets. The residential areas, with their small apartment buildings, were not in imminent danger, but the oceanfront area remained fragile. City leaders had not seen evidence that would change their minds. Ernie Martin and Ivan Rodriguez took action. With their encouragement, the county commission sued the city of Miami Beach for failure to comply with the county's historic preservation ordinance.

It was an issue of economics rather than philosophy. The city elders simply did not think that historic preservation had any upside. Some of them had lived in Miami Beach long enough to know that South Beach was never a glamorous area. They knew that a handful of architects drew up plans for a handful of builders, who slapped together a hotel or apartment building in five or six months. The quality of construction was good because that's the way things were built in those days, but they surely didn't see it as great architecture. They couldn't imagine how the area could become a booming tourist destination based on nothing more than fancy paint jobs.

Barbara Capitman decided to take another approach. With the backing of the quickly formed Art Deco Democratic Club, she entered the 1983 race for city commission, running against prodevelopment commissioner Leonard Weinstein. She blamed Weinstein for everything—catering to special interests, creating slums, increasing crime, declining tourism, even for the loss of trees and birds.[9] She promised the voters of Miami Beach a return to "romance." League members were expected to provide enthusiastic support for her candidacy.

Capitman held a campaign party for 250 supporters at the Versailles Hotel. The lobby and dining room were dressed up in glittering pink. Her pink gown was done by Andrea Freedman, who designed for Bill Blass. Guests partied among giant pink masks, lush flower arrangements and exotic plants, a gala spread of delicacies, and big band music.[10] The Imperial Hotel became the "Imperial People's Cabaret and Capitman Campaign South Beach Headquarters." On Saturday nights she promised a free cabaret featuring political satire. Capitman speculated in her campaign literature that "as the election goes into high gear it is expected that Miami Beach entertainers will create witty, droll songs and skits as commentary."[11]

Her campaign was filled with her customary hyperbole. Included in one handout was one of her favorite stories, about how she and high school friend Judy Holliday helped Betty Comden and Adolph Green organize New York's famous Village Vanguard Cabaret in 1941. (The folks at the Vanguard remembered it starting in 1938, and Adolph recalled that it happened purely by accident when Judy wandered in one day to escape the rain.)[12]

It turned out to be an odd election, even by Miami Beach standards. Former mayor Murray Meyerson ran on a progambling platform, in spite of repeated voter rejection of the idea. Mayor Norman Ciment suggested putting roadblocks on the causeways to keep out refugees; then he withdrew from the race. Voters overwhelmingly approved a referendum making it almost impossible to build new low- and moderate-income elderly housing facilities, a ballot initiative that was openly opposed by all the commissioners they elected.

The majority of Beach voters still had not warmed up to the idea of preserving the Art Deco district. Barbara Capitman's quirky personality and her confrontations with the city and developers had earned her a reputation of being contrary. She was seen as a single-issue candidate whose only interest was between Fifth Street and the Collins Canal. She spent $20,000 on her commission race and came in fifth in a field of five.

In a desperate effort to rekindle interest in the old South Shore redevelopment area, the newly elected mayor rechristened the area South Pointe, complete with the extraneous "e."

Miami Vice

Two good-looking guys in expensive clothes came driving up Ocean Drive in a Daytona Spyder with Leonard Horowitz's colorful hotels as the backdrop. It was a music video with a story line, accompanied by pulsating music heavy on the synthesizer, sun-drenched colors, beautiful people, quick camera cuts, palm trees, and sparkling blue water. It didn't look like anything that had been seen on network television before. It didn't look like the Miami that most people saw every day on their way to work. It certainly didn't look anything like the city the local cops saw while patrolling the streets of Dade County in their Crown Victorias. It was one of the "backdoor pilots," produced by studios each year, in a two-hour movie format to compete for a regular slot on the schedule.[13]

Miami Vice came to town with impressive credentials: an Emmy-award-winning writer and producer, clothing designed by Gianni Versace, music by Jan Hammer, Phil Collins, Glenn Frye, and Ted Nugent, and stars Don Johnson and Philip-Michael Thomas. On the screen, Miami became a city of navy blue nights, blinding white streets, and flamingo pink neon. It had all the fun and sex a city could offer two single guys who spent their work hours in the slimy cesspool of the drug world.

It was a far cry from the television shows that came from Miami Beach in years past. Steve Allen and Jack Paar brought *The Tonight Show* to visit the big hotel showrooms in the 1950s. Arthur Godfrey regularly broadcast his show from the Kenilworth and other hotels in the Bal Harbour area the same decade. Jackie Gleason moved into the Miami Beach Auditorium in 1964. The network morning shows were regular visitors, often setting up in Lummus Park, and the Super Bowl added the sports networks to the list of temporary resident broadcasters.

Miami Vice passed the final test and appeared on NBC's 1984 schedule for Friday nights at 10:00 p.m., opposite the soap opera *Falcon Crest* and playboy private eye *Matt Houston*.

The chamber of commerce, tourism officials, and civic leaders wrung their collective hands in dismay at the area's crime problems being glamorized on national television. They decried the show as a bullet in the heart of what was left of the Beach's tourism industry. Travel agents warned that people would stay away in droves. They predicted that their growing overseas tourism business would vanish when the show made it to Europe.[14] They complained that the style, the scenery, and the cinematography couldn't overcome violence, sex, and graphically displayed crime being splashed across the family rooms of America every week. Just as they ignored how historic preservation boosted tourism in Savannah and Key West, city officials turned a blind eye to the Hawaiian tourism boost that resulted from *Magnum, PI* or the benefits that *The Streets of San Francisco* afforded its city.

Local authorities pleaded with the producers to change the name of the show to something more benign. They protested a script that they thought depicted police brutality. They tried to get the writers and directors to downplay the violence. The area already was suffering from its international reputation as a crime-ridden pesthole. Miami had made headlines when its murder rate soared and the county coroner had to rent refrigerated trucks in which to store bodies because he ran out of room in the morgue. A quarter of the annual deaths were attributed to the area's exploding drug trade. The people who spent hundreds of thousands of dollars each year to promote Miami's film and television industry cringed every time an item appeared in a trade paper about local officials meddling in the production.

Miami Vice became a megahit, and the Art Deco district became a popular setting. Its lead characters, Crockett and Tubbs, basked in the sunrise and sunset colors, posed against the quirky architecture. The camera loved the angles and curves and ziggurats and textures. Friends teased Horowitz that he should get a screen credit for set design.

Tourists streamed to the South Beach to see the buildings, the parks, the streets where much of the show was filmed. They congregated wherever the crew was filming that day. They were drawn by the cameras, the lights, and the excitement, and strained to catch a glimpse of the stars. Tour bus guides weren't being asked about the area's murder rate; they were being asked where Don Johnson lived. They also were being asked about *Golden Girls* and *Empty Nest*, both of which were set in Miami but filmed in California.

Miami Vice poured millions of dollars into the neighborhood. Locations were rented, local actors got work, caterers were hired, hotel rooms booked, and equipment rented. *Miami Vice* even paid some owners to repaint their buildings in the Caribbean hues for which the show and the town were becoming famous. The lobby and mezzanine of the Victor were a favorite location. The downstairs restaurant of the Waldorf Towers was shot from different angles to be used and reused as a restaurant in one show, a nightclub in another. Empty hotel lobbies were transformed into stores one week and back to a hotel lobby the next month. Empty stores became offices and bars. Espanola Way stood in for a variety of anonymous South and Central American towns. Michael Kinerk and Dennis Wilhelm escorted a friend home from a black tie event to her South Beach apartment one night and arrived to find *Miami Vice* filming at her building. As they watched, a man came flying through a second floor window, flipped over the railing, landed on the ground, ran across the lawn, was "shot" and "died" on the table in the courtyard where the friends had eaten lunch the day before.[15]

The interest stirred up by the television show didn't come soon enough for Andrew Capitman's seven Art Deco hotels. Most of his money was gone, along with most of his hair. Facing increasing financial pressures, his limited partnership outvoted him to sell the hotels in October 1983, a decision that left him with a debt of $6,500 in unpaid resort taxes and a lot of hard feelings.[16] The buyer was Cavanaugh Communities Corporation, doing business as the Royale Group. Its president was Leonard Pelullo, around whom rumors of organized crime connections swirled. Andrew Capitman agreed to stay on as marketing director for six months with Dona Zemo as his assistant.

Royale said it would restore the Cardozo with indoor and outdoor cafés, a restaurant, health club, two floors of hotel rooms, one floor of suites. It was scheduled to open in late February 1984. It didn't. They closed all the hotels in the summer of 1984, after promising a $5.5 million renovation. They also promised a summer festival. It never happened.

Things were not going smoothly for the league, either. One of its most active members, Nancy Liebman, was becoming a visible presence in the local preservation movement. Already chair of the Miami Beach Historic Preservation Board, she had been appointed to a countywide association of local preservation boards. Her firm but reasonable disposition and ready smile were readily received by the people at city hall and in the board rooms. Doors were open to her that were closed to Barbara Capitman.

The contrast was obvious the moment the two women entered a room. Liebman exuded health and energy. Her easy-care hairstyle was always neat, and she dressed in the current year's fashions from Bloomingdale's or Nordstrom's. She was past her hamster-wrangling years and her youngest child was heading to college soon, so Liebman had more time to devote to the cause. With the patience to negotiate small successes, she had confidence that they would add up to the big victory in the end. The league was drifting into two camps, and the two women scarcely spoke to each other outside board meetings.

Liebman reached out to preservation groups beyond Miami Beach. She attended national and state conferences to learn from the experiences in other cities and apply their ideas to the district. She spent summers in the Berkshires or at Chautauqua Institution in New York, where she soaked up energy and ideas in the surroundings of vital, functioning historic villages. One weekend she attended a conference that included a session on the development potential of a historic district and heard how a town drew developers in from outside the region. It gave her an idea. As soon as she returned to Miami Beach, she went to see Maria Pellerin, the new executive director of the Miami Beach Development Corporation.

There was some retail business activity on Washington Avenue, and a few apartment buildings were beginning to be renovated around Flamingo Park, but Ocean Drive—the jewel of the district—was stagnant. The ten blocks of hotels and apartments north of Fifth Street—with Lummus Park, the beach, and the ocean as their front yard—were inert. All but one Royale property remained closed. Everyone agreed that all that spectacular oceanfront property should be a magnet for investors and developers. Yet nothing was happening.

Liebman enlisted the help of Dade Heritage Trust, the county's oldest and largest preservation association, to propose a conference to be sponsored by the development corporation to attract developers to Ocean Drive. Maria Pellerin agreed and plans were made for a three-day conference to be held in April 1985.[17] The conference planners agreed that if they couldn't get the current property owners to get on board with the program, perhaps the answer was to get new property owners. The league was not invited to be an cosponsor.

The planning committee met in the corporation's new donated offices in a starkly modern medical center. Lists were made of properties for sale or considered available. A program of topics began to take shape. Possible speakers were identified and contacted.

One tool the conference planners could use was a new sixty-two-page city report. Unlike past city policies, this report supported creating a local historic district from Fifth to Fifteenth Streets along Ocean Drive and Collins Avenue and preserving the historic buildings. In this major break from the previous city position, city planners saw potential for a dining, entertainment, and hotel district based on the Art Deco style. With South Shore languishing, Ocean Drive seemed like the best hope. When the report was released, the reaction of Ocean Drive property owners and hotel managers was decidedly guarded. Supporters were thrilled at the prospect of bringing nightlife to the street. Hoteliers who relied on elderly residents to pay the bills were concerned about the noise that would be generated by entertainment facilities. In one hotel, the average age of tenants was eighty. Late night jazz bands would conflict with early bedtimes.

Three thousand invitations went out to investors, real estate syndicators, bankers, and developers with track records in restoration from all over North America. They targeted people from out of town, entrepreneurs who could see the feasibility of what could happen in the district, not the downside of what had disappeared. Success depended on creative viewpoints that were not shackled by memories or limited to high-rise condominiums.

When it came time to schedule the activities and events, the conference planners ran into problems. The lack of facilities on South Beach, the very situation they were trying to address, made it difficult to find locations that would dazzle the potential investors. The only space they could find that was large enough to hold the conference was in the same modern Alton Road building as the corporation's office. The Royale Group offered the Carlyle Hotel as the conference headquarters. Aging residents temporarily were moved out of the Tides Hotel lobby to set up an opening reception. A cocktail party following the first day's sessions, billed as a "hardhat party," was held in the rubble of construction materials in the Cardozo. They rented a sightseeing boat for a waterway tour. Two unrestored hotels provided facilities for a reception and a poolside breakfast. The attendees saw an artfully edited video about the district that the development corporation had produced. They heard from city officials, tax attorneys, consulting engineers, marketing experts, and the few developers who were restoring properties in the district.[18] As organizers watched participants take lots of notes and collect all the handouts, committee members hoped their message was getting through.

They chose a few rehabilitated apartment and commercial buildings to visit on a bus tour and served refreshments in the courtyard of a renovated apartment house near Flamingo Park. They couldn't find a restaurant that could accommodate such a large group, so they set up long tables and brought in deli sandwiches for lunch in a tenantless storefront in the new Deco Plaza on Fifth Street.

The MacArthur Hotel had occupied its location on Fifth Street for fifty-four years. It was one of the first large buildings people saw when entering Miami Beach from the MacArthur Causeway. The old hotel was one block outside the National Register Art Deco district and one block inside the old moratorium area. Once part of Abe Resnick's inventory, it was dilapidated and condemned. A few years earlier, city inspectors gave the more than 120 residents less than four hours to vacate the building and declared it unfit for habitation with its corroding plumbing and dangerous wiring.[19]

Then Marty Ergas and Neil Berman took a giant leap of faith and poured $1.7 million into re-creating the MacArthur as Deco Plaza.[20] They hired Leonard Horowitz as the project designer. Horowitz painted it salmon, gray, peach, aqua, yellow, lavender, and blue, highlighting every detail in a different color. The upper floors were redone as rental apartments, with retail space on the ground floor.

Berman and Ergas gave their renters free memberships at a new nightclub around the corner. The Cinema theater, where the league staged its first big media event and one of its first demolition protests, had undergone a $5-million renovation in 1984 and reemerged as Club Z. Its Deco chandelier, staircase, and chrome balcony railings were restored; the abalone shell-clad bar was still intact. Now renamed Club 1235, the building was frequently a location for filming *Miami Vice* episodes.

South Beach was getting younger every day.

Collins Avenue, looking north from Eighth Street, during South Beach's first heyday. At right is the spire of the Tiffany Hotel. Romer Collection, Miami-Dade Public Library

The Lincoln Road shopping district attracted wealthy winter visitors in the 1930s. The street was closed and made into a pedestrian mall thirty years later. Romer Collection, Miami-Dade Public Library

Then. A senior citizens morning exercise group met in beachside Lummus Park in 1975. Historical Museum of Southern Florida/Miami News Collection

Now. Parking spaces on Ocean Drive are filled, and early morning activity has moved across the street to the sidewalk cafes.

A detailed model of the South Shore redevelopment project proposal, which was unveiled in 1976. Historical Museum of Southern Florida/Miami News Collection

The Art Deco style of the Cardozo Hotel lobby was overwhelmed by contemporary furnishings before it was restored in 1979. Historical Museum of Southern Florida/Miami News Collection

An important part of social life on South Beach in 1981 was the afternoon gathering of residents on the front porches of hotels like the Senator. Historical Museum of Southern Florida/Miami News Collection

Demolition of the New Yorker Hotel in 1981 gave a rallying symbol to the Art Deco preservation movement on South Beach. Historical Museum of Southern Florida/Miami News Collection

Developer Abe Resnick promised to be a voice for business interests and the growing Hispanic community during his 1984 campaign for Miami Beach City Commission. Historical Museum of Southern Florida/Miami News Collection

Gerry Sanchez challenged other investors and developers to join him in the South Beach renaissance when he spoke at the January 1986 Ocean Drive Developers' Conference. By permission of Gerry Sanchez

The first wave of modest hotel and apartment renovations returned lobbies to their original sleek style, shown here in the Waldorf Towers in 1987. By permission of Gerry Sanchez

A demolition crew member was one of the last people to see the vaulted ceilings and ornate windows of the Biscaya Hotel in 1987. Historical Museum of Southern Florida/ Miami News Collection

Senior citizens played bingo in the 1980s in a South Beach retirement hotel that today houses a multilevel nightclub. Historical Museum of Southern Florida/Miami News Collection

The long battle to save the Senator Hotel in 1988 took a toll on the health of an exhausted Barbara Capitman. Historical Museum of Southern Florida/ Miami News Collection

Nancy Liebman (*left*) used her visibility as a preservation activist to launch a successful 1992 city commission campaign. By permission of Nancy Liebman

Left: Then. The Cleve-lander Hotel got its first facelift in 1986, with only cosmetic improve-ments. Historical Mu-seum of Southern Florida/Miami News Collection

Below: Now. In 2003, the Victor was under-going its third renova-tion, which gutted the interior of the building.

The Clay Hotel was a flophouse in the 1970s and housed Mariel refugees in 1980. It became the area's first youth hostel and today operates as a hostel and full-service hotel.

Prices for overnight accommodations on South Beach were as low as $5 a night in 1976. Today, upscale hotels, like the Tides, charge up to $5,000 for a luxury suite, and serve breakfast on the front terrace.

The old buildings south of Fifth Street are being overshadowed by high-rises such as the 44-story Portofino Tower.

Widening the sidewalks on Ocean Drive in 1989 made space for today's oceanfront cafes to spill off the front porches.

The small apartment buildings on South Beach were an affordable housing choice in the 1980s. Many have been restored and converted to condominiums or expensive rentals today.

The homeless have been left out of the economic transformation of South Beach.

Muralist Raida captured some of the key figures of South Beach in the late 1980s. Shown in this portion (*approximately, left to right*) are Leonard Horowitz, Nancy Liebman, Niesen Kasdin, hotel owner Sandra Cook, Maria Pellerin, banker Abel Holtz, Commissioner Bruce Singer, attorney Alberto Sanchez, Les Beilinson, Gerry Sanchez, Mayor Alex Daoud, Commissioner Sidney Weisburd, Commissioner Ben Grenald, investor Gerry Marder, Richard Hoberman, Barbara Capitman, Commissioner Stanley Arkin, and Abe Resnick. Also in the original were Michael Kinerk, Dennis Wilhelm, Ernie Martin, Commissioner William Shockett, Planning Director Judd Kurlancheek, City Manager Rob Parkins, Economic Development Director Stuart Rogel, investor Gerry Vitale, Assistant City Manager Dick Foesman, Miami Beach Development Corporation chair Alan Rauzin, and Miami businessman Manuel "Bebe" Rebozo.

SOUTH BEACH

LAKE
PANCOAST

22nd STREET
COLLINS PARK
21st STREET
20th STREET
19TH STREET
18TH STREET

CONVENTION
CENTER

CITY
HALL

GLEASON
THEATER

PARK AVENUE
LIBERTY

COLLINS CANAL

CONVENTION CENTER DRIVE

WASHINGTON AVENUE

DREXEL AVENUE

PENNSYLVANIA AVENUE

EUCLID AVENUE

DADE BOULEVARD

VENETIAN CAUSEWAY

17th STREET

LINCOLN ROAD

16th STREET

15th STREET

ESPANOLA WAY

14th PLACE

14th STREET

13th STREET

12th STREET

11th STREET

10th STREET

9th STREET

8th STREET

7th STREET

6th STREET

5th STREET

4th STREET

3rd STREET

2nd STREET

1st STREET

COMMERCE

BISCAYNE STREET

BAY ROAD

WEST AVENUE

ALTON ROAD

LENOX AVENUE

MICHIGAN AVENUE

FLAMINGO PARK

JEFFERSON AVENUE

MERIDIAN AVENUE

WASHINGTON AVENUE

COLLINS AVENUE

OCEAN DRIVE

LUMMUS PARK

ART DECO DISTRICT

SOUTH POINTE

BISCAYNE BAY

ATLANTIC OCEAN

to Miami

MacARTHUR CAUSEWAY

ALTON ROAD

SOUTH POINTE PARK

GOVERNMENT CUT

HD 8
HD 5
HD 1
HD 2
HD 4
HD 6

Map of South Beach.

CHAPTER 8

Against Their Will

Scottish-born Nan Bayard was facing her worst nightmare. She was one of more than a hundred people who were being evicted from eleven Art Deco apartment buildings and hotels near the old city hall on Washington Avenue in May 1983. The buildings were not in the redevelopment area, crime-ridden, or crumbling from neglect. They were simply small, inexpensive apartment houses and hotels, home to mostly elderly residents, that were in the way of where the city wanted to put its new $18 million police station.[1]

Nan Bayard and her neighbors weren't the only ones being moved against their will.

The Biscayne Collins hotel once was a favorite of guests who patronized the Miami Beach Kennel Club on the bay. Ladies attired in fine dresses and gloves and men in suits and ties relaxed with a cocktail in the glass-enclosed clubhouse or enjoyed the sea air from the grandstand. Dog handlers decked out in Bahamian-style military uniforms paraded the greyhounds down the track. Other entertainments enticed patrons elsewhere over the years and the kennel club fell on hard times. The dog track, with its private three-hundred-foot beach, was torn down as part of assembling the land for the original South Shore project.

The change in the neighborhood took its toll on the Biscayne Collins, which had become favored by the Mariel criminals. It became so dangerous that police officers were ordered not to enter without backup. By May 1983, the criminals had left the hotel to families who were working as chambermaids and laundry workers and other minimum-pay jobs, many of them in the Beach's hotel industry.

The rooms were infested with bugs, there were gaping holes in the ceilings and walls, and windows were broken. The city cited the owner for hundreds of building violations. He was fined twice by the state for sanitation violations. In April, he was given an ultimatum to pay $7,000 in delinquent utility bills.[2] On Monday, May 16, the water was shut off. Tenants had received eviction notices a week earlier, and about thirty-five families had moved out. Those who stayed behind didn't have enough money for a deposit on another apartment. Their rent was paid through the end of June.[3] They couldn't afford to move.

The next day, however, the remaining residents were packing their belongings into a caravan of vehicles, including a borrowed bagel bakery truck. They could stay no longer. The owner blamed the hotel's demise on the city; he claimed that the moratorium and the forced housing of the Mariel refugees had created an impossible situation. The owner was a former member of the redevelopment agency.[4]

Two years later a quite different scene played out only a few hundred yards away from the Biscayne Collins. Charles Cheezem, one of the developers involved in the original South Shore project, still believed in it. He planned a nineteen-hundred-unit condominium and hotel on the old dog track site. His luxury South Pointe Tower would be walled off from the surrounding neighborhood by landscaped berms and protected by an attentive security crew.

He was getting the land for a bargain price, part of the legacy of the failed deals made with various developers over the years of the redevelopment agency's attempts to build its dream project. He held an option to purchase the twenty acres of bayfront land for $13 a square foot.[5] Brickell Avenue in Miami, which overlooked the same body of water from the west side, was selling for $185 a square foot. At twenty-eight stories, Cheezem's building would tower over the old South Beach neighborhood. It had been ten years since the redevelopment agency unveiled its comprehensive plan. Cheezem's would be the first new building constructed.

The groundbreaking was spectacular. Cheezem hired the producer who staged the opening ceremonies for the 1984 Olympics in Los Angeles. A spacecraft lit the sky with flashing lights, and a laser flashed from the ship onto a man-made mound where fireworks erupted in a ten-minute show. Invited guests dined on $100,000 worth of oysters and pâté.[6]

The expensive promises for South Pointe were of little interest to sixty-two-year-old Lillian Levin. Nine months after the groundbreaking for the Cheezem project, she cooked a chicken and sweet potato dinner in room 165 of the Bancroft Hotel on Collins Avenue at Fifteenth Street. She had lived there for sixteen years. The next day she would be moving out. All fifty elderly tenants of the Bancroft, including Lillian Levin, were being evicted. They were given six days' notice. The hotel operated, like many on the Beach, under a lease arrangement. The owners had not renewed the manager's lease when it expired in November 1985. They had received a $100,000 option to sell the building to a developer. The owner of the building was an eight-person partnership headed by Abe Resnick.[7]

Resnick and his partners blamed the manager for the problems, saying that he turned the place into a shambles and stopped paying his bills, including payments to the owners. In turn, the manager blamed the owners, claiming that he built the business up over five years and that when he took it over there were motorcycle gangs in the lobby. Lillian Levin didn't know who was responsible, but it didn't really matter. "I can't find the adjectives for how traumatic this has been. The people who have done this to us are cruel and heartless with ice in their blood."[8]

Resnick had been busy in the previous few months with other matters. The depressed economic conditions were making life difficult for developers. He decided that one way to improve the business climate was to get elected to the city commission. He ran on a platform to simplify zoning, streamline the code enforcement laws, and make Miami Beach more attractive to developers. As a former member of the Planning and Zoning Board and a developer, he knew where the problems were.

Resnick had an engaging smile and manner that could catch even his harshest critics off guard. He didn't present himself as a rich man. His office was identified only by a small sign on a door next to the Indian Hardware Store entrance. The door led up a worn wooden staircase to a warren of rooms covered in fake wood paneling hidden by photographs, drawings, and maps of his development projects. He had a nice office at home, but often worked out of a construction trailer on the site of his current project.

Although local elections in Florida were nonpartisan, it was no secret that Resnick was one of the rare Jewish Republicans in Dade County. He was conservative in all things, including money. He didn't carry credit cards. He preferred to pay cash. He didn't sacrifice, but he didn't like to show off.

Resnick was a wealthy developer with an abundance of friends in the Jewish community. He could campaign in the Hispanic neighborhoods in fluent Spanish. He promised them a voice at city hall. When the November 1985 election was over, the city commission included a new mayor, two lawyers, a university registrar, a builder, a druggist, and Abe Resnick.

Lincoln Road

Carl Fisher had a profound admiration for President Abraham Lincoln. Fisher spearheaded the building of the Lincoln Highway, the first transcontinental highway. His first hotel was the Lincoln Hotel on Washington Avenue. His headquarters occupied the Lincoln Building. He built Lincoln Road as Miami Beach's principal shopping district. Lincoln Road was where Fisher's wife built the Miami Beach Community Church, the city's first, founded in 1921 in a picturesque Spanish Colonial–style building. It was a vital part of South Beach life, and a gathering place for everything from a senior citizens' Bible study to Diane Camber's Brownie Scout troop.

In the 1940s and 1950s, Lincoln Road was considered, by many, to be the finest shopping street south of New York. The street was well furnished with respected stores such as Saks Fifth Avenue, Sara Weinstock, David Allen, Bonwit Teller, Peck & Peck, Adrian Thal Furs, Elizabeth Arden, Greenleaf & Crosby, FAO Schwartz. Shoppers could stop for a bite at the Russian Bear tearoom in the Sterling Building or relax at the sidewalk tables outside Nunnalley's restaurant on the south side of the street. There were General Motors, Packard, and Chrysler showrooms. A shopper could buy an antique watch, gourmet foods, and an ermine coat without the chauffeur having to move the Bentley to another five-cents-an-hour parking space. Ladies could rely on Gertrude Teich to give them a proper fit at her corset shop so they would look their best in the ravishing evening gowns from Zelma Butler's. Exotic Gardens florists had a wall covered with small vials containing cattleya orchids for their corsages.

Jeanette Joya sold expensive linens to wealthy customers at Moseley's while the store owner, Joseph Moseley, handled the special orders that came in from around the world. Joseph Moseley was elegant, debonair, and always impeccably dressed. The women adored him. Moseley's customers were the carriage trade, those who spent the season at their mansions or at the Flamingo or Roney Plaza, who wanted hand-embroidered napery for a dining table that sat twenty-six comfortably. Mrs. Joya or one of the other sales people would bring out samples for customers to see and touch and examine before placing their order for bed linens that were the exact color of a favorite flower or their granddaughter's eyes.

The street was described in *Life* magazine, February 24, 1941: "By day, when the serious selling is done, Lincoln Road looks like the kind of shopping section Hollywood might think up. Down the middle of the wide walks run big plots of grass and a row of palm trees. Rich ladies step sedately out of limousines and sporty ladies hop out of bright roadsters. The clothes worn are carefree and the dogs led along it are often offensively well-bred."

In the evenings, Lincoln Road was alive with men wearing summer-weight suits, escorting ladies in the latest millinery and evening gloves. There was a movie theater on every other block. Miami Beach was a popular choice for movie premieres. Jimmy Stewart and his wife, Gloria, were there in 1954 for the world premiere of *The Glenn Miller Story* at the Carib Theater, owned by the Wolfson family's Wometco Theaters. They buried a time capsule under Lincoln Road containing a screenplay from the film, a strand of pearls worn by June Allyson in the movie, and a menu from the Delano featuring a roast prime rib dinner for $3.00 and baked Alaska for two for $2.50.[9]

In the late 1950s, merchants wanted even more exclusivity and convinced the city to close the street, creating one of the first pedestrian-only malls in America. It was three thousand feet long and a hundred feet wide, the longest and widest outdoor shopping mall in the country at the time. The city hired resort architect Morris Lapidus, who had designed the Fontainebleau, to close the eight blocks to traffic and install fountains, sculptures, curved benches, and lots of tropical landscaping. It became a place to gather, to spend the afternoon, to people-watch.

Before long, though, the popularity of Lincoln Road began to fade. In the 1960s came the suburban shopping malls. Landlords were blamed for renting to schlock stores during the 1970s, when Latin American tourists started buying electronics and clothing in bulk. President Jimmy Carter was blamed for allowing the Mariel boatlift to get out of hand. Walt Disney World was blamed. City politicians were blamed for giving city support to a competing shopping area on 41st Street, for permitting retail events at the convention center, and for moving an annual art festival to Middle Beach.

By 1986, Lincoln Road Mall was dead. There were still rich enclaves in the city, but the average household income had dropped to half that of the rest of the county. More than one-fourth of the stores on Lincoln Road were vacant. The vacancy rate reached 40 percent on the western end of the street. It was one of the few areas of Dade County where property values actually were going down. Police surveillance cameras, tilted at odd angles, were useless for their intended purpose of monitoring the mall for the purse snatchings, store robberies, and assaults that terrorized the street. Thieves kicked in the doors of the Community Church one night and stole the audio equipment used to tape Sunday sermons for shut-ins. The organ was vandalized. Someone stole the solid brass bell that summoned parishioners to services. Even the Bibles vanished. A man, sitting in the once-beautiful Lincoln Theater watching a movie, thought it was such a wonderful theater and wondered why there were only three people there, and the other two were wearing raincoats on a sunny day. The entrance to the mental health center was under the old Cadillac logo. The regional Social Security office had moved into one of the storefronts. The few places doing business were discount shoe stores and electronics outlets, the "dead canary in the mine" for a prestigious shopping area. About the only people walking down the promenade were the elderly, some bag ladies, a few stray drunks, and one or two people who seemed to have neglected to take their medication. A *Miami Herald* reporter quipped that it looked like "a reenactment of the Great Depression, with some of the original cast."[10]

A few of the old timers still were there. In 1986, Jeanette Joya was nearing her fortieth year working at Moseley's, still selling expensive bed, bath, and table linens. Their customers came from the exclusive islands in the bay and flew in from Europe so they could order custom sizes and custom colors, even if they had to wait two years to get an embroidered table linen service. South American grandmothers would send their granddaughters to Mrs. Joya for their linen trousseaux. Moseley's still manufactured its own linens in the United States and Europe, fine one-thousand-thread-count sheets, bath towels with custom-designed monograms, crests, or insignias. The shop designed linens for Princess Grace of Monaco. After her second order, she granted Moseley's permission to add the design to their regular line.[11]

The other exception on Lincoln Road was Woolworth's Store 2042. It had been in the top five Woolworth's stores in square-foot profits for nine years straight. It stocked three and a half times more items than a regular Woolworth's. It was the only one with a separate grocery store and delicatessen, the only one with a U.S. Post Office. It was number one in the chain in sales of children's socks and Christmas decorations.[12] Not bad for a store in the middle of a depressed neighborhood of elderly Jews and refugees. Much of the block-long store's success was a result of the number of South Americans who visited the Miami area each summer. They spent thousands of dollars for bags of cut-rate watches and sunglasses, wallets and blankets, cameras and stereos, then resold them for three times their cost when they returned home. A majority of the Woolworth's employees were Cuban, including four Mariel refugees, so it was easy for them to communicate with the Spanish-speaking customers.[13]

Merchants had petitioned the city to reopen the street. It would have cost $3.5 million, five times what it cost to close the road in the first place. The voters turned it down. All efforts to attract a major retail developer had faded. The city manager floated the idea of putting a roof over the eastern three blocks to create an enclosed mall. Another proposal connected the road to the Miami Beach Convention Center with an elevated walkway. Someone else, who thought that the mall was too wide and symmetrical, proposed narrowing it at some points and making other visual variations. The latest suggestion was to change its name to Lincoln-Marti Boulevard to play to the Latin market.[14] It was hard to find any agreement among the landlords and merchants, the city officials and customers.

Micky Wolfson bought the Sterling Building on Lincoln Road and was restoring it to house stores, offices, and a private women's dining club where, following an obscure British tradition, all the waiters were called

Michael.[15] The building was Deco-ized years earlier, which obscured its original Mediterranean personality, but Wolfson was a loyal league member and chose to restore the building to its Moderne look. A canopy overhead shaded window shoppers, and dramatic lighting highlighted its curving facade and glass block horizontal wraparound windows that looked green by day, blue by night.

Wolfson and others saw the street's potential, but using historic preservation as a tool to revitalize the road wasn't a widely discussed option, in spite of positions by experts such as economic development and real estate consultant Donovan D. Rypkema, who said, "I have never visited a downtown with a successful record of economic revitalization where historic preservation wasn't a key element of the strategy."[16]

The artists had found Lincoln Road in March 1985. They were being priced out of Coconut Grove, the traditional Bohemian center of activity in the Miami area. Artists were veterans in appropriating forgotten areas. When a onetime New York industrial district was saved from extinction in the 1960s by two women who recognized the value of its cast iron architecture, it was artists who began illegally moving into its vacant lofts—and SoHo was born. After their new discovery came into vogue, the artists were priced out of SoHo and pioneered the rejuvenation of Manhattan's tangle of streets, warehouses, and tenements known as TriBeCa. It was the same in cities across the country.

Coral Gables potter Ellie Schneiderman persuaded the city commission to authorize a $62,000 grant to help cover start-up costs. Her argument was based on the theory of "revitalizing a slum through the arts."[17] She talked five landlords into leasing her space at $3.00 to $5.00 per square foot, cheap even by Lincoln Road standards. It was dirt cheap compared to ground floor rents of $20.00 and up on Forty-first Street. After seven months in planning, the mayor and about sixty artists gathered at 942 Lincoln Road, its facade wrapped in paper, and started painting. The mayor cut through the instant mural and declared the South Florida Arts Center open.[18]

Painters, photographers, sculptors, and performance artists began moving into scattered storefronts and sharing a cooperative gallery. They moved out of efficiency apartments and basements and borrowed garages. They didn't bring a lot of money with them, but the young people had a spirit of energy that the street had been missing for years. Other galleries followed, an interior design trade magazine moved its offices to Lincoln Road, and a few new businesses opened, including one that sold artists' supplies.

Other arts also were finding Lincoln Road. In 1980, film buff Samuel Kipnis, a Russian immigrant who made a fortune from his National Container Corporation, bought the Colony Theater, originally owned by Paramount Pictures, and donated it to the city. The city thought it would make a wonderful intimate performing arts center to complement its larger Theater for the Performing Arts on Washington Avenue. The Miami Beach Development Corporation had inherited the project and went to work trying to raise one million dollars to add to the funds the city had set aside for the project. After numerous redesigns, setbacks, and budget problems, work began in 1985 to rebuild the stage, add dressing rooms, install new air conditioning and electrical systems, improve the acoustics, and restore the original black and white tile facade.

When the Colony reopened in November 1986, guests walked across a carpet based on the design of one in Radio City Music Hall. They nibbled on hors d'oeuvres and drank champagne before sitting back to watch tap dancers and ballet dancers perform on the new sprung wood floor.

In 1986 Lincoln Road received another boost. The Miami City Ballet, a fledgling troupe of nineteen dancers, under the artistic direction of former New York City Ballet principal dancer Edward Villella, moved into the former Bonwit Teller store. The corner store had expansive windows that once held dreamy displays of the latest fashions for the well-dressed club ladies. Villella decided to keep the windows uncovered. Pedestrians would stop and gaze at the dancers working at the barre, pirouetting, and leaping across the floor. Sometimes the observers danced along or applauded when a number was finished. It took the dancers some getting used to.

The Yuppies Are Coming

The city of Miami had grown around a nineteenth-century trading post at the mouth of the Miami River on Biscayne Bay. It could grow only north, west, and south. The growth was staggering. Housing tracts and shopping plazas occupied land in 1986 that only twenty years earlier was tomato and strawberry fields. Golf course communities were perched on the edge of the Everglades, resulting in occasional reports of a displaced alligator taking its revenge on a wayward poodle. The miles from Homestead to north of West Palm Beach had coagulated into one solid megalopolis. Commuting times from the outlying areas were mind-numbing. People living in the new southern suburbs faced forty-five- to sixty-minute drives in bumper-to-bumper traffic to and from their downtown Miami offices.

Miami Beach was a quick fifteen-minute jaunt over three beautiful causeways crossing sparkling Biscayne Bay. Instead of cookie-cutter town homes and look-alike three-bed/two-bath houses in developments named after the trees or the ridges that were bulldozed to build them, the Beach had the charm of sun-washed apartments cooled by ocean breezes. It appealed to those who wanted proximity and individuality and were willing to accept inconveniences such as higher crime rates, green Dumpsters piled high with rubble parked at curbside, and a lack of chain stores.

Flamingo Park was South Beach's backyard. It was almost ten blocks square, dotted with baseball and soccer fields, handball and shuffleboard and tennis courts. For kids growing up in South Beach in the 1950s and 1960s, their summer cabana was the Flamingo Park swimming pool. Boys met girls over archery, arts and crafts, tennis, and other recreation department programs. It was space to stretch out in a neighborhood where apartments and hotels were squeezed together to take advantage of every inch of precious real estate.

The streets around Flamingo Park were lined with about twenty thousand rental units in two-, three-, and four-story buildings with compact courtyards cooled by schefflera trees and landscaped with hibiscus and crotons. Narrow sidewalks led to tiled galleries with decorative ironwork; grassy areas were bordered with stark white concrete edging. It was one of the few neighborhoods in Dade County where walking and bicycles were considered normal means of transportation.

The Flamingo Park area had not deteriorated as badly as some other parts of South Beach. Most apartment buildings had become year-round residences soon after World War II, and they didn't suffer the economic fallout from the downturn in tourism of the hotels or the forced deterioration of the South Shore moratorium. A few had been demolished to build low-rise condominiums, but most of the neighborhood was made up of delightful Art Deco and Mediterranean Revival buildings, all of similar size and scale, which gave the blocks a friendly, cohesive feeling. Shady streets were still neat and clean. There wasn't enough street traffic to have attracted the prostitutes and drug dealers.

The city manager announced a change of direction in the city's approach to its future image. Miami Beach was in fiscal jeopardy from the hazards of stagnant property values, the tarnished image left by the post-Mariel crime wave, the continuing perception of the Beach as a retirement haven, and a still-declining seasonal tourism industry. The resort taxes and building permit revenue that fueled the city for so many years were gone. Its property tax base couldn't support the city in the style to which it had become accustomed.

It was time to diversify. The city seized on the obvious. More and more small hotels were being converted into condominiums and rental apartments, and there was renovation activity in the quirky apartment buildings that were packed into the center of the Deco district. Young people were appearing on the streets of South Beach. Renovated Art Deco apartments could be marketed as the new "in" spot for the young and well-educated with rising incomes who would live there year-round. It was a radical change from the prodevelopment mentality of the past decade.

A few developers were ready.

Don Meginley was a forty-six-year-old native of Clearwater on Florida's west coast. He was from a hotel family. His interest in historic rehabilitation took him to Boston, where he cut his redevelopment teeth in the city's South End. Meginley, who learned about the Art Deco district through an ad in a national preservation magazine, was planning to spearhead a $6-million investment in a dozen or so apartment buildings on South Beach. Difficulty in getting loans from local banks downsized his plans, but he completed one eight-bedroom unit and marketed it to young professionals.[19] Meginley also was delighting in the relative ease of doing business in Miami Beach. In Boston, it took him five weeks and greasing some palms to get an appointment with anyone in city government. When he arrived on the Beach, the mayor called and invited him over for coffee.

Robert Holland was an experienced developer who turned run-down apartment buildings in Washington, D.C., neighborhoods—Georgetown, Capitol Hill, and DuPont Circle–into chic housing for young government types. He was attracted to Miami by stories about trendy Coconut Grove. One look told him its days of opportunity were past. However, after joining the afternoon crowd at the Carlyle Hotel for a cool drink, he decided that South Beach had possibilities.[20]

In two years, Robert Holland bought eight apartment houses in South Beach's Flamingo Park neighborhood at a value of $3.5 million. When Holland's first two buildings were finished, they filled quickly. The average age of the new residents was twenty-nine. "Old Miami Beach is getting younger every day" became the company's advertising slogan.[21]

Holland lured flight attendants, dental hygienists, and young executives with buildings that had citrus-colored exteriors, landscaped courtyards, high ceilings, and hardwood floors for rents of $425 to $550 a month.[22] They were small units—four hundred to six hundred square feet—with a living room, one or two bedrooms big enough for a bed and one dresser, a tiny kitchen, and a bathroom often with only a shower, no tub. But they were light and airy and comfortable, with retro charm that couldn't be found for any price in the new suburbs. Many new arrivals were Jewish or Hispanic, drawn by the familiar cultural spirit of the neighborhood. Some had grown up on the Beach and liked being able to stay close to home while being out on their own for the first time. Others found familiar comfort in the kosher markets and synagogues. Those with children were drawn by the availability of Jewish education at the many private schools in the city. Most of them liked being a short commute to work and a short walk to the beach. Few of them were interested in becoming activists in the preservation movement.

Merrie and Dick Thomas were displaced New Yorkers, driven out of Manhattan by the high cost of living. They had fallen under the spell of South Beach while on vacation. She was a manager at a new South Beach restaurant; he worked for a Miami advertising firm. They liked the urban feel of a neighborhood where they could rent a renovated one-bedroom apartment for a third of what they paid on Manhattan's Upper West Side.[23]

The pioneer developers did not have an easy time of it. Most older apartment buildings in the Art Deco district were built for seasonal tenants or for small working-class families. They weren't wired for hair dryers and cable television in every room. Extensive work was needed to create apartments that would attract the 1980s housing market. The developers also were having difficulty obtaining financing. Robert Holland's company was earning a respectable 10 percent cash return on its investment in the Twins, the Bayliss, the Dixon, and others. Still, his vice president had no success when she went to twelve local banks trying to find one institution willing to put $1.2 million into South Beach. She eventually gave up and obtained the money from lenders in Washington, D.C.[24]

Skeptics felt that the area wasn't ready to support demanding year-round residents. There were no shopping malls, movie theaters, or family restaurants. A few stores started stocking wine coolers alongside the prune juice and plantain chips, but most Beach merchants continued to cater to tourists, the growing Hispanic community, and the elderly, despite their dwindling numbers. There were plenty of souvenir shops, kosher delis, and Cuban markets, but there wasn't a fast food drive-thru window in sight.

A lot of the activity sounded suspiciously like gentrification. Some residential buildings in South Beach had a vacancy rate as high as 60 percent. There were places for the elderly Jews displaced by the renovators to live, but a move was disruptive and particularly difficult for an aging memory that had spent the last fifteen years with the dishes in a cabinet on the right side of the sink and found it distressing to adjust to them being on the left. Even the city manager conceded that the poor and elderly would be impacted by a change that would benefit the greater community. "If anyone will suffer, it will be low-income individuals who used to rent a one-bedroom apartment for $128 including utilities."[25]

The fire department had closed the Beachview Apartments, where Bennie Mazor lived in his ten-by-seven foot room with newspapers on the floor and tar paper on the ceiling. Faulty plumbing and wiring, improper ventilation, and illegally added rooms were sufficient reasons for the building to be declared unfit for human occupancy. It was the seventh building to be shut down in two months. Another 350 residents were displaced.[26] Bennie was not going to be able to find another room for $475 a year.

A second Ocean Drive Developers' Conference was scheduled as part of Art Deco Weekend in January 1986. On the opening day, developer Gerry Sanchez told the audience, "When I was here last year, I was so impressed with what was happening that I went out during lunch and started buying buildings. You'd better hurry before I buy the rest of them."[27]

Sanchez was exaggerating, but not by much. He had taken the long list of properties prepared for those attending the April 1985 conference and checked off four of them. He started with the Waldorf Towers at the corner of Ocean Drive and Ninth Street. It was in sad shape, only about 10 percent occupied. The tenants were elderly, and the rooms were pitiful. It was owned by two Chinese men whose office was in the Betsy Ross Hotel near Fifteenth Street. Sanchez bought both hotels. Then he bought the five-story Clevelander at Tenth Street.[28]

Gerry Sanchez had worked a remarkable change on Ocean Drive in the nine months since the first conference. The conference planning committee realized just how much had changed when they were organizing the second meeting. Instead of the registration and the opening reception being held at a retirement hotel, the party was at the sparkling freshly painted Leslie Hotel. Instead of having to serve box lunches in an empty store, a luncheon was held in a newly opened restaurant. On Saturday night, they could attend a cocktail party in a new lounge at the Clay Hotel on Espanola Way or go to a speakeasy at the Clevelander. The waterway tour was repeated, but this time it could end with a tour of the new arts center on Lincoln Road Mall and a reception at Micky Wolfson's restored Sterling Building. They did the bus tour again, but now they could visit more renovated apartments, commercial buildings, and hotels.[29] Instead of rows of aluminum lawn chairs on every porch there was now a smattering of umbrella-shaded café tables filled with young people laughing and spending money.

Robert Holland and Don Meginley were on the program to give insights from their success stories, as were Neil Berman of Deco Plaza on Fifth Street and Dona Zemo from the Royale Group, which finally had most of its hotels open. And Gerry Sanchez.

Sanchez was a fast-moving Cuban who emigrated in 1961, another refugee from Castro's regime. He came to Miami Beach and got a job as a dishwasher. The job didn't pay much, but he thought that at least the restaurant would feed him. It didn't. They put him to work peeling hard-boiled eggs. For every three eggs he peeled, he ate one. He ate so many eggs that he became sick and had to be taken to the hospital. That episode ended his restaurant career, and he never again wanted to see Miami Beach or hard-boiled eggs. He went to New York and studied banking, accounting, business administration, and law at City University of New York. Then he discovered real estate. New York's real estate market was in the doldrums in 1976, and Sanchez took advantage of the opportunity to buy some rundown buildings in upper Manhattan, Brooklyn, and Queens. He didn't like the work of the contractors he hired to fix them up, so he learned the art of historic restoration.[30]

He set up business in Brooklyn and did restoration work on the New York Public Library, Trinity Church, and the U.S. Embassy in Warsaw. He built his restoration company into an international operation with five hundred employees and offices in New York, New Jersey, and San Francisco. He had made plenty of money, so he and his wife decided to move to Miami, buy President Richard Nixon's winter White House on Key Biscayne, and enjoy the life of semiretirement at the age of forty-two.[31] To have a little something to do, he opened an office in Hialeah and did some restoration work around the county, including Lincoln Road's Colony Theater.

Linda Polansky hired Sanchez's firm to work on the exterior of the Clay Hotel. He used an expensive new system from Germany to gently remove the fading cream-colored paint. A reminder of the street's earlier days of anti-Semitism startled residents when the letters spelling out "Gentiles only" emerged from under the old paint.[32] The phrase was covered quickly with a coat of peach paint. Sanchez highlighted each architectural detail, put green and white awnings over the ground floor windows, installed new French windows and wrought-iron balconettes.

When he saw Ocean Drive, he smelled money. He started with the Waldorf Towers, designed by Chicago-born Albert Anis, whose work could be seen up and down Ocean Drive and Collins Avenue. Sanchez rebuilt its cylindrical lighthouse tower that the city had ordered demolished in the early 1980s and encircled it with blue neon at night. He cleaned up the Clevelander, also designed by Anis, getting rid of the tired green and brown vinyl couches in the lobby. Next was the Breakwater, where bare-chested workers attracted attention while climbing over scaffolding to clean off years of dirt and grime. He bought eight hotels, two parking lots, an entire block of Espanola Way—a total of $15 million' worth of real estate. He followed his rule of paying no more than $22 a square foot or $5,000 per room. He calculated that those prices were less than replacement value.[33] He bought so many buildings that when his Rolls Royce was seen parked in front of a building people thought he was buying the property. Sanchez wanted to buy every significant building in the district. He predicted that when the season of the pioneer was over, the price of buildings would be incredible.

Tony Goldman had come to Miami in 1983. He strolled into Coconut Grove and bought $2.3 million worth of real estate.[34] The Grove had lost the artistic spirit that made it unique. Like Sanchez, he attended an Ocean Drive Developers' Conference.

Goldman grew up wealthy on Manhattan's Upper East Side. His mother's interest in the arts was reflected in the Monets and Renoirs on the walls, paid for by his father's business of manufacturing women's coats.[35] Tony Goldman, though, decided his destiny wasn't in the garment trade. Instead, he went to work for an uncle's real estate company. He was good at spotting undervalued neighborhoods. When people were still afraid to visit Manhattan's Upper West Side, much less invest there, Goldman restored five of its brownstones. When the neighborhood gentrified and became coveted residential property, Goldman made a bundle. It was the same neighborhood that Merrie and Dick Thomas escaped for South Beach when the rents rose too high. Goldman saw the artists taking over industrial lofts in SoHo in the late 1970s. He bought a garbage truck garage, and converted it into Greene Street, a restaurant and nightclub. His timing was impeccable.[36]

On South Beach Tony Goldman bought three hotels in the Art Deco district, including the seven-story Park Central on Ocean Drive. He moved into its penthouse and began renovating its shabby hotel rooms.

There was a lot of work to be done, but without banks that were willing to finance renovations, progress was slow. The plumbing wouldn't work. A water leak caused a ceiling to cave in. Sometimes the newly arrived developers cut corners. Problems were concealed instead of repaired. Their renovation budgets were tight, and shortcuts were needed to stay in business. But Gerry Sanchez and Tony Goldman made people see South Beach's assets and overlook the ratty carpeting, musty smells, and old vinyl furniture in the lobbies. These were businessmen, not idealists. They didn't become successful by being reticent. Buildings began sprouting "Polonia" banners, indicating one of Sanchez's projects, or

"Another Goldman Property," showing Goldman was in business at that location. Supporters of the Art Deco district saw them as valiant knights riding to the rescue. Their critics thought they were modern-day Parolles.

The old property owners saw a diminishing elderly clientele and empty rooms. The Tides entered the 1986–87 winter season with only 65 percent of its rooms occupied. In 1986 you could find a small room in an unrenovated Ocean Drive residential hotel catering to the elderly for $7 a night or a room in one of the restored hotels for $95 a night. Lena Rottenberg, eighty years old, couldn't understand all the fuss. "It's silly that the young people have conniptions over these buildings and think they're historic. The 1930s was a very depressing time. But hell, I'll join in. I'm going to take my boa out of my trunk. I'm going to drink martinis on one of these porches."[37]

In 1984, only four developers were actively renovating buildings in South Beach. By 1986, thirty-two developers had spent $80 million to buy and rehabilitate old apartments, hotels, and stores.[38] One half of the fifty-two buildings on Ocean Drive had new owners. Some of them had been sold twice. The residential streets had seen 127 buildings change hands in eighteen months.[39]

Other hotels and apartments were jumping on the bandwagon. Beiges and browns were being replaced by coral, green, lavender, and blue. One owner went against the tide and opted to paint her building white with green trim. She was concerned that the tropical rainbow would confuse visitors. One blended into the next. Which, of course, is exactly what Leonard Horowitz had in mind when he designed the palette.

The old Warsaw Ballroom on Collins Avenue was converted into the trendy Club Ovo. You could dine at a Lincoln Road café where each table was designed by an artist and could be sold out from under your goat cheese and watercress sandwich. There was a gelato place and a sushi bar. Music clubs ranged from folk to rock, blues to jazz, piano bars to dance clubs.

City officials were becoming believers. The city's public relations man said, "In the past few years when I'd bring the out-of-town press in to see Miami Beach, they'd politely remind me that I was showing them the same places over and over again. The perception of Miami Beach as

God's waiting room is now behind us."[40] After years of glacial movement, it seemed that the district had exploded practically overnight.
There were people on the streets and in the stores, there were porchfront
cafés and restaurants and nightclubs. Moving vans and U-Haul trailers
were bringing people in, not taking them out. A New York photographer
had spent three weeks doing a series on the life of the elderly Jews of
South Beach in the mid-1970s. When he returned in the mid-1980s, he
found that a lot of what he photographed was gone, including the
people.[41]

Beyond the pretty new paint jobs, the glowing neon, and the busy
cafés there were dirty lobbies and cramped rooms, there was sporadic
service, crime, and a lack of shops that met the needs of residents. "Old
Miami Beach," a name that never caught on, was replaced with the familiar, more comfortable "South Beach," and, for most people, it incorporated everything from Government Cut to Dade Boulevard, including the
Art Deco district.

What caught the attention of the ruling circle, though, was that Gerry
Sanchez was selling buildings. Sanchez wasn't a hotel operator. He knew
the money was to be made buying, renovating, and selling buildings, but
he didn't want to be tagged as someone who "flipped" buildings—buying
them, fixing them up a little, and reselling quickly. He hired people to
help run the scattered properties he had accumulated.

One day he was standing on the porch of the Waldorf Towers when a
woman approached him. She said that she wanted to buy one of his hotels. Sanchez said, "Okay, you can buy this one." She said, "No, I want
that one," and pointed up the street to the Clevelander, with its "flying
saucer" patio roof. She gave him her credentials, which included owning
two hotels in Jamaica. He thought she would be good for Ocean Drive, so
he told her he would sell it to her if they could close the deal in ten days.
Setting a price was easy for Sanchez. He was superstitious and wanted to
make a profit that was based on his age. At the time he was forty-five. He
earned a $450,000 profit on the Clevelander only months after he
bought it.[42] He sold the Waldorf Towers to Don Meginley for three and a
half times what he paid for it less than a year earlier.[43] Politicians and
business interests saw that there was money to be made and began hail-
ing Deco as the city's economic salvation.

Four years had passed since the city commission adopted its much-criticized historic preservation ordinance. There still were no regulations on the remodeling or demolition of buildings in the Art Deco district. The historic preservation board finally felt it had enough support on the city commission to propose two locally controlled historic districts. One was Espanola Way, an idea that won the immediate endorsement of Linda Polansky and Gerry Sanchez. The other covered the hotel strips of Ocean Drive and Collins Avenue north of Fifth, and would end at Sixteenth Street, just south of some Abe Resnick-owned properties on Collins Avenue.

The preservation board finished preparing the proposals and submitted them for consideration at the next meeting of the planning board as required. As soon as the meeting began, it was clear that something strange was going on. Abe Resnick was there, along with his business partner Dov Dunaevsky. As the board members plowed through the day's agenda, the two developers were reported to have pulled Resnick's former fellow board members aside, one by one, for private, hushed conversations. When the district issue came up, the planning board sliced the proposed Ocean Drive district in half. The move eliminated all of Collins Avenue, including two more Resnick-Dunaevsky properties. There was no discussion, only a quick, unanimous vote.[44]

CHAPTER 9

Deli Diplomacy

Everyone on Miami Beach had their favorite delicatessen. Phil's catered to the staff at the Mount Sinai Medical Center. The kosher King David drew the Orthodox Jewish crowd. Wolfie's was the favorite of celebrities and old-timers. All segments of Miami Beach society merged at the deli. There could be two love-struck teenagers sitting across from a priest next to an elderly Jewish woman who was seated across the aisle from some cast members touring with a Broadway road company. The waitress might be a Methodist from Indiana or a Holocaust survivor who had her concentration camp tattoo removed as her prize on a television game show.[1]

Both a good deli butcher and a good deli waitress were treasured. They knew to serve the matzoh ball soup extra hot. They knew to slice the corned beef lean for older customers, but leave a little fat on the pastrami for the younger crowd. They knew what kind of cold cuts to pack for BeeGee Barry Gibb when he was taking out his boat and that Muhammad Ali would want turkey, roast beef, and corned beef on his sandwich when he was in town. In an emergency, a good customer could call the deli to deliver a sandwich to Beach High if young Jason went off without his lunch.[2] Over the years, as many political deals were hatched out in Miami Beach delis as at city hall or Mel Mendelson's butcher shop. Delis were the places to go for anniversaries, birthdays, business deals, a date, making up, mother-daughter days out, and to celebrate Ceil's recovery from her gall bladder operation.

Wolfie's Restaurant owner David Nevel, a friend of both Barbara Capitman and Abe Resnick, invited the two combatants to breakfast at his restaurant during the 1985 city commission campaign. Capitman had agreed to get her preservation league members to support Resnick's bid for the city commission in exchange for his support for preservation issues and financial help for her private Art Deco Institute. The agreement was dubbed "The Wolfie Accords."[3]

After the 1986 planning board vote that reduced the size of the proposed historic districts, Capitman emerged with both guns blazing. She charged that Resnick had betrayed his promise and had lobbied the planning board to benefit himself. Resnick claimed innocence and said he had nothing to do with the planning board vote.[4]

The war was on again.

When it was time for the city commission meeting to consider the preservation board's recommendation for the two historic districts, friends and supporters were summoned from the mainland, preservation groups, the synagogues, the PTA. Hundreds of people wearing pink Deco ribbons spilled out the doors of the second-floor commission chambers. Two commissioners wore pink ties.

The lobbying, the phone calls, and the letters did their job. The commission approved the Espanola Way Historic District and rejected the planning board's changes. It approved the entire Ocean Drive and Collins Avenue district as originally proposed by the preservation board. Abe Resnick cast the lone dissenting vote.[5]

The echo from the gavel had barely faded before rumors of lawsuits were heard. Preservation programs were keeping a lot of attorneys busy. In Palm Beach, three lawsuits were filed after buildings were designated without their owners' consent. Miami Springs was being sued for designating one of its earliest hotels, once a health spa owned by cereal king John Harvey Kellogg and now used as a retirement home. The high-powered Miami law firm of Greenberg, Traurig, Askew, Hoffman, Lipoff, Quentel and Wolff was hired to try to head off designation of the 1912 U.S. Post Office and Courthouse in downtown Miami. They failed. Greenberg, Traurig reached a stalemate over the designation of the Art Deco DuPont Building in downtown Miami when the city and the owner couldn't agree on the fate of its windows. Traurig himself was representing the owners of the vast Charles Deering Estate in South Dade to challenge the county's designation of the property as a historic landmark.[6]

The National Trust for Historic Preservation tracked the legal activity and was pleased that most cases were decided in favor of preserving history. Many decisions hinged on the pivotal ruling by the U.S. Supreme Court in 1978 that upheld New York City's landmarks law against Penn Central's challenge to the designation of Grand Central Station. Writing the opinion, Justice William Brennan compared landmark designation to any other zoning law that restricts use of private property.[7] It echoed an opinion by the U.S. Fifth Circuit Court of Appeals in the 1974 case of Maher *v.* New Orleans that "ephemeral societal interests" must be considered in crafting zoning laws.[8] A strong body of law was being established and would serve Miami Beach well if its new historic districts were challenged.

The battle being fought on the streets of South Beach was without legal representation. The elderly saw their way of life being destroyed. Hyman Katz, an eighty-two-year-old retired New Yorker, told a reporter he regretted moving to South Beach. "Miami Beach is gone. It's finished. It will be dead for the rest of the century. Look at Flamingo Park. People used to go down there every day to play shuffleboard. You used to wait hours for a game. Now nobody's left to play. Everything is changing, and it's changing for the worse. Older people these days won't come here. You can't even give the condominiums away in this neighborhood. If I could, I'd leave."[9]

Dorothy Kohn had wintered in Miami Beach for fifteen years. She sat on the porch of her Ocean Drive hotel to get away from the noise of power saws inside. Dorothy and her friends thought of South Beach as their special place. Now they had a desk clerk who spoke Spanglish–a blend of English and Spanish that they couldn't understand. Construction workers started pounding hammers at seven o'clock in the morning. She was going to cut her annual stay short and wasn't coming back.[10]

Residents weren't the only ones affected by the changing demographics of South Beach. Quality-conscious customers no longer shipped their cars from the north by rail. The wealthy residents of Star Island and Pine Tree Drive had BMWs and Mercedes in their garages. Allen Smith's Rolls Royce garage had hung on for sixty years in the same location on Fifth Street. So had Allen Smith, known to all his customers as Smitty. The long concrete and Dade County pine garage was filled with the parts needed to repair the signal window on a 1932 Phantom II, the Stromberg carburetor in a 1949 Silver Wraith, the disc brakes on a 1967 Silver Shadow, or replace the air filter on a 1974 Corniche. The city declared the garage unsafe and ordered it demolished. Smitty and his young assistant, who was seventy-one, packed everything, including unmarked jars of nuts and bolts. At age ninety-five, Smitty was finally closing up shop.[11] There wasn't that much business anyway.

Dorothy Kohn's friend on the porch didn't like the changes. "All I see are young people. I don't know what has happened to our old friends. It's funny. My generation built this town and now nobody wants us here."[12]

Like most residents of South Beach, most developers who were restoring the hotels and apartments were from out of town, many from New York. Michael Harvey was a local boy who grew up in Miami Beach. Like many Beach kids, he thought of his hometown as a worn-out retirement haven for old people. As soon as he had the chance, he got out to seek his fame and fortune in the theater. He succeeded.

There was a Tony statuette on his mantle as producer of the 1982 Musical of the Year, *Nine*, directed by Tommy Tune. He produced *Kennedy's Children*, a revival of *Sweet Bird of Youth*, and *Happy End*, which was nominated for five Tony awards.[13] Harvey was earning his stripes in the real estate business, too. His first taste of being a landlord came when he inherited his father's Hollywood, Florida, shopping center. It didn't take him long to realize that the millions it cost to produce a Broadway play could buy a really nice building that wouldn't close the next day because of a bad review in the *New York Times*.

A friend coaxed him into taking a look at South Beach. It wasn't what he remembered. Now, it reminded him of the free-spirited atmosphere of Manhattan's East Village where he had bought several apartment and retail buildings.[14] He put together a group of investors and bought the Helen Mar Apartments, a seven-story building on Lake Pancoast across a picturesque arched footbridge from Collins Avenue and a bit north of the National Register district. The Helen Mar was a fashionable address in its day. Olympic swimmer and film star Esther Williams had lived there. It originally had a nine-thousand-square-foot penthouse.[15] The Helen Mar suffered from decades of sloppy repairs and redecorating. Harvey's architect spent most of his time uncovering its floral motif friezes and black Vitrolite racing stripes.

Michael Harvey didn't want a traffic-stopping paint job reflecting off the calm dark waters of the lake, so he painted the Helen Mar white and cream with warm highlights of sage green and soft coral. The lobby was brought back to its original tropical Deco look with fluted columns, a curved coved ceiling, a zebra-striped rug spread on the polished terrazzo floor, and a wallpaper of oversized banana leaves. He decided to convert the building into a condominium. A two-bedroom unit was priced at $62,000, a price that appealed to the younger market but was also attractive to some of the building's elderly tenants.[16] It was the epitome of the kind of project that could help South Beach live up to its expectations as a vital historic district. It was a quality renovation that provided reasonably priced housing for young and old. It didn't rely on gimmicks and offered a quality product for the money.

Then Harvey tackled a block of Washington Avenue storefronts. He became so enamored with the potential of South Beach, he began lobbying others to join him. One was Gary Farmer. Farmer was intrigued by a building formerly occupied by The Famous restaurant, once the most popular Jewish restaurant in the neighborhood. There was a time that The Famous served fifteen hundred dinners a night and had fifteen valet parkers at curbside.

Farmer renamed it The Strand. His architect hung simple globe lamps from the illuminated domes in the ceiling and used broad arches to create intimate dining areas. He refurbished the restaurant's large kitchen to produce a menu of New American cuisine that rivaled the finest dining spots in Dade County. Many South Beach regulars—including people from city hall, the league, developers, and business owners—were invited on opening day. Lynn Bernstein arrived early. Not many people were there when she started having labor pains. She hurried to the bathroom. The doorknob came off in her hand, but she made it to the hospital in time to deliver a healthy baby girl.

The Strand became an immediate success in an area desperate for quality restaurants. At noon, it was often busy with developers, some sharing tables. The competition that usually distanced developers frequently was moderated on South Beach. They all were out on the same shaky limb and needed to work together to keep from falling. Farmer made the 1987 list of the "87 Hot People to Watch" in *Miami/South Florida* magazine, along with developers Don Meginley and Tony Goldman.

Both Michael Harvey and Gary Farmer utilized some of the $2.5 million of grants and loans that the Miami Beach Development Corporation was using to jumpstart South Beach. The money had generated more than $7.5 million of private investment and created hundreds of new permanent jobs in the process. Nationally, dollars spent on rehabilitation created 3.4 jobs for each job generated by new construction.[17]

The development corporation also had ventured into the housing business with Gerry Sanchez. They joined forces to buy an apartment building on Meridian Avenue to be developed for moderate-income families. They hoped it would serve as a model for other developers to increase the amount of sorely needed affordable housing on South Beach. The project brought Sanchez and the development corporation into a direct confrontation with the powerful city code enforcement board. The building had accumulated $19,000 in fines under its previous owner. The board cut the figure to $6,000, but Sanchez and the corporation weren't satisfied. Sanchez warned the board that enforcing exorbitant fines against a new owner who was trying to improve the neighborhood would scare off other developers.[18]

Another joint project between the development corporation and Sanchez had an even more dramatic turn and surprising outcome.

Sanchez went to the corporation seeking a loan for the renovation of the Edison Hotel on Ocean Drive, across Tenth Street from the Clevelander. The Edison was a five-story Mediterranean-style building with an airy entrance arcade porch and an inviting swimming pool tucked in back. It had been overlooked in the rush to Deco, but it appealed to Sanchez's Cuban roots. Originally he told the development corporation's board that he would give his personal guarantee for the loan, but he changed his mind and offered only the hotel as collateral. The building already was heavily mortgaged. The board was feeling uncomfortable being at the bottom of the list of creditors and wanted to reconsider its approval of the loan.

Development corporation executive director Maria Pellerin was a strong leader. She had served as a private consultant to the board before taking the $62,000-a-year job on a permanent basis. Pellerin—thirty-five, dark-haired, pretty, and smart—had spearheaded the Ocean Drive Developers' Conferences that generated the flurry of investment in South Beach. She had come into conflict with the board on a few other occasions, and she felt strongly about supporting Sanchez, who many believed was the catalyst for the renaissance on Ocean Drive. On Friday,

February 13, 1987, probably not the most propitious choice of dates, Pellerin told the board that if they didn't give Sanchez the loan she would resign.[19]

Pellerin's contract had another six months to run. She had just purchased a house on the Beach, and she hadn't put out any feelers for a new job. The board called her bluff. The following Monday the board met again and accepted her resignation, effective immediately.[20]

Replacing her as director was Denis Russ, another hometown boy who was president of the Beach High student government and got his law degree at the University of Miami. Serving as legal counsel for the league for many years, he wrote bylaws and grant applications and had done the legal work to set up the corporation. He would have to steer the group through some rough water. The organization, recently under scrutiny from the Department of Housing and Urban Development for questionable accounting practices, was in danger of losing its federal funding.[21]

Even with the grants and loans from the corporation, financing remained extremely difficult for South Beach developers. The campaign for preservation of the district was being fought as much in the boardrooms of the area's banks as it was in the commission chambers at city hall. Hopes lifted when the chairman of Sun Bank of Miami went to South Beach to see what was happening and how his bank might become involved. At the end of his tour, he discovered that his car had been stolen from the city parking lot. It was located later, stripped of its radio, car phone, air conditioner, and, perhaps most painful of all, his golf clubs.[22] It was not a good omen.

The newly arrived developers believed in South Beach. Miami bankers believed in condominiums and suburban homes bordering golf courses. Just as the developers were coming from outside the Miami area, most of the $165 million that was invested in South Beach renovations in 1986 and the first half of 1987 came from out of state. Local bankers saw a cramped neighborhood with limited parking and hotels with small rooms, no fitness centers, no Jacuzzis, no brand names on the letterhead. They saw derelicts sleeping in doorways, crack dealers setting up shop in boarded-up buildings, and a population that still was largely old and/or poor. The out-of-state bankers saw hotels and apartments in a tropical landscape with water views no more than a few blocks from any spot in the neighborhood. They saw couples checking into $140-a-night hotel suites, ordering pricey wine at porch cafés, driving luxury cars, dining from expensive menus, and listening to music at places like Jazz at the Waldorf, Café des Arts, and The Tropics International in Sanchez's Edison Hotel.

Tony Goldman pumped $9 million into South Beach, none of it local money. Don Meginley lost three apartment buildings because he couldn't get local bank funds to renovate them. Gary Farmer tried to raise money for The Strand locally but ended up having to get it through business associates in New York. Saul Gross of Streamline Development had to use the influence of New York business associates to get a loan from a Boca Raton savings and loan for a renovation. One economic development consultant tried to create a loan pool to share the risk. The banks weren't interested. Even when banks were willing to lend money, they would lend only about 65 percent of the appraised value as opposed to the typical 80 percent.[23] Plus they wanted personal guarantees.

The investments came with risk. The city prescribed the most meager of controls for its new historic districts. There were no comprehensive use guidelines to prevent the area from being overrun with tacky souvenir shops and noisy bars. Design guidelines didn't regulate interiors. Old zoning laws often were in conflict with the intent of a historic district. The preservation board served only an advisory function. There was minimal protection against owners impetuously demolishing a building. The code enforcement department seemed to prefer pushing demolition to encouraging renovation. Most of the National Register district was not covered by any local controls. The business owners and residents—old and young—were being pulled along with the flow. Although city hall had come a long way, it was clear that the focus was on the economics, not the aesthetics.

The revival of South Beach was still quite fragile.

The End of an Era

Eight years after the Mariel boatlift, a neighborhood that had been 75 percent Jewish was now 65 percent Hispanic, many of them also elderly. The Marielitos who had been resettled in the decrepit apartments in the redevelopment area had been replaced by families, aunts and uncles, grandmothers and grandfathers. The Stanley Myers Community Health Center, which opened nine years earlier with a clientele that was 98 percent elderly Jewish, now was filled with crying children. A tiny satellite office nearby still had a doctor who spoke Yiddish.

Like all of Dade County, crime was part of daily life. The elderly were afraid to go out after dark. Lillian Tepper took a cab the five blocks from her home to the bank. It cost two dollars, but she was afraid to walk.[24] Merchants complained about drunks and pickpockets who lurked around bus stops. The police department received fifty or more narcotics complaints on an average day.[25] So when a police car cruised past, it didn't catch the attention of the few elderly residents slowly working their way down the sidewalk or the drivers of the delivery trucks on the street in the early morning hours.

Officers Buddy Petit and Tony Holt stepped out into the still-cool February day and gave the old hotel a cursory glance. The uniformed officers approached the faded building, warily stepping through the high weeds that concealed a decade's worth of broken glass, rusted cans, hypodermic needles, and other debris. It was the way they started every day, searching through crumbling, boarded-up buildings.[26] They would retrieve stolen purses and radios, empty bottles of cheap wine, soda cans cut into make-shift crack pipes, and arrest four or five vagrants in the process. Most of the homeless who found shelter in the buildings took off before the officers arrived. They knew the schedule.

Petit and Holt had plenty of buildings from which to choose. From Dade Boulevard to the tip of the island there were more than 105 boarded-up or abandoned buildings.[27] Most of them were in the South Pointe area. The failure of that project, the collapse of the condo market, and a continuing depressed tourism business sentenced the buildings to economic purgatory. The cast-off buildings were a magnet for criminals and the homeless. Drug users, robbers, arsonists, and drifters all moved from one to another without concern for being bothered. Neighboring property owners and residents complained. Preservationists knew that each day of neglect made it less likely the building would be saved. In a two-year period, the city had ordered more than thirty buildings closed because of open sewage lines, leaking gas pipes, vermin infestation, inadequate plumbing, and dangerous wiring. At least ten families were relocated more than once.[28]

There was no law against a building being closed and boarded up by its owner. The city staff was stretched to the limit inspecting occupied buildings, especially with more and more buildings subject to the forty-year mandatory inspection rule. Abandoned buildings usually had to wait until a complaint was made. Fifteen buildings had been demolished in the previous three years under the authority of the county's Unsafe Structures Board. Several property owners took the city to court to contest ordered demolitions.

Marty Sherman was one who fought back. He bought the Rosemont Hotel in the old redevelopment area three years after the moratorium was lifted and three days after the Unsafe Structures Board ordered that it be repaired or destroyed, take your choice. There was no question that the Rosemont was a mess. Plaster was flaking off the walls and ceilings, revealing the lathing underneath. Bare lightbulbs hanging from exposed wiring supplied the only illumination. His plans to convert the three-story hotel into offices were stymied by one obstacle after another. His engineer had difficulty assessing the condition of the building because city hall couldn't find the original 1925 building plans. When bankers learned about the demolition order, they slammed the door on his application for a construction loan. His renovation timetable was rejected by the city.[29] By 1987, Sherman realized that no matter how he approached the problem, the city was determined that the building would be demolished.

Arthur Unger's family had owned the Royal Palm Hotel on Collins Avenue since his grandfather built it in 1939. As the old man's health deteriorated, so did the hotel. Unger was thirty-three years old in 1985 when he inherited a crumbling building with a million-dollar mortgage, five annual tenants, a bookkeeper who spent at least part of each day in a nearby bar, and a baker who spoke an unintelligible form of English.[30]

Unger couldn't bear to let it go. He saw a bright future for the beach and didn't want to miss out. His life was tied to the Royal Palm. Unger and his wife decided to bring the place back to life. An airbrushed mural was exhumed from beneath old wallpaper. From under the Formica on the front desk he excavated marble and neon. The exterior was given a fresh coat of paint, pink of course. The number of year-round residents began to grow.[31] The Royal Palm began to return to being a cheerful place where spry retirees played cards and danced and joyfully complained about the food.

Unger suffered a 40 percent drop in business for the 1987 winter season. Guests' rooms had been burglarized. Several families of mice took up occupancy. An unidentified man was beaten to death in the abandoned Poinciana Hotel that stood only a few feet away from his building.[32] His tenants were horrified. Unger blamed the derelict Poinciana next door for the problems. Unger decided that since the city wasn't doing anything about the Poinciana, he would do it himself. He sued its owners for $350,000. There already was a court order to fumigate the building. The judge found the Poinciana's owners in contempt of the city's cleanup order and slapped them with a five-hundred-dollar-a-day fine while he considered Unger's damage suit.[33] Ironically, Art Unger served on the panel that oversaw the city's program to board up derelict buildings.

The Biscaya was beyond the pale, at the edge of the moratorium area and just outside the Art Deco district. It was the last of the Carl Fisher–era grand hotels and one of the few buildings designated to be spared in the original South Shore redevelopment plan. Originally named The Floridian, the Mediterranean-style 242-room hotel occupied an enviable spot on the edge of Biscayne Bay at the southern entrance to the city. It opened in 1926 with a gala dinner-dance for five hundred notables. Guests in the plush rooms on the east side of the hotel could see the sun rise over the Atlantic every morning. Tourists watched from the mezzanine as luminaries of the day registered in the lobby's rotunda, where tall windows encouraged ocean breezes to gently cool the interior. From the two-story loggia on the west side they had views of the mansions on the nearby islands and the rapidly growing skyline of the city of Miami. There were balconies off the end units on each of the ten floors. The elevators did not go to the very top where the gambling room was located.

Sidney Saltz, who was the captain in the three-story dining room from 1936 to 1940, remembered fresh flowers on the tables, finger bowls, fine china and silver, and big band music for dancing every night.[34] Sophie Tucker had starred in the supper club for a New Year's Eve celebration that included dinner, dancing, breakfast, favors, and music by "Freddy Hamm and his recording orchestra" for ten dollars per person.[35]

The beginning of The Floridian's change in fortune came when it, along with many other Beach hotels, was taken over by the military as barracks for troops training for service in World War II. By the time the troops moved out, the profitable resort business had moved farther up the beach. In 1956, The Floridian became one of the city's first retirement hotels. Unable to make his mortgage payments, the owner lost the hotel to foreclosure. It was bought by Harry Goodman for $10.00, and an $800,000 mortgage. He renamed it the Biscaya.[36] Then came the South Shore moratorium.

The Biltmore, a sprawling Spanish Mediterranean hotel in Coral Gables, had a similar exciting and tragic past. Despite the 1926 hurricane and the end of the 1920s real estate boom, The Biltmore hung on until the early 1940s. It served the war effort as a military hospital, then as a Veterans' Administration hospital and the University of Miami School of Medicine until 1968. It sat empty and decaying for years until the city was able to acquire it from the federal government. Developer Earl Worsham, who was part of the original South Shore development team, was selected to carry out a $36-million restoration to return The Biltmore to its original use and beauty. The Biscaya was the only other major resort hotel from the twenties in Dade County that recalled the days when tablecloths were smoothly pressed linen and dressing for dinner meant more than "shoes required." All the others had been demolished.

The Biscaya's size and prominent location made its dilapidated condition a real thorn in the side of city officials. Everyone crossing the busy MacArthur Causeway from the mainland saw the windowless hulk as they entered Miami Beach. Firefighters feared having to battle a blaze started by a vagrant or arsonist in the crumbling structure, although the fire chief admitted it was "a classy old building."[37] Police were tired of making regular sweeps to clear out the drug addicts and their paraphernalia. It was the symbol of everything that was wrong with the city, a daily reminder of the failed redevelopment and a city whose prime had passed.

Harry Goodman announced plans to restore the Biscaya to its former beauty. Despite its abuse, the public rooms had survived with no significant alterations. The vaulted and beamed ceilings had not been touched, the decorative windows in the second-floor lobby were not destroyed.

The city responded to Goodman's plans by asking the county's Unsafe Structures Board to declare the building a hazard. The board complied in January 1984 and gave Goodman six months to renovate the Biscaya or demolish it. Goodman said the order scared off investors, and he went to court, where he obtained one delay after another. The city finally decided to pull the plug and, in November 1985, approved a contract to raze the hotel.[38]

The mayor was exuberant at the prospect of finally ridding the entrance to his city of what he considered an eyesore. Preservationists saw a chance to extend their revitalization of South Beach beyond the boundaries of the Art Deco district and to save an irreplaceable old Miami Beach landmark.

Goodman went back to court. Sid Borden went to the Biscaya.

Sid Borden was a cab driver from North Miami Beach with a soft spot for pussycats. Two years earlier, Borden had discovered that several stray felines had found a home amidst the broken glass and rotting furniture of the Biscaya. He stopped at the hotel every day to give them some food and loving care. With the threat of imminent demolition, Borden worked feverishly to find someone to help him round up the kitties and find new homes for them. A local animal aid society came to his aid and relocated seven of them to a new home on a big wooded lot with a woman whose cat needed a buddy. Several more cats and a litter of newborn kittens were rescued in the next few weeks.[39]

After several more rounds with the attorneys, the circuit court issued a restraining order that postponed the demolition, and Goodman took his case back to the Unsafe Structures Board. The board ruled against him again, but he continued his fight in the courts and won an eight-month reprieve from the demolition order. In the meantime, Goodman supported the nomination of the Biscaya to the National Register. Because it was south of Sixth Street and west of Alton Road, it was not included in the Art Deco district listing. The nomination reached the Florida Historic Preservation Office in May. The staff determined that it met the criteria, and the application was scheduled to be submitted to the state review board within twelve months, the standard time limit.[40] Preservationists again had hope that the Biscaya would be saved.

Harry Goodman was worried that he couldn't pull off the restoration. He called Gerry Sanchez to plead with him. "I know you are already busy, but you're the only guy who can save it. You're respected, a preservationist." Sanchez couldn't resist the challenge. He brought in an engineer who said the hotel could be saved and offered Goodman a contract to buy and restore the hotel.[41] He put up scaffolding and hung his Polonia banner above the Biscaya's name over the entrance. His architect, Les Beilinson, began preparing plans to convert the hotel into apartments. Sanchez was moving at breakneck speed. The city's patience had run out. Another demolition contract was put out on the hotel. Once the building was exterminated for rats and mice and some asbestos was removed from the boiler room, it would be demolished.

At 4:13 p.m. on Tuesday, February 10, 1987, the final day of the eight-month court-ordered reprieve, Les Beilinson went to city hall carrying the plans for the Biscaya's renovation. The Miami Beach City Attorney deemed the plans inadequate, claimed that they were not as detailed as required, and instructed that the demolition order be enforced immediately.[42] Neither Sanchez nor Beilinson was informed of the decision.

The next morning at 7:00 a.m., police officers entered the Biscaya to roust the dozen or so squatters who had taken up occupancy in the old hotel. Getting in was easy. Time, weather, and vandals had removed most of the first floor doors and windows. Tobias McHenry had left the hotel early that morning. His meager belongings still were strewn around the mattress he called home.[43] The police left them there, along with the flattened Old Milwaukee six-pack carton someone had tossed on the floor.

Thirty minutes later, the officers gave the all-clear signal to the heavy equipment operators who were waiting in front of the hotel on West Avenue. Only fifteen hours had passed since the city attorney rejected the renovation plans, a rare display of municipal efficiency. The city crew was sent to clear the area surrounding the Biscaya and do some preliminary work to prepare the building for implosion by explosives. They worked deliberately, the big machines creaking and groaning as they lumbered around the grounds of the lifeless hotel.

Word spread quickly. Angry preservationists began to assemble in front of the 7-Eleven convenience store across the street. Their fury at city officials increased with each swipe the bulldozers took. Only a month earlier, they had dined and danced in celebration of the reopening of the newly restored Biltmore in Coral Gables, a stunning success in a city that cherished its older buildings. League president Richard Hoberman was at work when he got the call. He raced across the MacArthur Causeway. Don Meginley heard what was happening and called Nancy Liebman, who called some of her Dade Heritage Trust friends and also sped to the scene. The crowd swelled with news crews and curious onlookers. They gasped as a front-end loader wantonly smashed into the side of the Biscaya, knocking loose huge chunks of masonry. Among them was McHenry, the homeless man who had left early that day. "My stuff's still up there," he complained. "I didn't get no warning. I hope I can get in tonight to get my clothes."[44]

Don Meginley and his eighteen-year-old daughter rushed over from Ocean Drive. They hadn't planned to do anything dramatic. But as a front-end loader approached the ornate entrance to the building, they defiantly stepped in front of the growling machine. Meginley's wife, Beverly, watched as her husband and oldest daughter, Kate, stood their ground, ignoring orders to move out of the way. She would have joined them, but she had to pick up their other daughter at school later in the afternoon, and she could anticipate what was about to happen.[45] Police moved toward Meginley and Kate and order the pair to leave or face arrest. They refused to budge. Again the police commanded them to leave. The bulldozer operator waited. Meginley and Kate stared at him, unmoving. The crowd held its breath and waited.

The officers glanced at city officials standing nearby, took their cue, handcuffed the hotelier and the pony-tailed teenager and led them away as the crowd cheered their admiration of the pair's dedication and courage. It was the classic preservation protest, including the defiant speech to the television cameras as the handcuffs were clasped around their wrists, classic except that Meginley was a hard-nosed businessman, a self-proclaimed conservative, and had never been involved in any kind of political protest in his life. As Meginley and his daughter were driven away in a police cruiser, the crowd's cheers turned to moans as the machine's sharp-toothed shovel gnawed off the graceful double switchback staircase leading to the main entrance. City administrators and officers stood to the side near the neighboring boatyard, satisfied with the progress. One was City Commissioner Abe Resnick, the man who demolished the Boulevard and the New Yorker.

Sanchez learned about what was happening from a reporter who phoned him to get a comment. Shocked, he raced to the site where broken pieces of his next planned project were being amputated from the building. Sanchez was seething. "This is unfair! This is backstabbing!" he screamed.[46] He argued with city officials in vain, then sped off to try to find a legal way to stop the bulldozers. At midnight, Sanchez left a judge's house in Hialeah with a three-day restraining order against the city.[47] It was too late to save the loggia, too late to prevent the front-end loader from chewing up the balustraded stairs that led to the once-elegant ballroom.

The next day, league members and friends wearing "Save the Biscaya" tee-shirts again gathered in front of the hotel and the piles of rubble. Meginley was back, released after his arrest and just as determined. Some held candles of protest. They vowed to stay all night, standing guard against another stealth attack. Someone suggested they hold a mock trial of the city attorney who ordered in the bulldozers. The attorney was found guilty of demolishing a historic structure. They hung an effigy of him, clad in a plaid jacket, striped tie, polyester pants, and a jaunty hat, from the chain link fence surrounding the building. (The city attorney later told Sanchez that the only part of the episode that made him really mad was that they dressed the effigy in polyester. He hated polyester.)[48]

Looking at the damage, Sanchez feared that the Biscaya already was lost. Beilinson was concerned that so many of the hotel's significant architectural features had been demolished that the project would no longer qualify for the federal tax credits that made it economically feasible.

Sanchez wasn't ready to quit, though. The action returned to the courthouse. Two weeks after the first assault on the Biscaya, to the dismay of Sanchez and the preservationists, the judge sided with the city's five attorneys and lifted the injunction, giving Sanchez twenty-four hours to appeal. The expense of a protracted legal challenge and the loss of the tax credits were too much. He had other restoration projects that required his resources. Reluctantly, he surrendered the project.

The deathwatch for the Biscaya began only eleven weeks after preservationists celebrated what they thought was a successful plan to save the once-luxurious bayfront hotel. The demolition crew went to work, placing explosives in strategic locations and knocking holes in the interior floors to wire the charges together. More than a thousand people lined the MacArthur Causeway on Sunday, March 15, 1987, as the thin light of dawn revealed the outline of the Biscaya. They smoked, double-checked their cameras, chatted with strangers who shared their curiosity. The earth made its final imponderable turn, and sunlight washed the top floors of the Biscaya one last time. At 7:30 a.m., Coast Guard vessels moved in to turn back boaters who were trying to get a closer view. It was rumored that the city's political publicist was hosting a champagne party for city officials at his office, with a view of the doomed hotel.[49] Nancy Liebman was one of the few league members among the onlookers. Most stayed away, unable to witness the ultimate loss and unwilling to be part of the morbid spectacle. Hundreds of cameras were pointed at the doomed hotel.

On a signal from their radios, police officers slid into their cruisers and maneuvered them across the roadway to block traffic. The crowd started honking horns, blowing whistles, encouraging the demolition team to push the button. Near the Biscaya, the crew was making one final safety check. At 7:44,[50] a puff of smoke came from a seventh-floor window, and a unison gasp was heard from the crowd. A series of muffled concussions like mittens clapping rippled across the water. Five seconds later, the center section of the Biscaya plunged to earth. The ends tumbled into the resulting vacuum. The only thing left was a cloud of dust staining the blue sky and a pile of rubble on the shore.

CHAPTER 10

Save the Senator

The dust had barely settled from the demolition of the Biscaya when the Royale Group, which was enjoying brisk business in its Ocean Drive hotels, announced the unthinkable. They planned to demolish the Senator, a three-story hotel on Collins Avenue at Twelfth Street.

The Senator was not iconic like the New Yorker or a solitary landmark like the Biscaya. The Senator represented the very essence of the district as a significant collection of like buildings. It was one of four hotels on consecutive corners on the east side of Collins Avenue with curving facades that gave an animated tempo to the street. Its architect, L. Murray Dixon, had moved from Georgia to Miami during the building boom of the twenties. He started designing Art Deco buildings in the thirties and contributed dozens of buildings to the South Beach skyline, including the soaring Tides and Ritz Plaza.

The Senator was considered a "must-save" building. It featured circular glass windows etched with egrets, banana leaves, palm trees, and cute little fish blowing bubbles. It had a towering finial above a two-story curved bank of windows over the entrance. There were frescoes of mermaids beside that desirable South Beach feature: a swimming pool. The multilayered geometric keystone fireplace was the lobby's focal point. During the 1960s and 1970s, its wraparound front porch was populated each day by ladies with sculpted hairdos, brightly patterned dresses, a necklace or nicely tied scarf adorning their throats, and each with a substantial handbag at her side or in her lap even if she wasn't planning to leave the building.

For the Miami Design Preservation League, this one was personal. The Senator was one of the hand-picked hotels bought by Andrew Capitman in the early 1980s when they were trying to kick off the South Beach rejuvenation. It also was personal for Leonard Horowitz. He had lived in the Senator for a while. One hot summer night a bunch of the league regulars met there for a party. The heat in Horowitz's room was intense so they went out by the pool and wound up in a water fight, squirting each other with old-fashioned blue seltzer bottles.[1] League members had a lot of memories wrapped up in the Senator.

The hotel had been closed in 1984 when the Royale Group took it over, and it was still closed three years later. The Senator was within the Ocean Drive Historic District and would be the first test of the Miami Beach Historic Preservation Board's limited powers to try to save a building under the 1986 regulations. The Royale Group claimed that it had no choice. They were desperate for parking for their Ocean Drive hotels. They needed to demolish the forty-eight-year-old Senator and two adjacent, less meaningful buildings, for a parking garage. A Royale spokesman explained, "We are on an island. When people come here they have to drive cars. Where are they going to put the cars?"[2]

Parking consumes 40 to 50 percent of the land space in most commercial areas, disrupts the retail streetscape, and puts pedestrians at risk from cars crossing the sidewalk at ingress and egress points. Finding a place for cars was a problem faced in many historic districts. New Orleans, Boston, and San Francisco all struggled to find sufficient space to park underground, behind old facades, or on the edges of historic areas.

Miami Beach had trolley service from the mainland in the 1920s along the county causeway (now the MacArthur Causeway) with a trolley station at the foot of Fifth Street. A trolley loop ran the length of South Beach until 1939. In the 1930s, railroad passengers could journey from New York City to Miami in thirty hours on the Silver Meteor express.[3] Gas rationing during World War II reduced travel by car. Parking first became an issue when motorists began crowding Miami Beach with their Studebakers and DeSotos in the late forties. Most of the elderly who populated the neighborhood in the sixties and seventies didn't drive, so parking ceased to be a concern. Every proposal for new mass transit links to downtown Miami or within Miami Beach had either already been rejected or was still under discussion.

Tourists wanted to have the freedom to explore other attractions in the Miami area during their vacations. Without any form of mass transit except city buses, most people coming across the causeways drove. There was plenty of parking on South Beach, but most of the large lots were west of Washington Avenue. People visiting the Art Deco district from the suburbs were accustomed to parking near the door of their destination. Parking was manageable during the day. But the fledgling nightlife scene was drawing crowds. It was a far cry from the time, only a few years earlier, when a news photographer posed Deco leaders standing in two Ocean Drive parking spaces with only a handful of cars and a U-Haul truck visible in the background.

The city's top planner downplayed the importance of the Senator. Demolition of one historic structure would "not mean the end of the Art Deco district" he said, adding that he didn't believe the Senator had that much significance.[4] The historic preservation board could not have disagreed more. The strength of the Art Deco district was in the numbers. Like supporting walls of a building, each structure in the district played a vital role in creating the result and removing strategic ones could cause its collapse. The board voted to delay action on the Royale Group's request for the maximum six months permitted under the new district regulations.

The debate raged on into fall 1987. The Royale Group rejected several offers from the city to utilize nearby municipal parking facilities. Barbara Capitman and Richard Hoberman took the fight to that year's National Trust for Historic Preservation conference in Washington, D.C., where they handed out postcards bearing a picture of the Senator to as many of the 2,500 delegates as would listen to their story. Trust members were dismayed at the news, but when the Washington-based preservation group issued its annual list of the eleven most endangered historic sites, the Senator wasn't on it.

By January 1988, the ruckus over the Senator gave promise to something the preservationists had only dreamed of achieving. A change to the local historic preservation ordinance could give the Miami Beach Historic Preservation Board the power to permanently block demolition of significant buildings, with the only appeal to the city commission.

The ordinance change passed unanimously. City commissioners, who had grown up with the Art Deco buildings of South Beach and held a rather low opinion of them, finally realized that the district was the best thing that had happened to Miami Beach tourism in a long time. Even Abe Resnick signed on. "We have experienced in the last few years a response—not just from our community but worldwide—that Art Deco's giving the city a lot of glory and vitality."[5]

The new law was not retroactive, however, and the Senator's demolition delay would expire soon. The city manager was instructed to try to engineer a swap of the Senator for some city-owned land two blocks north that could be used for parking. Royale executives responded favorably to the idea, and negotiations began in earnest. Barbara Capitman was so certain of triumph that she devoted the opening page of a book she was writing about the district to the Senator. She called it "a beautiful mute symbol of district success" and sent the manuscript off to the publisher.[6]

Meanwhile, the Royale Group's financial problems began to come to light. Their hotels were more than $48,500 in default for resort taxes owed to the city. A lender filed a foreclosure action against the corporation in federal court, which revealed that Royale owed almost a million dollars in contractors' fees, taxes, and insurance premiums. The mortgage company did not ask for an injunction to stop the demolition of the Senator.[7]

A one-week vigil of protest had been orchestrated at the Senator in March. With the situation in question again, protesters resumed their watch the week of June 19. Sixty protesters responded. They took shelter on the Senator's front porch during intermittent rain showers, which prompted the inevitable comments about having enough sense to come in out of the rain. They noisily marched up and down Ocean Drive and Collins Avenue, stopping along the way to give media interviews.

In July, the code enforcement board acted on its own and tossed the final straw on the back of the Royale Group's camel. During the four years it was closed, the Senator had gone without regular maintenance. The pale green and white paint was worn away. The pool was littered with trash. Awning windows were broken and boarded up. The board issued an order to Royale that the property had to be cleaned up. Royale responded that the building would be gone in thirty days.[8] The preservationists were appalled that the code enforcement board would take action that was at cross purposes with what everyone else was trying to achieve.

A new agreement was announced August 17. The Royale Group agreed to hold off demolition until mid-September to give the mayor time to seek a public referendum for a bond issue to finance four new parking garages. It was just for show. No referendum was scheduled.

Barbara Capitman took refuge in her home. She had run out of options that might save the Senator. The wrecking company was standing by. Matti Bower tried to rent the parking meters on the streets bordering the Senator to park cars there so the bulldozers couldn't get close enough, but the barricades were already set up. A few protestors continued the vigil at the hotel.

The last residents of the Senator were evicted on the morning of October 12, 1988. They were two tiny kittens, one a gray tabby and the other black and white. A woman on the demolition crew carefully tucked them into her truck to take them home with her.[9] Nancy Liebman was at the league's office on Ocean Drive when a hysterical telephone call came in, "They're touching the windows!" She ran down the street and started yelling at the man who was maneuvering a backhoe into position. He was unswayed. She dashed back to the office and made frantic phone calls to anyone she thought could help, but it was too late. By the time she returned to the Senator, a crowd had started to form.

Capitman, dressed in a black caftan that resembled a judge's robe, stoically stood at the front entrance. Her face showed the toll that the fight had taken on her. When police arrived to clear the building, she was escorted from the porch and departed for an undisclosed location, leaving behind league members, neighbors, news reporters, and some curious tourists.

Minutes later, the backhoe sitting on Twelfth Street reached its long arm over the wall around the pool and smashed into the glass-enclosed veranda. Some onlookers wept; others stared in disbelief. Richard Hoberman couldn't believe it was happening. One woman looked as if she were going to be sick.[10] Almost a third of the Senator was gone by sundown. It would take about ten days to finish the job because there was limited space on which to pile debris, and it had to be hauled away truckload by truckload. The candlelight vigils were over. The phone calls were done. There would be no more letters. All that was left was the media coverage.

The morning after the demolition, Miami Beach's Saint Francis Hospital issued a press release announcing that Barbara Capitman had checked in with heart problems. The next day, newspapers reported that she was taken to the hospital immediately after being escorted away from the doomed building. She called Dennis Wilhelm and asked, "How did you like my heart attack?" Among the phone calls she had made before the demolition were to hospitals looking for one with a publicity department that would work with her. Saint Francis Hospital apparently had agreed to her plan. But the crusade to save the Senator had ground her down. She had been hospitalized several times in the last few years. Wilhelm and Michael Kinerk didn't realize how much. She hadn't had a heart attack, but she was gravely ill.[11]

The demolition of the Senator was an enormous blow for the league, as devastating as the loss of the New Yorker. It would not be the end of the Art Deco district, as some predicted. Other buildings had been lost with less attention from the preservationists and the media. Each time a major building was lost, it sparked new interest in the district and was used to force through new, more protective legislation. It was a steep price to pay.

A Model Business

A classic Thunderbird was parked in front of the Beacon Hotel on Ocean Drive, the building that had caught Leonard Horowitz's attention in 1976. Leaning against the car was a slightly pudgy man wearing a vivid green blazer, tight black pants, sunglasses, and a straw hat. A video production crew was scurrying around him.[12] Elton John had come to the Art Deco district to film a new music video while he was in town to perform at two sold-out concerts the next weekend at the Miami Arena. The Art Deco district served as a great backdrop.

Film, music video, and still photographers followed *Miami Vice* to the district. The activity reached such a level that the *Miami Herald* published a daily listing of filming locations so fans and tourists could choose which ones to watch and so that residents knew what areas to avoid on their way to work. A popular Ocean Drive pastime was sitting at one of the new cafés, watching thousand-dollar-a-day models posing for photographers, strolling down the street, playing volleyball on the beach, or engaged in idle conversation over a plate of lettuce at the next table.

Fashion photographers made up the bulk of the business. The images they took graced magazine pages in Berlin and Rome, filled subway ads in London and Toronto, arrived at people's homes in mail order catalogs, and appeared in airport waiting areas all over the world. They became print and video ads for American Airlines, Sears, JCPenney, Bally of Switzerland, Yoplait, Bloomingdale's, and Spiegel. They appeared in *GQ, Vogue, Parade, Cosmopolitan, Life, Elle,* and other magazines. The music videos were regular viewing on MTV.

Fashion designer Calvin Klein started the flood in 1986. Rather, his photographer, Bruce Weber, did on the day he scrupulously posed four male and two female models, all of them completely nude and well-oiled, on the roof of the Breakwater Hotel on Ocean Drive for an Obsession for Men ad. Weber was transforming fashion photography with his edgy, erotic poses just as Bethann Hardison of the CLICK modeling agency was redefining how fashion models should look. There was a quest for the exotic and the dramatic. The colorful exteriors, the curves and angles of the architecture, and the slightly shabby look of South Beach lured photographers who always were on the search for new and interesting locations.

It wasn't just the Art Deco district that was attracting them. The Miami area offered an abundance of picture-perfect scenery—from the majestic Italian Villa Vizcaya to the ultracool buildings designed by Miami's Arquitectonica innovative designers to the untamed Everglades. They came for the remarkable natural light and the extraordinary blue sky. But most of them came to South Beach. From September to April, there were hundreds of them. Many came from Europe. Miami's warm winter months were the perfect time to shoot the following year's summer and fall fashions to meet publishing deadlines. *Select* magazine, the bible for people who spent their careers booking fabulous sites for photographers, had profiled South Beach as the next great production location in its 1986 location reference guide.

There was big money in all those dauntingly thin models and busy camera crews. A team for a typical fashion shoot included six or more models, a photographer, an assistant, an art director, clothing, makeup and hair stylists, all of whom needed rooms and food and cars and entertainment. There was a growing local pool of talented support services and agencies and location coordinators, but most of the photographers and models came from New York or Europe. Props, such as the yellow Thunderbird, added to the budget. One photographer spent $1,700 to have a sleek white yacht floating in the background for one shot.[13] As the 1989–90 season began, it was anticipated that the fashion business would spend almost $45 million on location shooting in Miami Beach that year.[14]

Business was so brisk that Don Meginley, who had gone to work for the Royale Group, transformed the Cavalier into a fashion hotel. Before dawn, people began straggling into the lobby looking for coffee. Sleepy-eyed models stumbled into the makeup rooms to be painted and powdered and polished, their hair curled, smoothed, and sprayed. Racks of next year's freshly pressed styles were rolled out of the elevator and parked next to the potted palms in the lobby. Photographers checked their cameras and equipment. Crew members called instructions to each other in a half dozen languages. Meginley, dressed in a polo shirt and khakis, supervised his staff, making sure the models and photographers had their preferred brands of bottled water, calling to double-check when the 1948 red Dodge would be there so actress Isabella Rossellini could nonchalantly recline against it for a shot for Italian *Vogue*.[15]

Outside, lights were being set up, translucent umbrellas put in place, cables strung, reflectors positioned, props readied. When the sun ascended to provide the desired light, the entire entourage simply walked across Ocean Drive to a lifeguard station painted an unlikely combination of yellow, green, red, blue, and purple and went to work. Vans and mobile homes carrying other crews scattered out across the neighborhood to photograph models in improbable poses in front of sherbet-colored buildings, prancing in the surf, or turning and posturing in the middle of a blocked-off street. It was great street theater for the tourists.

Another type of entertainment had arrived on Lincoln Road.

The New World Symphony was the dream of conductor Michael Tilson Thomas. For years, Thomas had said in interviews that it was a pity that the United States didn't have a national orchestra to train new musicians. Thomas realized that such a massive undertaking would require public financing, which seemed unlikely to happen. The idea piqued the interest of Carnival Cruise Lines magnate Ted Arison. He asked Thomas how much it would cost. Thomas waved off the question. "You'd have to be like the tsar of Russia to do something like this." Arison, unruffled, replied, "Well, I'm pretty close."[16]

The musicians for the New World Symphony were plucked from the outstanding graduates of the country's finest music conservatories. It was the only professional symphony orchestra in the nation without a permanent company of musicians. The youngsters were granted three-year fellowships to continue studying and honing their talents under Thomas's tutelage and offered a chance to showcase their talents for conductors always listening for new musicians to fill the chairs in prestigious symphonies around the country.

Providing housing was part of the arrangement to attract talented young string and woodwind players to the organization. The orchestra couldn't pay much, but they could give the kids somewhere decent to live so they wouldn't have to worry about finding apartments, security deposits, annual leases, and the other problems inherent in setting up house in a new place.

On a November evening in 1987, the beginning of the winter tourist season, most of the elderly residents and guests of the Plymouth Hotel on Twenty-first Street were gathered in the round lobby with its tufted padded leather wall and its Ramon Chatov mural of a tropical beach scene. It was bingo night. They sat on Naugahyde sofas concentrating on the numbered cards. After the game, Luigi was coming to play the piano, which was not quite as out of tune as his striped jacket and abstract tie. It was the favorite night for Lillian Raizen and the dance club she had started to keep her active. They loved to do the polka when Luigi played.[17]

The news came during the bingo game. "We are sorry to inform you that the Plymouth Hotel is sold." They were being evicted.[18] Young people were coming. The hotel had been purchased by the New World Symphony to house its young musicians. The beach was two blocks away, it was a short walk to Lincoln Road, and Collins Park was right across the street. It was large enough to house almost all the musicians. It had wide hallways to accommodate bass viols and harps and ample public areas where they could practice in small ensembles. The symphony administration thought it would be best if the old tenants moved elsewhere so the music from practicing percussionists and trombone players wouldn't bother them.

Like most elderly, the residents of the Plymouth did not like change, especially sudden, forced change. Moving to a new place would be an extremely stressful experience. The symphony reconsidered its decision and told the residents with leases they could stay until May, the customary end of the tourist season. As a result, twenty-five elderly residents would be sharing the hotel with fifty-five young oboe players and flutists and violinists. The musicians didn't know what to expect. They certainly didn't expect the warm reception they received from a white-haired delegation cheering "Hello! Hello!" as they moved in toting their luggage and instrument cases. The musicians and residents gathered that Saturday night for a barbecue by the swimming pool. The musicians talked about how exciting it was to join the orchestra. The residents talked about ways they might volunteer to help.[19]

Three months later, the new orchestra made the trip across Biscayne Bay to downtown Miami. The glorious old Olympia Theater had been donated to the city of Miami in 1975 by philanthropist Maurice Gusman. The magnificent atmospheric movie palace had been beautifully restored as the Gusman Center for the Performing Arts. Members of the New World Symphony took their positions on the Gusman stage for their first public performance. Michael Tilson Thomas, energetic as a young colt, strode onto the stage to great applause and anticipation. The musicians lifted their instruments and waited for their cue. At the stroke of Thomas's baton, they burst into "Bamboula Beach—The Miami Bamboula" by Wourinen. Ted Arison was in the audience. "When they started playing, they were absolutely incredible. I started crying. Lin [his wife] started crying."[20]

Arison wanted the symphony to have a permanent performing home. He bought them the Lincoln Theater on Lincoln Road in South Beach. It had become a second-run barn of a movie theater with rotting seats and the stench of disuse. The first time Thomas stepped inside "the smell was so horrible you could hardly stay in there more than a minute."[21]

The Lincoln Theater gave the symphony a 796-seat theater, rehearsal space, a percussion studio, music library, private practice rooms, and administrative offices. It was smaller than was ideal and even with acoustic modifications you could hear jets flying over and sirens going past. But the architecture, the location, and the price were perfect.[22]

The entire theater had to be redone. At first there was only enough money to do the performance hall and the first two floors of the office building. A pre-opening performance for an invited audience was scheduled for the night of the October 12, 1989. The acoustical paneling was not yet up. The musicians sat on a temporary plywood stage since the birchwood flooring had not been installed. The Art Deco tiles in the lobby were not completely restored. Conductor Thomas was nervous. Lincoln Road was a no man's land at night. Would anyone come?

They came, and heard the liquid sounds of Aaron Copland's "Appalachian Spring" fill the newly renovated hall for the first time. The following night for the official opening the symphony's chamber group, woodwind quartet, and brass choir gave preconcert performances on the mall outside the theater, finely dressed concertgoers clustering in the warm night as though listening to bands of traveling troubadours. The chaser lights on the marquee were running again as the audience filed into the lobby. Settling into their seats, visitors saw the new theater for the first time. They knew the New World Symphony had found a home when the trumpet players lifted their horns and opened the program with Stravinsky's soaring "Fanfare for a New Theatre."[23]

Changing of the Guard

The Art Deco district was beginning to come to life. Nancy Liebman had worked her way from grunt volunteer helping put together Art Deco Weekend to being named to the preservation league's board of directors. In 1988, the group needed a new executive director. Its unstable finances and internal squabbling made keeping an administrator difficult. That year's budget allocated only $15,000 for the job, which wasn't enough to attract a nonprofit professional. Liebman offered herself for the position. She reasoned that as executive director she could continue doing everything she already was doing and more. She worked well with Richard Hoberman, who was president that year, and the board seemed enthusiastic about the idea.[24]

The appointment did not come without controversy. Matti Bower, whose fiery temper often ran unchecked, resented that a rich doctor's wife was going to get paid for work that both of them had been doing for free for a half dozen years.[25] But Liebman was viewed as a strong advocate for preservation, level-headed, creative, pragmatic, and politically savvy. She could get people to do what she wanted and make them think it was their idea. And she would do the job for $15,000 a year.

As executive director of the league, Liebman became the spokesman for the Art Deco district. The media turned to Liebman for quotes on current issues, deflecting the spotlight from Barbara Capitman. The resulting conflict between the two women was inevitable. They both cared passionately about the Art Deco district, but they had a basic philosophical difference. Capitman saw the Art Deco district as a tribute to design, a place for the elderly and young to live peacefully together and a destination for tourists, drawn there by a controlled setting of vintage 1930s style. Liebman viewed preservation as a tool to be used to stabilize and improve a living city through guided capitalism.

People were reluctant to criticize Capitman openly. She had "discovered" tropical Art Deco as an architectural style, she started a movement, she created a National Register district. In the dark years when the effort seemed hopeless, she single-mindedly rammed the cause forward by overcoming tremendous opposition from city hall, the business community, and, sometimes, even from within the league. She deservedly was called everything from the "Duchess of Art Deco" to "Art Deco's Grande Dame." She alternately was called crazy, brilliant, argumentative, a visionary, strong-willed, a master manipulator, and a genius, by both her enemies and her closest friends. She drew people in with her passion and drove people away with her tactics. Even her most devoted supporters disagreed with many of her methods. But without her, there would have been no Art Deco district.

Liebman also had her critics, who felt that she didn't take a strong enough position on league issues while she was chairman of the Miami Beach Historic Preservation Board and that she was too quick to compromise. Few detractors knew that the Liebmans were among the investors who helped Andrew Capitman get his Art Deco Hotels group started in the early 1980s.

The league had a more immediate concern, though. Leonard Horowitz had been there from the beginning when the idea for the Art Deco district was conceived. He transformed the look of South Beach from beige and brown to a tropical rainbow. He drove ten thousand miles across the country in a Chevette with Barbara Capitman spreading the word about tropical Art Deco, a trip he likened to "crossing the Atlantic in a kayak."[26]

Most pioneer developers hired Horowitz, sometimes to design the paint job for the facades of their buildings, sometimes to design interiors. His enthusiasm was contagious. He involved no-nonsense businessmen in serious debate over the difference between coral and salmon. He painted Tony Goldman's Park Central periwinkle, khaki, lavender, and white. Horowitz knew the colors were not historically accurate, but after more than sixty projects, his concept of what would make people take notice of the district and fight to protect it was an unquestioned success.

Horowitz and his work began to grow more subdued in 1987. That was when he learned that he was HIV-positive. He took the test in secret and kept it that way. He started packing on a few extra pounds, in case he needed them later. He was feeling fine, although he had some trouble sleeping. He was still seen around the district, excited at its daily transformations. Then one day he collapsed while going into the league's offices.[27] He was scared. He didn't know what was happening to him. Late that summer, he checked into the hospital with pneumocystis pneumonia. Then he became paralyzed from the waist down.[28]

Ernie Martin and Tony Goldman organized a special meeting of the league in November at the Park Central. Horowitz, forty-two years old, who was openly, profoundly gay, had developed AIDS. It was time for the league to use its organizational experience to help one of its own.

Gays were a major force in the preservation movement nationwide. Since most gays and lesbians did not have children, a preserved building or neighborhood was a legacy they could leave to future generations. Depressed areas that were prime opportunities for revitalization often were populated by ethnic minorities who didn't have suburban prejudices. Gays did not have some of the concerns of the traditional American family that worried about the quality of schools and the safety of playgrounds and latchkey kids. They had pioneered the revival of marginal neighborhoods all over the country. Gay men had been active in the South Beach district from the beginning. They weren't there because they were gay. Many of them still were in the closet. Being gay was no more the reason for their involvement than if they were vegetarians or had brown hair. There was no organized movement within the gay community to support the Art Deco district. They were there because they were designers, architects, decorators, collectors, planners, property owners, and interested volunteers who were actively helping to save South Beach.

South Beach also drew the artistic and cultural crowd, including the symphony, the ballet, the South Florida Arts Center, and the fashion industry. With them came a sense of style and the money to buy or rent apartments and fix them up. They found a tolerant neighborhood of other displaced minorities who didn't mind having a few more single men in the neighborhood.

But with the gay population in the 1980s, AIDS followed.

Leonard Horowitz didn't have money. When he did have cash, he would splurge on something extravagant, like the time he cruised to London on the Queen Elizabeth II and flew back on the Concorde. But he had an army of battle-hardened fighters behind him. Fifty people came to the emergency meeting. This was one issue on which the league members could agree. They would do everything that was needed. Ernie Martin sent a mailing to the league's six hundred dues-paying members, and they responded generously.[29]

The league took over responsibility for some of Horowitz's bills, although collection agencies continued to hound him. Goldman provided an apartment in one of his buildings. A live-in attendant was hired. South Beach restaurants delivered dinners to him three nights a week. Liebman brought him chicken soup from the Epicure Market every week. Some friends took him on a powerboat outing one sunny afternoon. Members did his shopping, and food markets helped by donating groceries. Saul Gross, another pioneer restoration developer, took Horowitz out in his wheelchair to inspect the latest renovations. One of Horowitz's few complaints was that no one ever took him clothes shopping.

He met someone while he was in the hospital with another bout of pneumocystis in January, but he was too sick to pursue a relationship. "I'm looking for somebody I can just hug or something," he told a reporter. "You know you just need that. Just somebody to love and hug. That's all we were really looking for in the first place. It wasn't all the sex and everything. We just wanted to find someone to be with, like everyone else."[30]

Slowly he began to regain strength. He was able to discard the wheel-chair and walk with a cane. He resumed his social schedule. Then suddenly in April 1989, his health began to fail dramatically. Leonard Horowitz died on May 8, 1989, at the age of forty-three. He was not the first member of the South Beach crowd to die of AIDS. He would not be the last.

Barbara Capitman was deeply saddened at the loss of her friend, but she also was becoming increasingly concerned at the direction the district was taking. She saw the elderly being forgotten and shoved aside as gentrification took hold. She kept busy debating at commission and planning board meetings, protesting in front of buildings threatened with demolition, standing before the television cameras, and cornering print reporters. By spring 1990, she was working on another book on Art Deco architecture with Kinerk and Wilhelm. She had moved into a fifty-three-year-old house on Thirtieth Street, next door to Lynn Bernstein. She finally got a computer to replace the old Olympia typewriter and was starting up her public relations business again. She was excited that the whole family would be coming to Miami Beach for her seventieth birthday. Bernstein called her one evening to talk about the guest list. They laughed about one person who had been invited that Capitman didn't particularly like.

Barbara Capitman was taken to the hospital the following day. Her sons and their families quickly rearranged schedules and arrived as fast as they could. There was an article in the newspaper about her upcoming birthday, and Dennis Wilhelm called her at the hospital that night to tell her about it. She told him, "Wait until you see the story tomorrow."[31]

She died the next morning, March 29, 1990. The league had lost two of its founders in less than a year.

Kinerk and Wilhelm organized a memorial service. Barbara Baer Capitman was raised Jewish, but it was no longer a relevant part of her life. That aside, Kinerk called the mayor and told him they needed Temple Emanu-el, a magnificent synagogue across the street from the Theater of the Performing Arts. The rabbi was out of the country, but the mayor said he would take care of everything. John Capitman was opposed to having the service in a religious setting, but Kinerk and Wilhelm overruled him, with Andrew Capitman's concurrence. Kinerk and Wilhelm thought of themselves as Capitman's "third son." The service was standing room only. That afternoon, the mail that was delivered to Capitman's home included the city's historic landmark designation report for Temple Emanu-el.[32]

Kinerk felt that it would be appropriate for the city to honor Capitman in some way for her contributions to its revitalization. Suggestions included naming a major street after her, or a plaza, or turning an old Art Deco building into the community and educational center for senior citizens that she had always wanted. The commission voted six-to-one to rename one block of Tenth Street between Ocean Drive and Collins Avenue as Barbara Capitman Way.[33]

Commissioner Abe Resnick cast the dissenting vote.

CHAPTER II

The District Grows Up

Richard Hoberman invited some potential investors to lunch at an Ocean Drive hotel restaurant on an autumn Tuesday in 1990. As chairman of the league he planned to spend the time pitching the virtues of the Art Deco district, trying to persuade them to join the resurgence. As he waited for his chicken salad to be served, he surveyed the setting that made the area a tourist magnet from its earliest days. The remnants of Tropical Storm Klaus were whipping through the trees in Lummus Park and kicking up waves in the Atlantic. Hoberman looked up toward Fifteenth Street where the Jefferson Hotel stood at the head of Ocean Drive. He saw smoke. The abandoned Jefferson, a concern of preservationists and adjacent property owners for years, was on fire.[1]

His guests were speechless. They heard sirens approaching. There was nothing they could do. So they stayed at the table and finished their lunch, although Hoberman knew that a burning building was not going to impress investors with the promise of the district.

The firefighters radioed back to the station that there was light smoke coming from the hotel. A few seconds later they radioed again, "Make that heavy smoke." Less than a minute later, they made another call, "Make that a code one fire." The first and second floors were fully involved in what appeared to be multiple fires.[2] The forty-mile-per-hour winds off the ocean incited the fire in the long-vacant 1939 hotel. Firefighters hauled huge hoses from their trucks, and ladders were lifted to reach the flames leaping through the roof. The many windows broken during years of disuse created a flue that sucked the inferno through the building. A city order for the owner to board up the building had been ignored. The adjacent Bancroft Hotel, still empty five years after Lillian

Levin and her neighbors were evicted, was equally unprotected. Fire crews aimed water jets on the Bancroft trying to keep the flames from spreading. Clouds of smoke, spreading to buildings across Collins Avenue, forced residents out of their apartments and hotel rooms with cloths over their faces. One woman who evacuated had jumped to safety from the second floor of another hotel to escape a fire only six months earlier.[3] By 12:30, firefighters were resigned to limiting their efforts to damage control of the surrounding area. The Jefferson could not be saved.

Fires were all too frequent in the Art Deco district, particularly in abandoned buildings. There had been earlier fires at the Jefferson, the St. Moritz, the White House Hotel, and others. Arson on Miami Beach had hit an all-time high in 1985. There had been several deaths. Only a month earlier, the owner of the Shorecrest, immediately north of the Jefferson, pleaded with the city commission to demolish the Jefferson and the Bancroft hotels or to see them properly secured. There had been small fires in both hotels, and each attracted a steady stream of unsavory-looking characters. Homeless people had set up housekeeping in the drained Bancroft pool, complete with easy chairs. The issue was scheduled for discussion at the next city commission meeting.[4]

The city's building director estimated that, in the Art Deco district alone, at least seventy-five vacant buildings remained unprotected in defiance of city orders. The city had the power to contract for the necessary work and place liens against the building for the cost of the repairs, but it would cost a half million dollars to seal all the abandoned buildings in the city.

Some empty buildings belonged to the Royale Group. The company had ridden into town on a cloud of promised multimillion-dollar renovations, strong commitments to historic preservation, and an eagerness to be the linchpin in the revitalization of the Art Deco district. The city and preservationists alike had looked to them as the key to launching new investment on Ocean Drive and Collins Avenue.

In June 1989, eight months after the demolition of the Senator, Leonard Pelullo, chief executive officer of the Royale Group, had been indicted on forty-six counts of wire fraud and one count of violating the RICO (Racketeer Influenced and Corrupt Organizations) Act for allegedly misappropriating funds from an Ohio savings and loan association.[5]

The feds claimed that Pelullo was engaged in a series of illegal schemes to defraud both his own company and the Ohio lender by diverting money from a Royale subsidiary.[6] The charges stemmed from loans made to a separate Pelullo-controlled company that was renovating the Beach hotels. The assistant U.S. district attorney in Cincinnati alleged that a part of the loan proceeds was used as a kickback to an officer of the Ohio lender and that an unidentified amount found its way into one of Pelullo's personal bank accounts.[7] Anger toward Royale because of the demolition of the Senator was so intense that it was hard to find anyone in the district who was sorry to hear the news of Pelullo's downfall. Private speculation swirled that Royale had bought the hotels only in the anticipation that casino gambling would be legalized and they would enjoy a windfall.

In November 1990, a federal judge ordered a foreclosure sale of the Royale's hotels. The debt on the hotels was more than $35 million.[8] They were sold on the courthouse steps on a busy downtown Miami street. The winning bidder was the main mortgage holder. It paid $9.95 million, just over a quarter of the value of the mortgages.[9] It was anyone's guess who would buy the hotels from the lender or what would happen to them.

Whoever bought the Royale's properties would have stronger regulations to observe when doing renovations. Preservationists had been piecing together local historic districts that would bring the entire National Register district under the protection of the city's landmarks ordinances before any more buildings were demolished.

Creating a local historic district was a long and tedious process that included public hearings, meetings, and votes by the historic preservation board, the planning and zoning board, and the city commission. In 1990, the preservation board succeeded in pushing a third historic district through the city commission. The Flamingo Park Historic District cut a wide swath through the center of South Beach, and most of the residential area of small Art Deco and Mediterranean apartment buildings was now protected. Combined with the Ocean Drive/Collins Avenue and Espanola Way districts, 85 percent of the eleven-year-old National Register Art Deco district had been brought under local preservation regulations. Some areas remained unprotected. Most of the area north of Fifteenth Street including Lincoln Road, the neighborhood around the Bass Museum of Art in Collins Park, and the upper half of Collins Avenue, which included the Art Deco signature Delano, Ritz Plaza, and Sands hotels were fair game.

The Collins Avenue hotels were of particular concern. The city's convention center was undergoing a $92-million expansion that would make it one of the ten largest such facilities in the world. No major new hotels had been built in Miami Beach since 1967. The city craved a new convention hotel that would attract the top meetings and exhibitions. Every few years the subject would emerge, be discussed with great fervor, and then return to hibernation.

The city identified fourteen possible sites for a convention hotel in 1988. With specific properties in mind, it might finally attract a developer interested in building the long-sought project. Five of the sites would require demolition or severe alteration of historic hotels. Two suggested locations were near the Bass Museum, a neighborhood that preservationists envisioned as a European-style village of hotels, shops, and cafés that would offer the convention-goer an alternative to the environs of the traditional big hotel.

The site that generated the biggest protest from preservationists was on Collins Avenue, one of the most recognizable strips of major Art Deco hotels in the National Register district. It included the Bancroft that had survived the Jefferson fire, the St. Moritz, the Shorecrest, Art Unger's Royal Palm, the Poinciana site, and the Sands. Abe Resnick had sold the Sands and the neighboring empty lot where the New Yorker had stood to investors, who had plans to buy the entire block from Fifteenth to Sixteenth streets and raze the historic buildings to create space for a 1,200-room hotel.[10] If the district was to be maintained, then local protection was needed quickly.

By 1991 a proposal to overlay the entire National Register district with local historic district designation was before the Miami Beach Historic Preservation Board. Nancy Liebman had her hands full. Her three kids were out on their own, so she and her husband decided to sell the big house on the canal and move to an apartment on the Venetian Islands. The house sold quickly, and she had six weeks to pack up twenty-three years of accumulated furniture and books and her husband's paintings and her files and their memories and all the stuff the kids still had stored there. Then her husband had to have surgery in Philadelphia, and she flew there to be with him for several days. Her older daughter was expecting her first child. Liebman had a lot of distractions, but designating the rest of the Art Deco district was a goal she had worked toward for ten years. As chairman of the historic preservation board, she needed to guide it through the process.

Liebman was speechless when she was told that she should abstain from voting on the final district recommendation because of her position as executive director of the league. She didn't own any property in the area, and neither she nor the league would realize any monetary benefit from the designation. She had voted on other equally sensitive issues without challenge. She felt that her integrity was being impugned. A $15,000-a-year job wasn't worth the insult.[11]

At the same time, her position with the league was on shaky footing. After Barbara Capitman died, many members had expected the media spotlight to shift to Michael Kinerk. He had been Capitman's right hand and confidante for years. But he was limited in his role as a spokesman because he worked for the *Miami Herald*. Liebman, already established as executive director and a quotable spokesman, had a strong personality that left scant room for another voice. During her tenure, she had gone from working alone in a cubbyhole office in the back room of a storefront to supervising a professional staff.

Internal politics and financial struggles could have been the league motto. It tacked between boom and bust. The fat days when there was a big grant in hand always gave way to scratching for funds to pay the phone bill. It had four employees, nearly a thousand members, and some serious money problems. Most of their income came from sales of merchandise and programs during Art Deco Weekend. The league's Welcome Center store, where visitors could buy "I Dig Deco" sand pails, posters, tee-shirts, and Deco related books, had not turned a profit in the three years it had been open, and board members laid the blame at Liebman's feet. The league finished the previous two years at a deficit, and the reserve fund withered to less than $20,000.[12]

The money crunch came to a head in October 1991. The board fired all of Liebman's hand-picked staff and brought in an accountant to take over the finances. It was going to try to do the work of the staff with volunteers. Liebman was incensed. She could not continue the league's existing programs and activities with only volunteers to help her. Between the question of her eligibility to vote on the preservation board and the bitterness in the league's board room, Liebman knew that something had to give. The day after the Art Deco Weekend in January 1992, their most successful event ever, was Liebman's last day as executive director of the Miami Design Preservation League. The press reported that she resigned, and, to save public face, the board appointed her as its spokesman and chair of its governmental affairs committee. She barely had time to clean out her desk before she was on the battlefront again.

Liebman was looking out the window from her Venetian Islands apartment a few weeks later and saw bulldozers rolling up Collins Avenue. She immediately got on the phone to the Sands' new owner, who explained that Abe Resnick's son Jimmy had told him that he would never be able to sell the site for new development if he didn't tear down the hotel. Even with the resurgence of interest in South Beach, the Sands was worth more dead than alive. The building's assessed value was less than a million dollars. The land beneath it was worth more than two million.[13] Although it was within the National Register district, the Sands still had no local protection.

Jimmy Resnick had taken over many of the daily responsibilities for the Resnick operations. He had grown up on South Beach as a typical American kid, spending his time at Flamingo Park playing basketball, baseball, soccer. He married a Miami Beach girl and was raising three sons in his hometown. He shared his father's opinion about other people telling him what he could do with his own property. And he didn't like old buildings.

Liebman sprang into action by habit. The next day protestors were standing on the sidewalk in front of the Collins Avenue hotel shouting "Save the Sands! Save the Sands!"[14] Young people, old people, children, people on bicycles, and tourists in shorts and tee-shirts stopped to look. On the south side of the Sands stood the St. Moritz, a slender building with a soaring tower, also vacant. To the north was the site where the New Yorker had been. A tall crane was positioned behind the hotel, on the ocean side, hidden from the street. Moments later, the crane swung a heavy ball into the upper stories of the northeast corner of the hotel. A little girl on the sidewalk stuck her fingers in her ears to muffle the noise. The Sands was added to the list of historic buildings that had been lost.

The Park Hotel on Ocean Drive didn't wait for its owner to request a demolition permit.

Restoring the aging hotels was like walking across a minefield for architects and contractors. The architect never knew what hidden surprises were not reflected on the building records at city hall. There were clues. A wall that looked like drywall but felt like wood, baseboards that changed width halfway across the room, uneven floors, a horizontal bulge in a wall were all signals to inspect things more closely. When he exposed the ceiling he might discover that the floor deck above wasn't concrete, as expected, but an ancient Roman system using red hollow clay tile.

Replacing the plumbing and wiring was relatively simple, and the wood usually was in good shape unless moisture had been allowed to seep into the building. Terrazzo floors could be covered with plywood during construction, then polished to a new shine. Fireplace surrounds were removed and stored temporarily, murals covered to avoid damage and then restored by an artist. Windows were reglazed, or, if inappropriate replacements had been installed, windows similar to the originals were ordered. The architect could work around interior columns and load-bearing walls to create new spaces. Construction of a new addition required excavation and trying to keep out the water until the foundation could be poured.

The real problem was concrete. During the grim years of the 1970s and 1980s, many property owners didn't have the money to maintain their buildings properly. Moisture intrusion corroded the reinforcing bars and beams and caused the concrete to spall and begin to crumble. Soil tests had to be conducted to determine whether the concrete foundation was strong enough. If the underground concrete failed the test, then a geotechnical engineer had to be found who was willing to vouch that repair techniques could be used to mitigate the damage. If not, the building had to be demolished. The league constantly fought to prove that reinforcing buildings was possible and economical.

The Park Hotel had been finished in time to survive the historic 1926 hurricane. It was one of the handful of buildings on Ocean Drive designed in the Mediterranean Revival style. It had some serious structural problems. Workers needed to reinforce the hotel's supporting columns using Gunite, a concrete forced into forms under high air pressure. Threaded rebar and reinforcing screen were used to give the Gunite a good foothold on the old exterior walls. A couple of men were inside the building spraying the material on the columns of the south wall and several others were outside manning the compressor, mixer, and other equipment.[15] The crew inside heard a low, loud creaking sound coming from above them. It didn't stop. It grew louder. They didn't know what it was, but they knew it wasn't good. They dropped everything and started running as fast as they could toward the front of the building. They had just reached safe ground when the south wall caved inward, bringing down the roof right where they had been standing.

Luckily, no one was injured. Engineers sadly pronounced the Park Hotel dead on arrival. The wrecking ball finished what gravity and time and salt had started. It raised a question that had been lurking at the edges of the restoration movement for a long time.

The extent of renovations had changed dramatically since the early days of the South Beach revitalization when developers slapped on some pastel paint, exterminated the rats and roaches, threw out the smelly mattresses, put some wicker furniture and potted palms in the lobby, and doubled the rent. Prices for South Beach properties were rising; standards for the finished project were higher; more money was on the line. There were no preservation controls over interior renovations. Nothing prevented a developer from eviscerating the building, leaving only the original shell, and putting in a new interior dressed up with the old front desk and elevator to give it a hint of authenticity.

The company that was setting the new standard of balance between restoration and remodeling was Dacra Companies, owned by brothers Craig and Scott Robins. Although their father was a longtime Beach developer, the Robins brothers cut their South Beach development teeth with Tony Goldman. Older brother Craig began working with Goldman after graduating from the University of Miami law school. They did several projects with Goldman before the brothers set out on their own.

Dacra entered the district on Collins Avenue, which was beginning to come into its own. For several years, the street had been playing second fiddle to Ocean Drive and Washington Avenue, which ran parallel on either side of it. They turned a former drug den, the Webster Hotel, into commercial space to rent and luxury apartments for themselves.[16]

The Robins brothers used a tough-love approach by maintaining architectural exteriors while gutting the insides to create dazzling accommodations inside the historic shell. Their approach echoed that of Barbaralee Diamonstein in her book *Remaking America* in which she wrote, "Preservation does not, and emphatically should not, mean merely restoration."[17] It was expensive, but it was getting results and getting attention. Their properties were attracting a wealthier clientele that demanded spacious rooms with designer furnishings and well-lighted bathrooms and expected more than a few luxuries to justify the jarring charge on their platinum cards. It opened a lot of eyes about the attainable profits of the old hotels.

Their partner in some of their projects was Island Trading, a development company headed by Chris Blackwell, the music maven who made stars of Bob Marley, U2, and Grace Jones. The two companies teamed up and hired local architect Les Beilinson and English designer Barbara Hulanicki to renovate the Marlin Hotel on Collins Avenue, with a heavy dose of cosmopolitan sleek, a resident modeling firm, and its own recording studio.[18] They brought celebrity glamour to the district and gave it the glitz that quickly was elevating South Beach to a *haute* destination.

The Art Deco district had outgrown the days when everyone knew everyone else and hung out on the porch at the Cardozo talking about how they were going to change the world. Success was in the air. The historic preservation board pressed harder to put the final piece of the puzzle in place to bring all of the National Register district under local regulation.

Hurricane Andrew

At 6:00 a.m. Saturday, August 22, 1992, the late-night crowd was heading home from the South Beach clubs. Cafés and diners were serving breakfast to their early morning regulars. A few apartment dwellers were slipping outside in their bathrobes to retrieve the morning paper. Ocean Drive was quiet. At the National Hurricane Center in Coral Gables, word came in that Tropical Storm Andrew had reached sustained winds of seventy-five miles per hour. It was upgraded to the season's first named hurricane.[19] It was headed straight for South Florida.

Summer was almost at an end. Public schools would open in ten days, and South Beach parents were going across the causeways to K-Mart and Office Depot and the mall to shop for clothes, notebooks, and new shoes.

Weekend gardeners were ripping out weeds that had taken liberties with flower beds of lantana and liriope. Golfers with summer memberships were squeezing in another eighteen holes on the links. Children were going to birthday parties or spending the afternoon at the Flamingo Park pool. Off-season tourists were joined by local residents enjoying a day at the beach.

The activity level at the Dade County Office of Emergency Management was one of controlled nervousness. Kate Hale, the office's director, was in communication with local, state, and federal agencies in preparation for a 6:00 a.m. Sunday meeting. If the storm stayed on track, everyone needed to be ready for action.

Red and black hurricane warning flags were raised Sunday morning, and all of South Florida switched into hurricane preparation mode. Owners of Dade County's almost sixty thousand boats scrambled to get their vessels to safe harbor before the bridges were locked down to facilitate residents' evacuation. Dialysis patients hurried to hospitals for treatment, not knowing when they would be able to get there again. Homeowners put up hurricane shutters and stored lawn furniture and trash cans in their garages. Supermarkets were jammed with people buying bread, diapers, kitty litter, batteries, pet food, and bathroom tissue. Shelves were emptied of junk food, beer, and bottled water. Service stations had lines of customers filling their cars and trucks. ATMs ran out of cash. Churches canceled services to batten down their buildings. Building supply stores opened trucks full of plywood in their parking lots to try to keep up with the demand. Horses were taken to safe shelter. Booms of cranes were lowered and secured, and construction materials tied down. Officials at MetroZoo herded animals into pens and marshaled the flamingos into the public restrooms for protection. Pregnant women who were within three weeks of their due date were urged to check into a hospital because the low barometric pressure associated with a hurricane often caused babies to arrive ahead of schedule. Cruise ships at the Port of Miami raced to get their returning passengers to the airport and to board their outbound passengers in time to get the ships out of harm's way. Radios and televisions everywhere in Dade, Broward, and Monroe counties were tuned in for the latest updates.

Bob Sheets, director of the National Hurricane Center, gave the bad news to the local weather reporters. If Andrew stayed on track, a storm surge of more than ten feet would wash over homes, condos, and hotels near the coast at whatever point the storm came ashore. There was one glimmer of hope for the Miami area. A high-pressure system off the Georgia and Carolina coast might ease up enough for the storm to veer north. Instead, the storm sped up, reaching sixteen miles an hour forward motion.[20] It would strike South Florida stronger and earlier than expected.

The evacuation order went out. Residents of Miami Beach, Key Biscayne, and other coastline communities were instructed to leave immediately. Those who refused were asked for the names of their next of kin. City crews and fire fighters knocked on the doors of people who had signed up as needing assistance to leave. Ten percent of the Beach's residents were considered "frail" and posed special evacuation problems. Metrobus operated a shuttle to assist those who did not have their own transportation. Some checked into inland hotels or went to stay with friends or family. Others were among the 84,000 people taking refuge in the emergency shelters the American Red Cross set up throughout Dade County.[21] They had to take their pets to kennels before they would be admitted. Traffic ground to a halt on major roads as people tried to flee to northern counties. It was after noon on Sunday before Governor Lawton Chiles threw open the toll booths on the Florida Turnpike to allow cars to move through more quickly.

City workers tied down light poles, shuttered city buildings, removed coconuts and dead fronds from palm trees, and took trash cans and other portable objects to warehouses. The city hurricane command post was readied in a windowless fourth floor room in city hall. The mayor planned to spend the night there. Miami Beach hospitals moved five hundred patients inland but remained open with those who were too ill to be moved.

Diane Camber knew what a big storm could do to Miami Beach. Her parents were there during the 1926 hurricane. She remembered the story her father told of swimming up Collins Avenue to see if her mother was okay. The house her father built had withstood other hurricanes, so she decided to stay put and invited Richard Hoberman over for a prehurricane dinner. Lynn Bernstein gathered up precious items from her mother, grandmother, and great-grandmother and left with her husband and daughter to stay at a friend's home in South Miami. Michael

Kinerk and Dennis Wilhelm, who had moved to the beach in 1986 up the street from Bernstein and three blocks from Abe Resnick, took refuge at the *Miami Herald*, a structure built to withstand 150 mile-per-hour winds. Liebman was with her family spending the month in the Berkshires. Her mother-in-law called to tell them a storm was coming, but Liebman thought she was overreacting.

By nightfall, Miami Beach and its neighboring communities had hunkered down. South Beach streets were deserted. Parking lots were empty. Restaurants were dark. A few hurricane parties hosted and attended by people who had more beer than sense were getting under way. Andrew strengthened to 150 miles per hour and drew a bead on Dade County.[22] It had been twenty-seven years since a major storm hit the Miami area. A majority of the population had never experienced the wrath of a category-four hurricane. The new suburbs of South Dade never had been tested, nor had the high-rises of Miami Beach and the office towers downtown. The only question that remained was exactly where the eye of the storm would make landfall, who would take the direct hit.

The wind started to intensify by midnight. Hoberman woke up at 2:00 a.m. At first he was a bit miffed; he thought Camber had given him regular coffee instead of decaf. Then he realized that it was the moaning wind that woke him. Wilhelm watched from the *Herald* building as the lights on the MacArthur Causeway thrashed about wildly. High-rise condominiums lurched noticeably. Bernstein was huddled under the stairwell in her friend's house with her husband, daughter, and their dog.

Andrew's winds exceeded 165 miles-per-hour before the eye came ashore just south of Miami and directly east of Homestead Air Force base at 4:55 a.m. as a category-five storm.[23] By then, power was out to most of the county. Battery-operated radios and televisions were the only sources of information for the millions of people who were huddled in hallways and bathrooms listening to the wind scream. Police and fire dispatchers took more than five thousand emergency 911 calls between 2:30 and 4:30 a.m., mostly from people who realized they had made a terrible mistake to stay where they were. It was too late to help them. By 4:30 a.m., 164 mile-per-hour gusts were battering the National Hurricane Center in Coral Gables. Its rooftop radar system was gone. A section of its ceiling collapsed. Forecasters had to rely on satellite images from phone lines to keep feeding vital information to the media.

The fury subsided on South Beach by 8:00 a.m. Monday. Trees were lying across flooded roads and resting at rakish angles against buildings. Streets were awash in glass from broken windows of stores, hotels, and apartments. Traffic signals were lying useless on the pavement. Street signs littered sidewalks. Camber and Hoberman emerged from their homes to find fallen limbs and trees but no serious damage. A few cars that were left on the streets were dented from flying debris. At the Burdines department store, mannequins had tried to escape through shattered display windows. Coconut palms were scattered around Lummus Park. Awnings were shredded. On the south tip of the beach, the winds stripped the stucco from the upper story of the old hotel that W. J. Brown built in 1915 revealing the original name for the first time since 1936. There was no electricity, no running water. Houseboats bobbed upside down in Indian Creek. Golf courses were swamped, tennis court nets were in tatters, swimming pools were filled with debris. The beach was littered with the detritus of an angry ocean.[24]

Long lines of traffic backed up on the causeways as Beach residents and business owners anxiously waited to return and see how their property had fared. Tempers began to flare as they learned it would be at least 5:00 p.m. before they would be allowed back on the island. The streets weren't safe because of downed power lines and trees blocking the roads. Most of them hadn't seen a television or a newspaper, although the *Miami Herald* managed to get out a limited edition that morning. When they were able to pass the barricades, Kinerk and Wilhelm returned home to find five trees uprooted in their yard and one broken window. Bernstein's front door was blocked by fallen trees, and her roof was leaking from damage done by flying debris. It was much worse farther south.

There was no power to 1.3 million of Dade County's homes. The death toll was twenty-three. One hundred eighty thousand people were homeless. Officials predicted it could take up to two weeks for the county's water system to be in full operation again. In the Country Walk subdivision in South Dade, roofs were gone, and houses had collapsed. Three-quarters of the county's 2,400 traffic lights were out. Exterior walls were ripped from apartment buildings and shopping centers. The trees in the state park on the tip of Key Biscayne were lying on the ground, every pine tree laid out pointing due west. A 210-ton freighter had been lifted from its anchorage and deposited five hundred feet inland. A sailboat landed on top of Vizcaya's neatly trimmed hedges. Curtains fluttered from broken windows of the Dade County Courthouse, and shards of glass littered the sidewalks in downtown Miami. One man, whose wife had been after him for years to get a tool shed, woke up to find that he suddenly had one in his backyard. In Homestead, it was hard to find a building that wasn't damaged. Every block of Florida City had at least one building demolished. Gas station pumps were ripped from the ground, and an eighteen-wheeler was lodged in what was left of a concrete building. The trunk of a palm tree was pierced through by a sheet of plywood. The zoo was missing three hundred of its birds, and the koalas were hungry because the eucalyptus trees were destroyed. A state official said "Homestead Air Force Base no longer exists." Hurricane Andrew cut a path of destruction twenty-five miles wide across the entire peninsula. There was more than $25 billion worth of damage, including more than a billion to the county's agriculture industry.[25] Metro-Dade emergency services, the agencies that were supposed to help everyone when something like this happened, lost helicopters, fire trucks, rescue vehicles, and fire stations, losses that severely hampered their ability to respond.

South Beach dodged the bullet. It was bloodied but unbowed. Ocean Drive was coated with sand. There were broken windows, downed signs and trees. But by Thursday, South Beach was back in operation. In spite of a 7:00 p.m. curfew and police roadblocks scattered around the city, people reappeared on the streets and in the cafés. The Beach rolled out the red carpet. The state tourism office ran an advertisement in *USA Today* proclaiming "Florida: We're Still Open." Hotel owners and merchants applauded their employees for getting reopened so quickly. Labor Day weekend was coming up, and South Beach wanted to be ready for people looking for a break. The scheduled school opening was delayed two weeks, which gave students time to help clean up yards, deliver food to the homebound, and sort and pack donated goods.

Within a few days, the Art Deco district began filling up with homeless residents, insurance adjusters, scam artists, and out-of-state power and telephone crews. Residents of storm-torn parts of the county came to escape their ravaged neighborhoods, to get away from the smell of rotting garbage and standing in line four hours to buy a bag of ice, from living in tents and spray painting their address on what was left of their homes in hopes that an insurance adjuster would show up, from the whine of chain saws and the groan of heavy equipment of six huge construction companies hired by the Army Corps of Engineers to help clear the debris, from thousands of National Guardsmen and federal troops wearing camouflage, from the twenty-four-hour-a-day throbbing of helicopters overhead ferrying relief supplies to the hardest hit areas.

Vacant apartments in renovated and unrenovated buildings instantly became prime real estate because they had a roof, a door, and electricity. Those looking for long-term shelter weren't finding any bargains, though. Florida had laws to prevent price gouging, but they didn't cover rental housing. Prices soared overnight. A man looking for a rental for his family found a two bedroom/two bath apartment on South Beach for $1,600 a month. When he called back the next day, the price had gone up to $2,700.[26]

The Last Piece of the Puzzle

League members heaved a collective sigh of relief that South Beach had survived the storm intact. After everyone cleaned up their downed trees, broken windows, and torn awnings, they focused attention on the preservation board's new proposal that would give local historic district status to the entire one-square-mile National Register area. As the recommendation worked its way through the board meetings and public hearings, it became clear that a compromise would be necessary to get a majority vote of approval from the city commission. An agreement was hammered out that put the league in the uncomfortable position of agreeing to a provision that would accommodate construction of a convention-sized hotel within the district. The league agreed to help a hotel developer incorporate historic oceanfront hotels on Collins Avenue north of Fifteenth Street into a new design. The preservationists despised idea of mammoth hotels for people who wanted to stay in shiny new rooms and look out at the Deco buildings like monkeys at the zoo. But the city was determined to have its new hotel.

The league wanted to get the final piece of the district designated before the National Trust for Historic Preservation's annual conference came to Miami in early October 1992. Having the National Trust conference held in Miami was considered a major feather in the caps of the South Florida preservationists. When the idea of bidding for the meeting originally was floated by Dade Heritage Trust in the early 1980s, it was summarily dismissed by many national and state preservation leaders who didn't consider the Miami area ready to host the annual national event. In 1986, the leaders of Dade Heritage Trust decided to submit an invitation anyway. Its members arrived at the National Trust's annual meeting in Kansas City that year armed with a supply of tiny pink embroidered flamingos, which they affixed to their own lapels and the clothing of anyone else who was willing to walk around wearing a pink flamingo. They actively lobbied to secure the national meeting for Miami. They wanted to generate enough interest and enthusiasm to influence the National Trust board when it came time to select its meeting site for 1992. It worked.

Florida had built one of the most respected historic preservation programs in the country. The state, city, and local education programs, the level of state and local funding, the numbers and enthusiasm of the members of preservation groups around the state, the organization, and the visibility were envied by many. More than two thousand preservationists from around the country were heading to Miami in October 1992. Some of them planned to stay in South Beach hotels, although transportation was difficult to the convention headquarters in downtown Miami. The Art Deco district, which just had been dubbed by *Travel and Leisure* magazine as "the hippest hangout on earth" would play an important role in the week's program. The league hoped that the presence of so many preservationists would underscore for city commissioners the importance of their treasured Art Deco buildings and the need to preserve them.

Dwight Young, a senior communications associate with the National Trust, wrote in the preconvention issue of the *Historic Preservation News*, "I'm going to stroll up the street, along that incomparable blocks-long row of hotels. I'll hear the music and the cash registers ringing. I'll notice the new neon signs and the fresh paint jobs and the lines of cars looking for parking spaces. And somewhere I'm going to stop in the middle of the sidewalk and shout, 'Barbara Capitman was right!'"[27]

The Miami area had a lot of success stories to put on display. The Venetian Causeway from Miami to Miami Beach had been rebuilt as a historic roadway after plans to "modernize" it were defeated. The Charles Deering Estate in South Dade had been acquired by the county and undergone a careful restoration under the guidance of Ivan Rodriguez. There were historic districts springing up in inner-ring neighborhoods and suburbs as residents began to understand how to employ preservation to stabilize property values and revitalize the neighborhood. There were more than fifty sites and three thematic districts in Dade County listed on the National Register. The members of the National Trust for Historic Preservation wouldn't see the 1907 Redlands schoolhouse or the 1898 Richmond Inn at the Deering Estate or Lowry Anderson's blacksmith shop built in 1912. They were flattened by Hurricane Andrew. Dozens of historic wood-frame buildings from the early 1900s were demolished or heavily damaged. Vizcaya had sustained injury but would be presentable. It would take a lot of work, but the conference would go on.

Ten days before the Miami Beach City Commission meeting to vote on the final section of the completed local historic district, things started unraveling at city hall. Two commissioners would be out of town on the day the vote was scheduled. Two others felt they needed to abstain from the vote because they or their families had interests in the area. That left only the mayor and two commissioners, two shy of the five votes needed.[28]

The city attorney finally ruled that the conflicts of only one commissioner who owned property were sufficient to preclude him from voting. Another commissioner flew back from a trip to Chicago. One was awakened from his regular afternoon nap to cast his vote. Commissioner Abe Resnick was out of town. The ordinance passed five-to-zero. Ten years after the city's historic preservation ordinance was adopted, and thirteen years after the Art Deco district was added to the National Register, the one-square-mile local historic district was complete.[29]

CHAPTER 12

The Final Knockout

There was a time when Miami Beach was as famous for boxing as it was for its sunshine. Most of the credit went to Chris Dundee, a boxing promoter from Philadelphia.

Chris Dundee arrived in Miami Beach and opened the Fifth Street Gym in 1950. It wasn't glamorous. It occupied the upper floor of an old block-long building at Fifth Street and Washington Avenue. Dundee was going to promote fights at the Miami Beach Auditorium right up the street.

The key to putting together a fight card every Tuesday night was to have an abundance of local talent. Bringing experienced fighters in from out of town cost money for transportation, housing, food. If the guy lived right across the bay, then all you had to pay was bus fare. His family could feed him. The Fifth Street Gym was Dundee's training school. Everybody who was a boxer or had a dream to be a boxer showed up at the Fifth Street Gym to see if he had what it took. Maybe he would make it, maybe he wouldn't, but he was there.

The door was guarded by a cranky troll named Sully. Sully didn't look good even when you dressed him up. Because Sully's salary came from the two bits admission everyone was charged to enter, he made sure everyone paid. Visitors and fighters and trainers alike climbed a creaky staircase to a room that was larger and dirtier than everyone expected. The Florida sun strained to make its way through the grime on two walls of windows. The room was filled with sounds of people involved in intense physical activity.[1]

The place was a dump from the beginning, but that's what Dundee wanted. Clean and shiny didn't suit the world of boxing. It needed to be raw and gritty. It smelled like all gyms smell: an unmistakable blend of sweat, rubbing alcohol, and leather. They kept patching the floor where it had been skipped raw by soft leather soles but the plywood wore out faster than the hardwood. The pharmacist in the drugstore on the first floor lived under the threat of being leveled by a plummeting heavyweight. The air in the gym was thick with dust, smoke, and hope. It was dedicated to the single happy proposition of building champions.

Miami Beach, like all of the Greater Miami area, was racially segregated when Chris Dundee opened his gym. Public facilities had separate bathrooms, separate water fountains. Famous black entertainers performed for rich white audiences in the Beach hotels, but they couldn't eat in the restaurants or stay in the hotel rooms. If a black fighter needed something from the drugstore downstairs, someone like Sully would have to go get it for him. When Dundee walked down the beach with his dog, Brandy, the black fighters couldn't accompany him. Dundee's training center couldn't be in one of the black neighborhoods because the white fighters feared for their safety. It couldn't be in one of Miami's white neighborhoods because the residents wouldn't tolerate it. South Beach was Jewish; they were more tolerant.

African-American fighters from out of town had to stay in the Liberty City or Overtown neighborhoods of Miami, usually at the Mary Elizabeth or Carver hotels. If the fighter was a real contender or would be staying for a month or so, Dundee would put him in an apartment. Fighters began showing up on South Beach when the gym opened at 11:00 a.m., but the black fighters got on the back of the bus and left town as soon as training ended at 3:00 p.m. People from Overtown who saw the fighters coming back to the Mary Elizabeth from the gym every day, who lived next door and went to church with them, had to sit in the balcony at the auditorium to watch them fight.[2]

Promoting a fight took more than putting a few ads in the paper and pasting up posters around town. Dundee usually was at his desk, odd-sized papers littering the cracked glass top. He would take the lock off the dial and start making calls. "I'm sending two tickets over to your house. Have a check for $50." "How many you want? Six today?"[3] He was a busy man. Dundee needed someone else to manage the fighters. He brought in the one person he could trust: his kid brother Angelo. In the ring, Angelo Dundee was one of the best. But Chris made the business decisions. When a guy called and wanted them to train a young fighter named Cassius Clay, Angelo thought the kid had talent. Chris wasn't sure. They were offered $150 a week or 25 percent of the fighter. Chris Dundee took the $150 a week.[4]

When Cubans began arriving in Miami, the Fifth Street Gym became the home for a string of proven Cuban champions and every Cuban kid who wanted to box. It probably was the most integrated spot in Dade County—white, Hispanic, and black fighters trained together. The boxers who trained there filled the hall of fame: Muhammad Ali, Joe Louis, Archie Moore, Sugar Ray Robinson, Sonny Liston, Joey Maxim, Roberto Duran, Carmen Basilio, Willie Pastrano. Celebrities wearing thousand dollar designer suits and sports reporters wearing frayed jackets from Sears all came to be part of the excitement. Fans came from all over the country and from Europe. The Beatles dropped in and clowned around for a photo op with Clay before his 1964 fight with Sonny Liston and before he changed his name to Muhammad Ali. People from South Beach didn't come, except some young boys from south of Fifth. The neighbors barely acknowledged that the gym was there.

One man sat in the front row at the auditorium on most Tuesday nights. He started chatting with Angelo Dundee between fights. Angelo found out that the guy was a doctor. One night, a fighter broke his hand. Angelo asked the doctor if he could take a look at it. His name was Ferdie Pacheco, and he became known as "the fight doctor." He had one office in the black neighborhood and one in the Cuban neighborhood, just what the Dundees needed. He also was very unhappily married and would do anything to get out of the house. He accompanied Dundee contenders to London, Rome, Sweden—wherever Chris Dundee would send him.[5]

By the 1980s, the boxing business had changed. The promoters and the fighters followed the big-money box offices to Las Vegas and Atlantic City and the bigger-money lure of pay-per-view-TV. The city commission decided to open the fight promotion business on Miami Beach to others and revoked Chris Dundee's exclusive rights to promote matches in the city. There wasn't enough freelance boxing talent to fill another card. Dundee threw in the towel.

The neighborhood also had changed. The gym was at the northern edge of the redevelopment area, surrounded by hotels filled with Cuban refugees and Jewish elderly. The drugstore on the first floor closed in 1981. Dundee was paying $900 a month to rent the old gym. In January 1982 he sold his lease to Felix "Tuto" Zabala, who sold it to a Miami contractor who moonlighted as a fight promoter.[6]

Big-name fighters still came to the Fifth Street Gym, drawn by its history, hoping a little luck was still hanging in the air. Tommy Hearns trained there in 1985, Gerry Cooney in 1987. But where there used to be forty fighters crowding the dusty gym, there now were a dozen on a busy day. Octogenarians eased themselves into the two rows of red theater seats and reminisced about boxing history, claiming some measure of fame in their past associations with champions. Fight placards from the gym's days of glory were yellowed with time and cigar smoke. The heavy bags were scarred with years of leather gloves making hard contact. The bell that used to ring every three minutes to help fighters time their sparring sat silent. A naked hundred-watt bulb was the only light above the ring. The water fountain didn't work. Two ceiling fans struggled to move the stale air.

The Beach started to come back in the 1990s, but the gym didn't. By 1993, the grocery market downstairs had closed, as had the liquor store and the tavern. The building was rotting. People joked that if the termites stopped holding hands, the place would fall down. What was left of the Miami fight game moved to newer, more modern facilities. The New York owners of the building decided to tear it down and replace it with something new.[7]

The building wasn't architecturally distinctive, but it was arguably one of the most historic buildings on South Beach. The Fifth Street Gym had produced twelve world champions. But it was a block outside the National Register and local historic districts. No nomination had been made to designate it as a local historic landmark. No red flags went up in the building department when the owners requested a demolition permit and there was no legal excuse for city hall to delay or deny it. The owners didn't volunteer to be heroes. They didn't think it made economic sense to repair the structural problems. They were getting hit with constant fines and penalties for code violations. No one in the boxing world stepped forward to save it. Sports fans had moved on to the Miami Dolphins, the Miami Heat, the new Florida Marlins, the championship University of Miami football and baseball teams. A community that was still recovering from a devastating hurricane only nine months earlier didn't have the energy or resources to worry about an old boxing gym.

The Monday morning sun already was heating up the day as forty-three years of world boxing history sat on the executioner's block in May 1993. A backhoe crouched nearby. A few blocks away on Ocean Drive, the South Beach regulars were working on their tans on the sand and on their social lives at the sidewalk cafés. A handful of people who wondered what was going on collected on Fifth Street. Ferdie Pacheco stopped by for a last look. He found out about the demolition when a newspaper reporter called him for a comment. "We just don't have respect for our past. The city of Miami Beach is historically brain-dead. Sports in South Florida will never be the same."[8] While a television reporter was interviewing him, Pacheco's new wife could be seen in the background helping carry Ali's training table to safety. It would have been appropriate if a referee wearing a black-and-white striped shirt issued a ten-count, but the backhoe simply lumbered over and landed a fatal punch to the face of the old pink building.

Join the Circus

The Fifth Street Gym wasn't the only knockout in 1993. Miami Beach Mayor Alex Daoud had not been a vigorous advocate for preservation, but he kept the city commission busy with other matters and allowed the district to seek its own level.

Daoud was a tall, good-looking, charismatic young man when he was first elected to the Miami Beach City Commission in 1979. He had a smooth style, an ingratiating manner, and a knack for being on the popular side of issues. He reminded elderly women of their grandsons. By the time he became mayor in 1985, he had kissed most of the babies in Miami Beach, attended hundreds of bar mitzvahs, weddings, and funerals, and smiled and lovingly patted the hands of just about every elderly person in the city.

He was equally busy behind the scenes. It started at the waterfront mansion of a Miami banker. Sitting on the smooth green lawn, Daoud admired the banker's beautiful pool and his beautiful Italian yacht. He wasn't being handed a bag full of money in a back alley. He was told he had "great potential" and was offered a thousand-dollar-a-month legal retainer. He thought, "I'm just as smart as he is, so, therefore, I'm entitled to this, and I'll probably vote that way anyway."[9]

A federal grand jury issued an indictment in 1991 accusing Daoud of extorting money and property from contractors, developers, labor unions, and others, and of filing false tax returns. The forty-one-count indictment was the result of an ongoing probe into political corruption in Dade County municipalities by the U.S. attorney. Daoud was the third mayor in Dade to be indicted in two years. The mayors of Sweetwater and Hialeah already had been convicted.[10]

It was well known that Daoud trolled the habitués of the Miami Beach *haut monde* and schmoozed his way into thousands of dollars in gifts. The federal government didn't think all of those gifts were given without strings attached. One charge in the indictment involved money received by the mayor after he persuaded the city commission that CenTrust chairman David Paul should be given a special exemption to build an enormous teakwood dock for his Italian yacht shortly after that afternoon meeting on the banker's back lawn.[11]

Daoud went to trial in 1992. When the jury finished its deliberations, it acquitted the mayor on ten counts, deadlocked on twenty-four, and returned one guilty verdict for taking a $10,000-bribe from a drug dealer. The prosecution planned to retry the unsettled charges.[12] Daoud made a deal that would avoid a retrial on the twenty-four deadlocked charges and the six untried tax evasion counts. That's when the prosecutors and the judge learned that Daoud had a pipeline to the grand jury and that two of his secretaries lied for him on the witness stand.[13] In the end, Daoud pled guilty to four charges: bribery, money laundering, tax fraud, and obstruction of justice. The judge accepted Daoud's negotiated plea and sentenced the former mayor to five years. He got out two years early for his assistance in helping to convict the banker.[14]

Daoud was not the first sensational politician in Miami Beach history, although he was the first to sustain a federal conviction. In 1953, the publicist who was managing the mayoral campaign for Harold Shapiro rented a few rowboats, decorated them with "Vote for Shapiro" signs, and moored them in Biscayne Bay. Then he paid the owners to let him sink them.[15] He let the newspapers assume that the other candidates sank the fleet, a tactic that smeared all of his opponents at once. Elliott Roosevelt, who was elected mayor of Miami Beach in 1965, was photographed by his publicist to emphasize his resemblance to his father, President Franklin D. Roosevelt, and sent out mailings using Eleanor Roosevelt stamps. The ploy was highly effective. A woman was overheard telling a friend, "Sadie, he was a wonderful president. He'll make a great mayor."[16]

One of the most recent was Commissioner Abe Hirschfeld. He was unhappy with the *Miami Herald*'s coverage of his financial affairs. One day he walked up to one of its reporters and spat in her face. She turned to leave, and he did it again. He said later he was proud of it.[17] Apparently he liked the *New York Post* better. After a $3 million investment, he was named its chairman of the board in 1993.[18]

Into this pantheon of political history stepped Nancy Liebman. She announced her candidacy for the city commission in the 1993 election. She felt she had done all she could with the league and the historic preservation board. The decision delighted her friends. For years they prodded her to run, but she always laughed them off by saying that she didn't want any part of the circus at city hall. Finally, she decided it was the best way to use what she had learned to make an impact on all the issues that would make Miami Beach a more livable city. A lot had been done for the tourists and the business community. The residents needed a stronger voice at city hall. South Beach was growing out of control and becoming a hangout rather than an historic resort. It was drawing the oxygen out of the city and overshadowing other issues that affected all city neighborhoods. There was no question which seat she would seek. Abe Resnick had been a thorn in her side for years.

Resnick irritated a lot of people during his eight years on the city commission. He asked for "courtesy warnings" for commissioners who were about to be cited for code violations. He was in conflict with the city manager from his first month on the commission. He wanted each commissioner to be given a portfolio, to put each of them in charge of one city department, bypassing the city manager's authority. At the same time, he was extremely well liked by the voters, especially in the Jewish and Cuban communities. Resnick had a vast network within the two ethnic groups. He could make three phone calls, and five hundred people would show up for a protest. He took a hands-on approach to being a city commissioner. He would get up and walk out of a meeting at his business office where a multimillion-dollar development project was being discussed to go help a woman who had a problem with garbage collection.[19]

His true passion, though, was talking about the Holocaust. He was determined to keep the memory alive, to help adults and children learn what happened so they would make sure nothing like it ever happened again. Among his treasured possessions were letters from schoolchildren who wrote to thank him for teaching them about the Holocaust on field trips. He was seeking funds for a Holocaust memorial at the Garden Center on Dade Boulevard, a controversial location that caused difficult feelings between Resnick and the ladies of the garden club. He remodeled an old storefront for the Or Chaim synagogue, named after his father.[20] His family sometimes criticized him for giving too much. He countered that he had money twice before in his life. His family lost everything they had in Lithuania; then he lost everything he had in Cuba. Not having it again didn't worry him.

Even Liebman admitted he could be charming.

Before the campaign could get started, Abe Resnick, age sixty-seven, decided not to seek reelection to a fourth term. He had succeeded in getting more Hispanics on city boards and in the police and fire departments. He felt he had accomplished his goal of making the city more friendly for developers.

For Nancy Liebman it was a four-decade journey from New Jersey schoolteacher to the overseer of the Art Deco district. She had been president of Temple Menorah and become politically seasoned as president of both the Miami Beach High and Biscayne Elementary parent-teacher associations. She steered the historic preservation board through its first tumultuous years and won her most sought-after victory when the commission voted to protect the entire National Register district under local regulations. She was on the board of trustees of the county's largest preservation group, and she was on the National Trust for Historic Preservation's board of advisors, which gave her a national voice. Her husband thought she was nuts, but her candidacy was okay with him as long as they still could go away for at least a month in the summer. She drafted an ambitious agenda: crack down on underage kids in the South Beach nightclubs, continue working for libraries, schools, and the arts, find a solution to the problem of abandoned buildings and code violations, upgrade the entertainment district, and address the needs of other Beach neighborhoods.

She started the campaign with $15,000 of her own money and, in a letter she sent to almost everyone she knew, she announced her plans and asked for donations. As soon as they went out in the mail she thought, what if nobody contributes? What would she do? The day after the letters hit mailboxes around Dade County, checks started coming in from people she knew from PTA, Friends of the Library, preservationists, and city acquaintances.[21] The generosity she had shown to others over the years came back to her.

Lavender, red, and white signs advertising her candidacy appeared throughout the city. Her biggest challenge was convincing the voters that she knew and cared about more than the Art Deco district. Campaigning for city commission had changed a lot since the days when bagel parties and ice cream on the front porches of hotels and the card rooms of the condominiums were required campaign stops. She did her homework before she answered the questionnaires sent by various community associations, made the rounds for media interviews, and attended candidates' nights. She smiled and shook hands and sent out mailings.

Hers was the only contested race. She had three opponents for the seat. Crime, the parking shortage, the future of Lincoln Road, dilapidated buildings, and the city's efforts to attract the long-sought convention hotel became the main issues of the campaign. On election night, five hundred people gathered at an Ocean Drive hotel to await the results. They erupted in applause when she arrived. She had won.

One of the things Liebman wanted to do first was deal with the runaway nightlife scene in the Art Deco district. The ocean side of the neighborhood was turning into a party scene with the rowdiness of Bourbon Street instead of the lively sophistication the league had envisioned. It seemed nobody cared about the people who lived there. Liebman was ready to get tough.

A Victim of Success

Tony Kay came to South Beach with some pals from college one year for spring break. Most kids are content to come back from the annual trip with a couple of tee-shirts, a great tan, and a three-day hangover. Tony Kay bought a hotel. Actually he called his mother in Chicago and convinced her to come to South Beach and take a look.[22] She went up and down the street. Everything she liked belonged to Gerry Sanchez. She liked the Clevelander most of all. The carpeting was frayed; the vinyl furniture in the lobby was ripped. It was decorated in combative shades of green, yellow, and orange. But it had three amenities that were coveted on South Beach: a prime location, a swimming pool, and its own parking lot. She had agreed to the terms Sanchez set down in their meeting on the front porch of the Waldorf Towers in 1986.

The freeform pool was on the corner fronting Tenth Street in the dead center of the Ocean Drive strip. The adjoining outdoor glass-block bar was a few steps off Ocean Drive. Tony Kay and his brother Kent knew they could turn it into party central. The party started early in the day with a few beers while playing volleyball or flying kites on the beach across the street or hanging out by the pool. Live bands and disc jockeys blasted rock music into the night air. The Clevelander became a magnet for young people looking for a good time.

The success of the Clevelander attracted other music clubs. Penrod's, a spring break institution in Fort Lauderdale, followed with a restaurant and dance club at the south end of Ocean Drive. Rolling Stones guitarist Ron Woods opened Woody's, a dance club in an overhauled Art Deco hotel that generated complaints about loud music and rowdy patrons. Music blared from bars throughout South Beach. Each opening was hailed as a sign of success.

Ocean Drive traffic was bumper to bumper, which came to a complete halt when the guys in the rented Thunderbird going north stopped in midstreet to exchange phone numbers with the girls in the convertible going south. Police began regulating how many times a car filled with gawkers could drive up and down the strip fronting Lummus Park, especially on weekends. Sidewalks were clogged with people wandering from bar to restaurant to sidewalk café to another bar. Parking valets acted like carnival barkers trying to attract the people in passing cars. Ocean Drive, Collins, and Washington avenues became rivers of light, color, neon, music, and hormones.

New clubs debuted on South Beach with a celebrity guest list and an opening party that rivaled most awards shows and often went on for two or three days. These were parties to be bragged about by those who were there and by those who weren't but wanted their friends to think they were. The clubs hit it big for a few months, then gave way to newer, hotter, wilder spots down the street. Club designers spared no expense to outdo each other with light shows, multilevel dance floors, fog and mist, chrome and mirrors creating uninhibited atmospheres that encouraged uninhibited behavior.

The real action didn't begin until almost midnight. Hopefuls would line up outside the velvet rope at the door of whichever club was in vogue that week. Like hopeful new arrivals knowing that their future depended on passing the eye test at Ellis Island, they waited anxiously to be "approved" and admitted. It was all in the presentation. If the jeans and tee-shirt were by the right designer and you looked darned good in them, then you were chosen. If you were wearing khakis and a polo shirt, then you spent the night on the outside looking in no matter how much cash you slipped to the gatekeeper. The month's hottest promoters kept the lines long and eager with theme party nights that convinced people that attendance at drag talent night or island night or the incredibly successful gay nights was essential to maintaining their "cool" factor.

Inside was a writhing mass of bare-chested young men, barely dressed girls, drag queens wearing enough makeup to fill a Mary Kay representative's monthly minimum, and a few shocked librarians in town for a convention. It was a swirl of sparkles and spandex, thongs and animal prints, leather straps and black stockings. Alarmingly tall models in four-inch stilettos swept past, leaving model wannabes from the suburbs in their wake. Celebrities behaved badly, hardly noticed in an intoxicated swarm of teens made up to look as old as they claimed on their fake IDs and burned-out club regulars who were there every night because that was what they did.

Throughout the night the sidewalks were crowded with people stopping at cafés for a carbohydrate fix before going to their next stop. Stretch limousines and Harleys ridden by really big guys with tattoos vied for space at the curb. People stopped in at the Washington Avenue shops that stayed open late because customers actually shopped at that hour. In most parts of the country, "after hours" meant after the workday. Even in nightclub jargon, an "after hours" club in most cities would open about 2:00 a.m. and might keep the party going for another couple of hours.

South Beach was in a different time zone. Most of the clubs were open until at least 4:00 a.m. Then it was time for the second shift.

The late-night crowd entered through back doors off dark alleys. The clubs had perfectly good front doors, but the secret of knowing where the best party was and where the back door was added to the allure. The action became even more daring after hours. People would retreat into unisex bathrooms, emerging after a longer time than normally would be considered necessary. The energy level was enhanced by chemicals stronger than what they were serving at the bar.[23]

Most revelers headed home by 8:00 a.m. The limos had gone home, replaced by city garbage trucks picking up trash from the night before. On Washington Avenue a few shopkeepers already were working brooms against cigarette butts and gum wrappers that had been recklessly cast on the sidewalk the previous day. Hotel lobbies were showing their first signs of activity as maintenance men checked at the front desk for overnight complaints of burned-out lightbulbs and stubborn plumbing. Platoons of domestic workers and hotel chambermaids were landing at bus stops in each block. But there were no elderly gentlemen like Benjamin Levy walking slowly to the cafeteria for breakfast.

One club on Washington Avenue was particularly notorious. After numerous complaints, a city photographer visited the club with undercover police and taped the activity. Bare breasts and buttocks were the least of it. The video included a shot of two people having sex surrounded by a cheering crowd. Nancy Liebman showed it to the commission twice in an effort to get them to crack down. They refused to act.[24] Architecture critic Ada Louise Huxtable, criticizing New Orleans's commercialization of the French Quarter, wrote, "The city's mistake has been in treating the area primarily as a business bonanza rather than as an environmental trust, something not achieved automatically or guaranteed by aesthetic restrictions."[25] The Beach had come back to life, and the income to the city was too addictive to rock the boat.

It wasn't the South Beach that Benjamin Levy and Bennie Mazor and tens of thousands of elderly Jews called home. It wasn't the South Beach that the league pictured when it started its seemingly impossible quest in 1976. It wasn't the livable neighborhood Liebman fought to preserve and enhance. In the fifteen years since the Art Deco district won its place on the National Register of Historic Places, the area had been completely transformed. They were saving the buildings, but they were losing the struggle for the heart, soul, and character that was the point of the entire exercise.

It was not the first city to face the problem. The baby boom generation had an insatiable appetite for historic and cultural tourism, which generated 140 million visitors annually to historic districts and sites around the country. Key West cleaned itself up and rebounded as a tourist destination and a preservationist's paradise. Its popularity created a whole new set of problems, not the least of which was traffic gridlock. Tourists had more trouble finding the unique stores and homey restaurants associated with old towns, but they were overwhelmed by bars and chain stores and souvenir shops.

Seattle's Pike Place Market was threatened with demolition by a misguided 1960s urban renewal project. It was saved by heroic grassroots effort and turned into a seven-acre historic district. Over the years Pike Place became so popular with tourists that crafts vendors outnumbered farmers, and more stalls catered to tourists who wanted prepared food. Locals found it increasingly harder to shop Pike Place for fresh fish, fruits, and vegetables.[26] Cooperstown, New York, was the destination for tourists who came to visit the National Baseball Hall of Fame and its renowned summer opera company and delight in its charming restored nineteenth-century buildings. Cooperstown drew a half million tourists a year to a town of twenty-one hundred residents, which put tremendous pressure on local resources.[27] New Orleans's Vieux Carre, under protection since the Louisiana legislature acted in 1936 to preserve the brick, wrought iron, and history of its more than three thousand nineteenth-century buildings, was feeling the stress. It suffered a 30-percent drop in permanent residents between 1980 and 1990 and was turning primarily into a food court and shopping mall. High-rise hotels on Canal Street and other new construction on the district's edges were isolating the French Quarter from historic downtown.[28] Ybor City, the historic cigar-making neighborhood of Tampa, awoke from its decades-long coma after a long battle by preservationists to save it from urban renewal. It was struggling with many of the same problems as South Beach and becoming a giant outdoor daiquiri bar.

The problem was that Miami Beach never was a quaint little town with shops full of handwoven baskets, custom pottery, and cookbooks for famous local cuisine. It was built as a tourist town, complete with souvenir shops stocked with pink flamingo shot glasses and citrus-colored tourist clothing, cheap beach towels, picture postcards, and racks of Kodak film. Over the years, however, Miami Beach evolved into a neighborhood.

The old barber shop and fish market and drugstore that carried sickroom supplies were gone, succeeded by Banana Republic and Kentucky Fried Chicken. The restaurant run by the lady who wore tricolored eyeshadow in the colors of the Italian flag was replaced by bistros with low lighting and high prices. In a little more than a year, almost forty new businesses, including fourteen restaurants, opened on Washington Avenue. Older businesses who had survived the aging of the population, the crime wave, and the lean years were going under as rents doubled and tripled practically overnight.

Incomes had crept up, tourism was increasing, and many retirees had been displaced by a younger population, but South Beach was still not an affluent neighborhood. Plenty of waiters and paralegals were renting apartments on Meridian and Euclid Avenues and mixing in with the young executives moving into the condos and the celebrities visiting the newest watering holes. Shops on the high end were struggling to find enough customers. Stores on the low end were having trouble paying the rent. A shopper on South Beach could find a $450-pair of designer jeans or a $2-pair of thrift store denims, but not a basic $35-pair of Levis. Renovations were scattered. Vacant, boarded-up buildings sat next door to swank newly remodeled hotels. Stein's Hardware and the dollar stores were surrounded by Venezuelan designer clothes and restaurants where the valet parking cost as much as the entrées. Most of the Deco furnishings and fashion stores that had opened during the early 1980s had disappeared. Elaborately restored apartment houses with manicured landscaping sat beside plain vanilla condominiums from the 1960s.

Locals avoided Ocean Drive, although they enjoyed going to Lincoln Road, where sidewalk cafés had usurped the center of the mall, different colored tablecloths providing the demarcation where one ended and the next began. Almost forgotten were the residents who needed to buy groceries, shaving cream, and fish food. It was a lot of sizzle and very little steak. Morris Lapidus, the ninety-one-year-old Russian immigrant architect of the Fontainebleau and the Lincoln Road Mall, was so fed up with the situation that he resigned from the league in a huff. He never had been a big fan of Art Deco, and his resignation letter to the board of trustees charged that the league was ruining the city and that Ocean Drive was "beginning to look like Coney Island."[29]

South Beach had become a mix of svelte models coming back from a fashion shoot, pale tourists in sandals, rollerbladers in tight shorts, singles seeking singles at late night clubs, Hispanic attorneys, mothers with toddlers, gay couples, and a few remaining elderly Jews trying to figure out what the heck happened to their neighborhood and the life they had created there.

The old redevelopment area south of Fifth was still littered with empty buildings and garbage-strewn lots. On any given block you found a wood-frame apartment house from the early days of the Lummus brothers, a rapidly aging Mediterranean Revival building from the twenties, a Deco hotel from the thirties, and a tedious condominium from the sixties, with a big vacant lot around the corner. The extreme tip of the island was off limits to developers. The Army Corps of Engineers abandoned the site in the seventies; it was deeded to the city and transformed into South Pointe Park at the intersection of the ocean and Government Cut.

The redevelopment agency still existed, but the role of the board was now filled by the city commission. Agreements made with developers during the ballyhooed days of the big plan still hung over the city. There was a new player in town. Thomas Kramer, head of the Portofino Group, arrived in 1993 with his wife Catherine, daughter of a German publishing scion.

Kramer was an arbitrage hellcat who traded his way to a fortune. He had pockets full of cash and big plans. He bought $20 million worth of South Pointe real estate in his first six months on the Beach and set about establishing a reputation as a womanizing party boy. He opened a nightclub named Hell. It closed a year later, making easy work for local headline writers. He was called everything from a carpetbagger to a greedy developer, and worse than that in private. He wanted to build a 262-foot-tall apartment building, ten times taller than most of its South Pointe neighbors.[30] The residents were only somewhat appeased when he brought in some of the world's best-known architects for a design charette to create a concept that would appeal to the residents of the rest of the Beach as much as it would to the buyers in his buildings.

After the city finally pulled the plug on the South Shore redevelopment project in 1982, the corporation that had been promised the contract to redevelop the city's marina took the city to court. A multimillion dollar judgment was awarded that obligated the city to build the promised parking lots and marina boat storage, repair the seawall, and pay for environmental cleanup, plus allow building development far beyond what was being permitted in other parts of South Beach.[31] Kramer and his Portofino Group had acquired the lucrative legal benefits along with his chunk of valuable property. To many locals, Kramer's plans were uncomfortably reminiscent of the original redevelopment agency's scorched-earth project.

A few developers were already taking tentative first steps into the area south of Fifth. Two old hotels were being renovated into apartments. A sixteen-unit townhouse project was expected to begin construction in early January. Zoning was approved for an eighteen-unit townhouse project. The Nemo Hotel, on Collins Avenue at First Street, which had generated more police calls than any other building in the city back in 1982, was purchased with plans to renovate.[32] Sitting on an empty lot at First Street and Jefferson Avenue was a sign advertising the Courts at South Beach. The pictures in the sales center showed luxury townhouses in a gated community described as resembling a Tuscan hilltown, an ambitious goal on an island that rose to only eight feet above sea level at its highest point. The price: $200,000–$660,000.[33]

The advertising did not mention that the Courts project was subsidized by the city as affordable housing. In 1988, the city offered to sell three blocks of land to developers who would build town homes priced about $80,000. The deal later was amended to drop the specific price figure in favor of "market rate." The city paid $6 million for two of the blocks and had an agreement to buy the third for $2 million. They would sell it to the developer for $4.43 million. The buyer would get some vacant lots, a few small houses, and two historic coral rock homes. One of them belonged to a Hungarian immigrant who couldn't understand why the Communists in Budapest left her alone, but the government in Miami Beach would confiscate her house. An elderly man had to leave the cottage he had moved into fifty-eight years earlier, with the fig tree out front where he had buried his parrot. Forced to move were the single mom who came to South Pointe so her son could attend a good school, the couple who prized their backyard garden, and the restaurant owner who had survived by fending off crack dealers with a baseball bat.[34]

The old South Beach was not included in the National Register Art Deco district for political reasons. The local overlay district did not incorporate anything south of Sixth Street. The redevelopment area had lost eighty-one buildings in five years, but some historic gems were still in danger. It was time to bring it back into the fold.

Even with the success of the Art Deco district and the failure to get the redevelopment program off the ground, the proposal to create an Ocean Beach historic district received a cool reception from its property owners. Some feared that it would further thwart the long-awaited renaissance of their "blighted" area. Developers strongly opposed anything that could limit their ability to build. Shortly after word got out that the planning department was drafting a proposal for an Ocean Beach district, eleven older buildings, including four historic cottages, were bulldozed by nervous property owners. Applications were filed for demolition of twenty more.[35] Many were owned by speculators who had bought them at bargain prices from owners who were desperate to get out after the moratorium was lifted.

The historic preservation board wanted all of old South Beach brought under local historic district protection as quickly as possible. Three committees and more than a year later, doubters still wavered. A neighborhood advisory board voted nine-to-two against the designation. It believed only a dozen buildings in the area qualified as historic and preferred individual designation of those buildings while leaving the rest of the area to redevelopment.[36] The district committee had 148 structures on its list.

The inclusions became secondary to the exclusions. Left out of the boundaries was Joe's Stone Crab restaurant, the highly successful culmination of Joe and Jennie Weiss's seafood shack. Several older hotels and properties that had already received approval for new construction were also left outside the gerrymandered boundary lines. Some who wanted to be excluded weren't. Thomas Kramer failed to delete two of his empty lots because the city thought a district called Ocean Beach should have at least some oceanfront property in it.

By a unanimous vote of the city commission in 1996, the area south of Sixth Street—the site of a failed coconut plantation, the "Jewish

Riviera," the target of a multibillion dollar redevelopment plan, the victim of the moratorium, the home to thousands of Mariel refugees, the survivor of a crime wave, and, by the end of the twentieth century, bereft of many of its original buildings—was designated as the Ocean Beach Historic District. Supporters hoped the magic of the Art Deco district would spread.

The magic was making life very hard for people like Selma Bushinsky. Around the corner from where elegant restaurant patrons had valets park their Volvos and Audis and dined on $30 plates of seared tuna, Bushinsky went to bed in a tiny efficiency apartment on Pennsylvania Avenue. There were two beds: one for Selma and the other for her forty-three-year old son Carl. Carl was suffering from a painful back injury and could not work. Selma had to cover her rent and other monthly expenses with her meager $380 Social Security check.[37]

People like the Bushinskys were victims of the area's success and soaring rents. The number of affordable single-room units had been reduced by a third. The city itself had contributed to the reduction of affordable units.[38] Goodman Terrace replaced twenty rundown cottages in old South Beach when it was built in 1952 to provide housing for blue-collar city workers. Three connected buildings held fifty apartments, including some three-bedroom units, a rarity in South Beach. Caught in the moratorium, the buildings had developed electrical problems, water leaks, and sewage backups. The city thought there must be a better use for a one-million-dollar piece of land. People who had lived there for thirty-five years, who paid only one-third of their monthly income as rent, were forced out. In 1990, Goodman Terrace had been razed.

The city had also crossed swords with the federal department of Housing and Urban Development over HUD allegations of racial discrimination in Rebecca Towers, the housing authority's senior citizen buildings on the bay front south of Fifth Street. Rent was only 25 percent of tenants' monthly income. Some of those displaced from land purchased for the South Pointe project had been moved there. Although the population of Dade County was 17 percent black, African-Americans represented only 1 percent of Rebecca Towers' residents. The housing authority had refused to open the Towers to anyone who did not already live in Miami Beach.[39] Even efforts to help developers build affordable housing had backfired. Grant money used to rehabilitate apartments required that a certain number be set aside as low-cost housing, but there was a three-year maximum on the rent subsidy. As soon as the cap expired, the apartments could be rented at the higher market rate for a renovated building.[40]

Selma Bushinsky dreamed of having a larger apartment, but it seemed unlikely. Her name was somewhere on the four-thousand-name waiting list for public housing assistance. The list had been frozen for more than four years. By comparison, the city of Homestead had a thousand on its waiting list. Metropolitan Dade County, which covered all the unincorporated area and all but four cities, had a list of only two thousand.[41]

Buildings that had been renovated in the 1980s as rental apartments were being sold as condos. Each one took moderately priced rentals off the market. Buildings that sold for $90,000 in 1986 were reselling for $270,000 six years later.[42] Renovation was turning low-income residents into urban refugees. They couldn't compete with the margarita crowd that partied until dawn. Out went the elderly, the single mothers, the sales clerks and clerical workers, the university students, and the artists. Economic gentrification had taken hold.

The number of elderly had shrunk by two-thirds since 1980. Streets that used to close down at 10:00 p.m. were just getting started at that hour. Hallways that used to smell of boiled cabbage now carried the aroma of freshly ground hazelnut coffee. Those seniors who remained had to adjust to a louder, livelier neighborhood. New Year's Eve was one barometer. The lobbies of South Beach residential hotels and apartments used to host spirited New Year's Eve parties with crepe paper streamers, long balloons hanging from the ceiling like sausages at the deli, shiny cardboard hats, and celebratory bottles of ginger ale on every table. There was music and dancing and reminiscing about seventy years of other New Year's Eve parties. Every year there were fewer parties. Finally there were none.

Matti Bower, then serving as a member of the board of the housing authority, felt that the city wasn't doing enough to address the need for affordable housing, that it continued to cater to developers more than the needy. People with good credit and full-time jobs but who were working for minimum wage couldn't afford a place to live. The housing authority offered a minimal rent-supplement program for the low-income residents displaced by gentrification.[43] The Miami Beach Development Corporation also recognized how the revitalization of the area was cutting into the supply of affordable housing and began a program to try to tackle the issue. They initiated a change in the county housing assistance program to allow scattered site housing, bought individual condo units and refurbished them using grant money, county funds, and loans. Most of them were bought from Jewish retirees or their estates. The group had assisted one hundred families to buy their first homes through one of its programs and renovated an apartment building to house people living with AIDS.[44]

The city commission wasn't enthusiastic about providing more. One city commissioner said he thought there was enough affordable housing on the Beach for its residents. He didn't think they should do more because he was concerned that the city would become a "magnet" for low-income people.[45]

One of the lucky residents was school counselor Sandra Maji. Two years earlier, Maji and her daughter had lived in the Lincoln Plaza Apartments. The city condemned the building and gave its dozens of low-income tenants twenty-four hours to move out. The owner of several other South Beach apartments bought Lincoln Plaza to rehabilitate it. The city's housing program matched his $250,000 investment.[46] The 1925 building had its facade restored to its original Mediterranean Revival beauty. Hidden details were uncovered and highlighted with color. Now the building blended smoothly with one across the street that had been converted into luxury condos. Inside, apartments were totally renovated. Eighteen of the apartments were dedicated for low-income housing for at least seven years. Sandra Maji attended the ribbon-cutting ceremony. She was moving back into Lincoln Plaza, into a sunny corner apartment with her now-sixteen-year-old daughter.[47]

Even more ignored were the homeless. They ate what they could find, went to the bathroom wherever they were, spent the day dozing in doorways and back alleys. They hung out in South Pointe Park and parking lots. One man spent every night under a Miami Beach welcome sign. A woman slept in front of an Amoco station. Homeless advocates estimated at least four hundred homeless people were living on Miami Beach.[48]

Across the bay, the homeless could get a hot meal, a bed, medical care, a shower, and a change of clothes. There were no such services on the Beach. The city gave the bulk of its federal funds for the homeless to the city of Miami for its homeless shelter program. Homeless encampments at Flamingo Park and South Pointe and the Bass Museum parking lot had been cleared out. More than two hundred people were moved into shelters across the bay and seventy-five were "reunited" with family or friends outside the state.[49] The only food for the homeless was a once-a-week bag lunch run by Temple Beth Sholom. About 150 people lined up on Sunday mornings when volunteers handed out packages of fruit, juice, a bag of chips, and maybe a meat sandwich. They used to serve the bag lunches in a park on Washington Avenue. The neighbors complained so they moved to a community center on Sixth Street. Those neighbors complained. Now they were on West Avenue, but not for much longer. That property was about to become the site of a new apartment building.

Mona Cohen, eighty-nine years old, was living in her third residential hotel. She had been evicted when renovations began on the others. "The other hotels don't want us. The young people spend one hundred dollars a night. It's more profitable. This is the last outpost for seniors. They can't dump us in the ocean. They gotta put us somewhere." She saved money by bringing home the leftovers from the community center where she ate lunch every day. Cohen proudly claimed she hadn't cooked a meal in twenty-five years. She didn't have as many partners for the dances on Monday and Wednesday nights. "They're all dead except for one and he doesn't dance anymore."[50]

CHAPTER 13

Casa Casuarina

Alden Freeman discovered the first stone for the foundation of Casa Casuarina in Santo Domingo, capital of the Dominican Republic. He spotted it in the ruins of the Alcazar de Colón, former home of the Columbus family. Yes, *that* Columbus. Christopher's oldest son, Diego, was named admiral and governor of the West Indies in 1509 and built the expansive villa soon after his arrival on the island of Hispaniola. At the time Freeman liberated his stone, the crumbling Columbus mansion was thought to be the oldest Spanish-built building in the Western Hemisphere.[1]

Freeman had plans for the stone. He enlisted Charles Boulton for a building project on Ocean Drive in 1930. The ornate Spanish Colonial style of Diego Columbus's original house would blend comfortably with the village of Espanola Way, the opulent waterfront mansions, the Mediterranean flavor of Carl Fisher's grand hotels, and the only two other buildings on the street, the nearest one being two blocks south. The 1926 hurricane had left Freeman's building lot devoid of vegetation except for a gnarled casuarina tree, known locally as an Australian pine, not looked on fondly as a landscape specimen. W. Somerset Maugham had just published a book of six stories about life in the tropics, *The Casuarina Tree*, which added a nice literary touch. Freeman planted his souvenir from Santo Domingo as the cornerstone, and Boulton christened the building Casa Casuarina.

Jac Amsterdam bought the building five years later and gave it the eponymous name Amsterdam Palace. Residents loved the open courtyard, ringed with the sculpted busts of an eclectic collection of "influential" faces including Gandhi, John D. Rockefeller, Julius Caesar, Cleopatra, Mussolini, and Lenin. Dominating the courtyard was the Homage

Tower, a replica of the structure where Christopher Columbus was held prisoner by King Ferdinand.

Like the rest of South Beach, the Amsterdam Palace began to decline, but residents felt it still was important to keep up appearances. Ladies freshened up and put on cool dresses and gentlemen donned tropical weight jackets before assembling on the wide stone terrace to sip cocktails while the sky blushed pink as the sun retreated toward the Gulf of Mexico and the Goodyear blimp *Mayflower* made its way back to its mooring on Watson Island at the end of the day. Even in the dark days of the late 1970s and early 1980s, authors, painters, sculptors, bartenders, and other free spirits felt privileged to pay $325–$600 a month to live in a building with flaking paint, cracked plaster, and a legend of a resident ghost attired in white pajamas who frightened away unwelcome guests.[2] There was a long waiting list for the apartments, even though the copper-domed observatory atop the third floor no longer revolved, and the elevator hidden in the tower was a bit unsteady.

When the league began hosting Art Deco Weekend on the street outside the front gate, the residents of the Amsterdam Palace opened their doors—quietly. Those "in the know" would rap on the seahorse-shaped iron doorknocker to be admitted through the towering arched doors to the terrazzo-floored courtyard. There would be beer and tours for a dollar a head. Guests could stroll along the two tiers of shaded loggias. They climbed the rickety stairs, marveling at the stained glass windows and the mural of Christopher Columbus landing on a generic Caribbean island. They wandered through apartments cooled by the ocean breeze through twelve-foot-high French doors. They peeked into the yellow-and-white tiled kitchens. It was a cloistered sanctuary from the spirited street fair outside. As evening dimmed the natural light, lanterns hanging from wrought iron brackets on the supporting columns of the first floor arcade illuminated the scene. The enterprising residents used the money for their party fund.

Everyone wanted to get inside the Amsterdam Palace. When art *mondain* Andy Warhol visited South Beach, a herd of news reporters and photographers tagged along, shoving microphones and cameras in Warhol's face as Diane Camber and Lynn Bernstein took him and two busloads of his entourage on a tour of the building.

Every developer on South Beach wanted to buy the Amsterdam. The absentee owners lived in France and frostily declined to respond to inquiries. Gerry Sanchez was determined. He had a burning passion for anything involving Christopher Columbus. In typical Sanchez style of living large, he talked of erecting a statue of Columbus in the park across the street from the Amsterdam Palace, a sculpture taller than the Statue of Liberty. After an exhaustive search, Sanchez tracked down the owner's agent in the Netherlands Antilles. It took a year to set up an appointment. Sanchez offered him $1.3 million for the building. The agent made a counteroffer to sell it for $1.1 million, on the condition that a little something extra surreptitiously be deposited in cash in his personal Swiss bank account.[3] Sanchez accepted, although he didn't have any particular plans for the building. He was busy with $22 million' worth of other projects and tinkering with the Amsterdam Palace wasn't a priority. That was fine with the residents.

Sanchez had lost interest in the building by the time he sold it in 1993 to Italian fashion designer Gianni Versace for $2.9 million, netting him a tidy profit.[4] Versace was not a newcomer to Miami Beach. He created the Caribbean-toned *Miami Vice* look for Don Johnson and Philip Michael Thomas. When he discovered Ocean Drive, he moved into the Amsterdam and made South Beach a second home. Versace—walking down to the News Café every morning to pick up newspapers and magazines, frequenting the clubs—became a regular sight in the neighborhood. The city, dazzled by Versace's celebrity, had dreams of him bringing his *haute couture* empire to Miami Beach.

Versace's vision for the Amsterdam Palace was more dramatic than that of Alden Freeman. He would turn it into his private mansion in pure Versace style and restore the name Casa Casuarina. But something was missing—a garden, perhaps with a swimming pool. It wouldn't be an ordinary rectangular backyard pool with a two-foot-wide deck and a couple of scrawny croton plants. Versace's contractor described it as an open courtyard with towering Royal and date palm trees, dark green foliaged lemon trees, and silver buttonwoods surrounded by a two-story stucco facade lined with arched mahogany windows.[5]

The building covered the property from lot line to lot line; there was no space for a pool. Versace bought the Revere Hotel on the corner next door for $3.7 million so he could knock it down and build his garden.[6] A serendipitous result of the demolition would reveal the long-obscured view of Casa Casuarina's southern facade. Craig Robins owned the Flambeau and Victor hotels on the north side of Casa Casuarina. Robins had his own plans to renovate the 1936 Victor and demolish the nonhistoric Flambeau next to Versace's house, to build something new on the empty lot. The combination of Versace's and Robins's plans would mean an enormous disruption of the block.

Like many of the buildings in the Art Deco district, the Revere, while not a landmark on its own merits, continued the governing scale and harmony of the street. The preservationists thought that all of Ocean Drive was protected under historic district regulations. But the Revere was built in 1950. The original survey done by the league in 1978 covered buildings built before 1950 and had established the cutoff date incorporated in the district legislation. The city attorney determined that the ordinance did not cover the hotel. Nancy Liebman realized that they faced an insoluble problem and that a change to the ordinance was needed. Several buildings from the 1950s, like the Revere, were not distinctive, but they supported the integrity of the district. Any such change, however, would not be retroactive. Ironically, the Revere itself had replaced a two-story home built in 1922 and demolished before anyone thought of protecting the city's early structures.[7]

Word that there was a request for a permit to demolish a building on Ocean Drive set off alarms at the league office. The hardliners, led by Michael Kinerk, Dennis Wilhelm, and Matti Bower, were determined that every building in the district should be saved at all costs. Another faction, including Richard Hoberman and Bernard Zyscovich, who was the league chairman, was willing to cede the Revere in exchange for a tougher law protecting similar buildings in the future. Although not as active in the league since her election to the city commission, Liebman was in agreement with the moderates who felt that the Revere was not worth the expenditure of precious political resources. She had learned that preservationists had to pick their fights carefully. She cautioned, "The mission of preservation is not to keep every stone in place. It's not a museum, it's a living thing. It isn't just saving buildings. It's saving an environment and an atmosphere."[8]

The fight over the Revere threatened to wrench the league apart. A majority of the league's board members won a bitter vote to file suit to stop the demolition. Emotions were so caustic that Kinerk and Richard

Hoberman stopped speaking to each other; Liebman and Matti Bower did likewise. Zyscovich resigned as chairman in protest. A fierce chill enveloped board meetings.

Versace turned his Italian charm and his attorneys on the league board members. In exchange for the league withdrawing its lawsuit to protect the Revere, he would use his influence to help them amend the ordinance. The board finally relented and grudgingly agreed that the time and money would better be used for other purposes instead of a divisive court fight that they didn't have much chance of winning.

On Thursday afternoon, September 9, 1993, the pale pink silhouette of the Revere stood for the last time against a clear blue Florida sky. A faded red Mack truck from Shark Wrecking sat on Eleventh Street, its diesel engine spewing exhaust. The crane swung the pear-shaped wrecking ball, and Shark took its first bite out of the hotel. A disgruntled league board member grumbled, "The demolition derby is on full blast, and it's being brought to you by the preservationists and the Miami Beach government."[9]

Versace used the resulting space to full measure. The arcaded addition housed a gym, guest suites, and a Moroccan bath overlooking a swimming pool surfaced with glass mosaic tiles in an original Versace design. The baths were resplendent with gold-plated shower heads and marble tubs generously supplied with a supply of scented oils and Versace-designed towels. The new wing also housed a library with a wrought iron staircase tipped with gold filigree and etched windows.[10] Contractors ripped through walls of the old apartments to create four luxurious master suites, eight sumptuous guest rooms, two staff apartments, and common areas that visitors described as everything from "splendorous" to "vulgar." Jewel tones of ruby and turquoise and topaz stained the windows. Mosaics, smooth river stones, and chips of ceramic tile gave texture to walls adorned with works by Picasso and Modigliani. Fabrics and color schemes that were seen on fashion runways from New York to France to Italy adorned the media room, the bedrooms, the dining room. When it was finished, the mansion was estimated to contain approximately twenty thousand square feet of space including terraces and balconies.[11] Architecture critics and starry-eyed guests lucky enough to get an invitation thought it was magnificent. The preservationists hated it. Only the shell remained in its original form. One offended league member said there was no longer any suitable use for the building except as a Versace showroom.

Gianni Versace traveled to Europe in the summer of 1997 for the glamorous round of fashion shows. He presented his spring men's collection in Florence and Milan. Then he went to Paris to unveil his women's *haute couture* designs. The reviews were glowing. He flew back to New York and on July 10 settled into a first-class seat on American Airlines for the flight home to Miami.[12]

He slipped back easily into his South Beach daily routine. On Monday evening, he and two friends drove up to the Bay Harbour Islands theater for the early evening showing of *Contact*, starring Jodi Foster and Matthew McConaughey. He was still tired from the week before so instead of dining out as planned, they returned to South Beach and fixed a snack before turning in early.[13]

The next morning, July 15, Versace emerged through the Gothic front gates into the hot summer sun that already was spreading across the keystone front steps—the same steps where league volunteers gathered on that January day twenty years earlier to begin their first detailed exploration of the neighborhood. He turned south, but, instead of following his usual route on the west side of the street, he crossed and walked down the sidewalk along Lummus Park.[14]

Early beachgoers were filling the coveted parking spaces along Ocean Drive and its intersecting side streets. A symphony of American and European accents softly played as sidewalk cafés served surprisingly hearty breakfasts to people who were so thin. Versace stopped at the News Café for a cup of coffee, Italian newspapers, and fashion magazines. About 8:30 he strolled home, exchanging friendly greetings in Italian with a local artist along the way. A few minutes later, he walked up his front steps and began to unlock the gate to his lavish home. Andrew Cunanan walked up behind him.[15]

Moments later, Officer Calvin Lincoln was driving his patrol car south on Ocean Drive. The driver of a passing car frantically flagged him down and shouted, "Someone's been shot!" and pointed down the street.[16] When Officer Lincoln screeched to a stop in front of Casa Casuarina, he saw a man on the third step, slumped to his left, his head in a pool of blood. Lincoln checked the victim for vital signs. There was no pulse. The fire/rescue unit arrived, along with a fire engine and the detective bureau. Two men who were in the house said that they heard shots. One of them had chased a man for a short distance until he turned and pointed a large automatic handgun at his pursuer.[17]

A few days later, Andrew Cunanan committed suicide as police surrounded his hideout to arrest him for the murder of the fifty-year-old fashion designer and the serial killing of four other men. More than seven hundred people packed into Miami Beach's Saint Patrick's Church for the memorial service, with hundreds more standing outside. Versace's ashes were flown by private jet to Milan, accompanied by family members, who made their way to a small cemetery near his lakeside villa at Lake Como and laid Gianni Versace to rest.[18]

A Matter of Taste

The loss of the Revere and the disagreement about Versace's renovations to Casa Casuarina illustrated a basic disagreement among South Beach preservationists over what changes to the streetscape and the buildings were acceptable. Trying to embalm an entire privately owned neighborhood in a bygone time had questionable economic viability and ran contrary to the direction of preservation nationwide, which was to recycle buildings, giving them new uses while maintaining the significant architectural elements that made them special. *New York Times* architecture critic Paul Goldberger wrote, "It is one thing to escape briefly into the time capsule of a futuristic Disneyland or a historic Williamsburg; it is quite another to attempt to live a real life, day in and day out, in a place so cut off from the continuum of time."[19]

Much had been lost on the road to success on South Beach. A survey taken by University of Miami architecture students in 1997 revealed that of the 259 hotels, apartments, and commercial buildings on Ocean Drive, Collins Avenue, and Washington Avenue included in the National Register listing, 10 percent had been demolished in the eighteen years since the Art Deco district was officially recognized. Another 11 percent had been altered beyond hope of restoring them to their original appearance.[20] Some buildings on the extinct list were heartbreakers such as the New Yorker and the Senator. Others were less noble, like the Revere, but each made its own unique contribution to the fragile fabric of the Art Deco district. The battle between architectural integrity and the almighty dollar was raging.

Almost half of the new development projects in Miami Beach in the past three years were within the district. Hotel firms, investors, and developers were swarming around the neighborhood like ravenous mosquitoes who spotted a fresh tourist. Unlike the South Beach pioneers, such as Gerry Sanchez and Tony Goldman, Robert Holland and Saul Gross, some newcomers were in hot pursuit of the free-spending pleasure seekers and had only a passing interest in the fact that much of the area was a National Register district. Preservation purists, residents, and city leaders in some communities were distressed at the loss of the genuine character of historic areas for the sake of commercial success. There was a growing national debate over whether adaptive use even should be considered historic preservation. The developers on South Beach were maintaining the original use of the hotels and apartments. Their adaptation was to the lifestyle and expectations of their customers.

The dread of having to deal with the city's review boards was so great that some buyers preferred to demolish their buildings than renovate them. Architects could be put through the wringer of drawing up detailed plans two or three times before they were approved, an exercise that drove up costs. The board was criticized for its seeming capricious decisions, sometimes contrary to the city's written guidelines. Writing in the *Journal of the American Planning Association*, John Forester explained how planning and zoning officials exerted tremendous influence and power in their interpretation of ordinances or the length of time they could take to review an application.[21] The process in Miami Beach seemed intentionally confusing to architects and developers.

Nationwide, property owners and developers complained more about historic property regulations than any other kind of city zoning laws. They understood and accepted setback minimums, fire codes, fence heights, and requirements for the use of certain building materials. But the cumbersome permit process in historic districts drew the ire of property owners and architects alike. Miami Beach created confusion with old zoning laws that encouraged development but conflicted with the goals of the district. The design review board rejected dozens of unacceptable alterations every month. It even turned down a project submitted by the city. The city solved that problem by promptly removing all municipally owned properties from the review board's jurisdiction.

Even restoring original features could pose difficulties. Most of the marble used in the 1930s was from Georgia and Tennessee, where it no longer was being quarried. The only company still making Vitrolite was in the Czech Republic. One clever architect solved that shortage by using oil paint on the interior surface of a sheet of glass; only very close inspection could tell it was not pigmented all the way through.

There were construction dilemmas. Tony Goldman decided he wanted his architect, Les Beilinson, to add a swimming pool to the Tiffany Hotel on Collins Avenue. Because there was no land around it, he decided to put the pool on top. Of course, the building wasn't designed to hold a big tub full of water on the roof, so Beilinson inserted a four-story structure through the interior of the building to support the pool.[22]

The stakes were getting higher as property sales prices soared and renovations became more elaborate and expensive. A dashing German tourism entrepreneur purchased the landmark National Hotel on Collins Avenue, a late Deco beauty with a bell tower that could have been the model for *Star Wars*' R2D2. The hotel had changed hands in 1988 for $3 million, again in 1993 for $4 million. When Hans-Joachim Krause bought the National in 1995 for $9 million, he started on a $5 million renovation project.[23]

Next door was the Delano, one of many hotels and apartments that had been damaged by arson during the dreary days of the 1980s. It had a finned tower that reduced every travel writer to metaphors of Buck Rogers or Flash Gordon. Ian Schrager, of Studio 54 fame, bought the dilapidated Delano for $4 million in 1993 and spent $22 million making it über-chic and adding private bungalows by the pool for the celebrity crowd.[24] Schrager hired Parisian *enfant terrible* designer Phillipe Starck to transform the Delano. The results won rave reviews from the *New York Times* and a spread in *Vanity Fair*. Superstars flocked to it.

The building's exterior was preserved, although it went against the pastel trend and was painted entirely white, including its famous spaceship fins, which conceivably made it one of the more accurate exterior restorations in the district. A maze of tall green hedges deflected prying eyes, and impossibly long white curtains were hung over the porte cochere to further protect the privacy of guests who didn't want to be seen getting out of their Lamborghinis.

The interior also was entirely white. The lobby, the rooms, everything was white. One unimpressed guest likened it to spending a week in the hospital. Starck masked the original terrazzo floors under planks of wood, ripped out the skywalk, and shrouded the octagonal columns in fat round white overcoats. He divided the lobby into a succession of spaces separated by two-story high white gauze drapes. The few pieces of furniture in the lobby were Homeric in scale, including a couch with a back that was nine feet tall and a bed that seemed to be hiding from the chambermaid.

The result was surreal and award-winning, but the awards were from out of town. The locals were incensed. The Delano was a Kurt Cobain guitar lick in the middle of a Duke Ellington dance tune. It became the poster child for inappropriate renovation. Schrager only made matters worse when he argued, "Those old motifs and designs were conceived of forty or fifty years ago. I am skeptical that they would be as much of a lure today as they were then. What is so great about South Beach is not so much the architecture but the scale of it. If you knocked them all down and built something else back to the same scale, South Beach would be just as special."[25] He was in agreement with the late scholar Walter Muir Whitehall, who complained, "Preservationists should try to keep America beautiful rather than to create little paradises of nostalgia."[26]

That kind of attitude had preservationists foaming at the mouth. Those who wanted to make their property "different" were missing the point. Randall Robinson, a preservation planner for the league, fumed that the Delano was a wonderful design but it was in the wrong place. It was a historic district, for crying out loud, and people wanted to see the real thing.

Some saw the Delano and the Robins brothers' Dacra hotels as proof that South Beach was growing up. Hotels were training their staffs how to cater to people who were accustomed to spending $2,000 a night for a room. Rooms were supplied with multiple phones, internet connections, European linens, and spa brand products in marble bathrooms. Locals wondered how many of the artifacts stripped from the hotels were destroyed and how many were being spirited away to be sold quietly into private collections.

Property owners began trying to out-paint each other. The pastels of Horowitz's palette were giving way to bolder colors. Instead of soft lavenders, greens, and blues trimming a pale background, buildings were being decked out in striking yellows, brilliant orange, and vivid coral, arguing with each other for attention. One property owner lamented that the focus was no longer about architecture but about paint. The son of one of the district's original architects said the painters made the buildings look like a basket of Easter eggs.[27] Kay Pancoast, widow of John Collins's grandson Russell and herself an architect, echoed Fontainebleau architect Morris Lapidus in decrying the entire Art Deco craze. "I'm appalled that they become so prominent. They were built cheaply, before a building code. Today they would not be allowed to be built."[28]

The desire to restore Art Deco buildings to the 1930s had been replaced by a goal of torturing enough space from a hotel lobby to add a shop or café or adding another story or dressing up the old facade. The rooms in the older hotels were small, plain, and unappealing to the upscale tourist of the 1990s. Developers such as the Robins brothers were gutting entire floors to create more spacious rooms, nicer bathrooms, bigger closets. New residents were buying apartment buildings around Flamingo Park and knocking down walls or building stairs to merge two or three small units into more comfortable spaces that fit contemporary lifestyles. Display windows were hacked into the walls to convert a Deco lobby into a bikini and sunglasses store. The Breakwater punctured the walls with new doors and railings to create balconies overlooking the courtyard and enlarged its windows for a better view. Bands of Vitrolite were wrenched off an apartment building. Modern railings, overplanted landscaping, and other design blunders were in danger of turning the Art Deco buildings into caricatures of themselves.

The question of historic building interiors vexed preservationists across the country. Adaptive use of derelict schools, warehouses, churches, railroad stations, and industrial factories required substantial alterations to convert them into condominiums, artists' studios, shops, and art centers. Even then, significant architectural elements were expected to be retained. Ripping out entire interiors and replacing them with modern rooms was anathema to the purists but the only practical economic answer to developers who wanted to maximize the return on their investment. They weren't catering to the bed-and-breakfast crowd that was happy in quaint, cramped rooms.

The early developers had, for the most part, left all of the original architectural elements intact and decorated around them using period furnishings. The competition for customers, to be the hippest and coolest hangout, was prompting hotel, restaurant, and bar owners to be more "creative." Art Deco lobbies were transformed into island hideaways or pared-down minimalist settings, walls were given faux marble treatments, fireplaces were ripped out or hidden. One popular nightclub put tepees on the beach. Stores on Lincoln Road were completely demolished except for the street facades. Once inside the front door, shoppers saw the same store they saw in Phoenix or Indianapolis. The hotel and apartment owners, the restauranteurs and retailers who arrived on South Beach after 1990 saw the crowds, the excitement, the flood of dollars pouring into the district. Hoteliers like Schrager overlooked the fact that South Beach was architecture's version of the Toastmaster toaster and the China Clipper and possessed a remarkable identity before the celebrities and party nights took over.

New construction on vacant lots in the district was another source of disagreement. At the 50th National Preservation Conference in October 1996, four high-profile Chicago architects had debated whether preservation guidelines actually promoted mediocre design. The symposium was moderated by New York Times critic Paul Goldberger. Three of the architects agreed with the thesis that design regulations had a "deadening effect" on cities and ignored the need for a city to evolve. One of them described forced design as "fake" historic architecture. They acknowledged that a dislike of much modern design had fueled preservation efforts nationwide, yet they wondered how to blend the old and new without having cities frozen in time.[29]

Les Beilinson had been tiptoeing along that line for years. Beilinson was a soft-spoken architect who contributed his expertise to South Beach as a member of the historic preservation board, a member of the league board, a member of the Dade Heritage Trust board, and he served with other organizations and committees. His biggest contribution, though, was as the architect for dozens of hotel and apartment renovations. He had worked for Sanchez, Goldman, Dacra, and almost every other developer who had a building on South Beach. He had helped develop the design standards for the district. But even Beilinson couldn't always figure out how to interpret them, as was demonstrated when his plans for a store for Ralph Lauren were rejected by the design review board for being "excessively neutral."[30]

The tourists were euphoric, snapping pictures of one peacock building after another and partying all day and night. The crowds increased the pressure and energized a new debate over the future of the district.

Cultural Awakening

In the glamour days of Miami Beach, the Washington Storage Company catered to the wealthy owners of the mansions that lined the oceanfront. When it was time to escape the snow of their northern estates, the rich and pampered called Washington Storage. The company returned precious belongings to the homes, placed the cleaned oriental rugs on the polished floors, hung the furs in the closet, set the silver mirror and comb on the vanity, had the phones connected, hired servants for the season, and readied the house for the owners' arrival. The Mathews family owned Washington Storage and its vast Spanish Baroque-style building remained in the family even after the call for their prestige services waned. Mike Mathews had been an active member of the league from its earliest days.

Micky Wolfson rented space at Washington Storage for years. His father passed away in 1982, leaving his children a substantial inheritance. Wolfson Jr. traveled around the world assembling one of the world's great collections of propaganda and decorative arts of the late nineteenth and early twentieth centuries. He tired of paying rent to store his extensive holdings, so he bought the Mathews' building. The Art Deco district was to have a new museum: The Wolfsonian. Poised out front on the sidewalk would be a stainless steel Art Deco bridge tender's house that once graced a span over the Miami River.

Wolfson's achievement was admired. It was unheard of in the 1990s for an individual to accumulate a collection, renovate a building to house it, hire a staff, bring in academics, and open it to the public. Scholars from around the world lauded the opening because it provided an opportunity to examine culture in a way offered by no other institution in the world.[31]

It was a fitting addition to South Beach. The arts had been part of the district since the beginning of the preservation movement. The earliest members of the league were designers, artists, collectors. It had been a dozen years since Ellie Schneiderman coaxed $62,000 of federal grant money out of the city commission and started the South Florida Arts Center. In those days, an artist could step outside his door onto the mall and be in the company only of seagulls and a few stray cats.

Bringing life back to Lincoln Road was not without growing pains. Like most cities trying to revitalize a commercial area, there were missteps along the way. Lincoln Road tried a farmer's market, a noontime concert series, a crafts festival, a *Carnaval*-type celebration, performances of Shakespeare, and belly dancers to attract businesses and shoppers back to the mall. In the end, it was the artists who made it happen. Lincoln Road had become the cultural hub of Miami Beach. There were sixteen art galleries and ninety artists working at the arts center. Space they had rented for $3 to $5 when they moved in had risen to $25 a square foot.[32] The street was the home of the Miami City Ballet, the New World Symphony, and a concert series at the restored Colony Theater. It had attracted smart restaurants, fashionable shops, and a substantial city investment to spruce up the landscaping, lighting, and public spaces. The clubby atmosphere of the early days had passed. Local retailers who had been in business for years were being priced out of their stores. Boutiques moved into spaces where the artists used to buy toothpaste and Tylenol.

The world of art also was experiencing growing pains at the Bass Museum (pronounced like the fish). John and Johanna Bass had donated some of their sugar fortune to create a fine arts museum in Miami Beach in 1964. They furnished the museum with a major portion of their extensive private art collection on permanent loan. The museum was housed in the city's former library, an Art Deco beauty faced with Florida limestone sitting in a park on Collins Avenue between Twenty-first and Twenty-second streets. The building was part of South Florida's introduction to Art Deco, designed in 1930 by Russell Pancoast, grandson of original Miami Beach planter John Collins.

The Bass sat at the nexus of the big draw attractions that brought tens of thousands of people to South Beach every year. The beach, the convention center, the Theater of the Performing Arts, the New World Symphony, and Lincoln Road were within a few blocks of the museum. The area had remained almost untouched in the developers' rush to the action south of Lincoln Road.

Diane Camber had left her job with the league and joined the Bass as executive director in 1980. At that time, the museum wasn't even accredited. By 1986, it was successful, crowded, and outdated. Seven years and several proposals later, the city grudgingly requested bids to increase the size of the museum sixfold. A Japanese designer was chosen, and the Bass was ready to move ahead with a $16.5 million construction project.

The city decided that if that much public money was to be spent, it wanted a stronger voice on the museum's board of directors. The museum was governed by a five-member board that included the city manager, two Bass sons, the chairman of the chamber of commerce, and the president of the Friends of the Bass. The city wanted the board expanded to thirty members. The Bass family heirs were so offended by that idea that they threatened to take their paintings and go elsewhere.[33] Alternatives were floated, discussed, rejected. The debate between the Bass family and the city raged for months in private conversations, in public meetings, in the media. Camber suggested a compromise that reduced the size of the expansion. Finally, in 1994, under threat of losing $1.7 million in state grant money, the commission conceded.[34]

They were well into the design process when things became more complicated. In a complex exchange, the city landed a windfall from the county that included a new regional library and approximately $20 million in long-term revenue. Among the things the city could do with the newfound money was help fund a building for the Miami City Ballet. The ballet had grown in size and reputation in its ten years. It was terribly cramped for space in its Lincoln Road storefront, and Lincoln Road was eager to return that prime corner property to commercial use. The ballet threatened to leave Dade County and move to West Palm Beach.

The main Miami Beach library was located in Collins Park, in front of the Bass Museum, but it was small. Eleven sites were suggested for the new regional facility. People in North Beach wanted it there. South Beach residents wanted it there. The planning board wanted it in North Beach.

The city commission wanted to keep the library near the Bass. Some people, perfectly happy with the current library, didn't want a new one at all. The county library advisory board recommended using the original library, now the Bass Museum, and expand it to create the new library. That would mean building a new museum. The funds from the state for the Bass expansion couldn't be used for a new museum. The Bass would still have its paintings but nowhere to hang them. Friends privately joked that Camber was so stressed out by all the indecision that she was wandering around the museum at night talking to the artwork.

One evening City Commissioner Susan Gottlieb was sitting at home doodling. The former president of the ballet trustees called to remind her that the ballet really needed a new home. Gottlieb kept doodling and suddenly said, "I have it!"[35]

The Bass Museum and its new expansion wing would be built as designed. The city would acquire property on the north side of the park for the new library and a new home for the Miami City Ballet. Miami Beach would have a cultural center.

CHAPTER 14

Art Deco Weekend

When the first Art Deco Week was held on Ocean Drive, the street was neglected and shabby. Twenty years later, the program for the 1998 event offered reprints of Woody Vondracek's original 1970s poster "Old Miami Beach; We still remember the vacation you never forgot" and his first poster for the Cardozo Hotel.

After its less than stellar inaugural in 1978, the Art Deco festival was moved to January and downsized to a long weekend. It continued to lose money with every attempt. Michael Kinerk called Ernie Martin to a meeting in a conference room at the *Miami Herald* building and exhorted him to take over the 1983 weekend and turn it into a money maker. Martin called some friends with the Little Havana Kiwanis to find out how they ran their highly successful Calle Ocho festival. They told him what permits were needed, how to work with contractors, how to negotiate with vendors, and all of the other nuts and bolts details. That year, the league made enough profit to pay off its debts from earlier years.[1]

Almost everything on South Beach had changed by 1998 except the people organizing Art Deco Weekend. Kinerk was chairman emeritus, having turned over the official chairman's duties to Matti Bower. But Kinerk and Dennis Wilhelm were working hard, as usual, to help coordinate all the elements and volunteers it took to put on the show.

Kinerk was an indefatigable worker on behalf of the league. He had served as treasurer, put out the newsletter, organized Art Deco Weekend, cowritten three books on Art Deco, chaired committees, helped restore a hotel, campaigned for city commission candidates, fought and made up with most other leaders of the group, planned conferences, served several terms as chairman of the board, and contributed his time and money for twenty years. During the final weeks of Art Deco Weekend planning, he spent as many as fifteen hours a day working on it. Two months before the 1997 festival, he took a leave of absence. The event would go on, but Kinerk was exhausted.[2]

He was back for the 1998 event, along with familiar names including Wilhelm, Nancy Liebman, Richard Hoberman, Diane Camber, and Denis Russ, joined by others who had become league stalwarts over the years. The year's theme, Art Deco fashions, was chosen months in advance. There was considerable work involved when 400,000 people were going to drop in over the weekend. There was a program to be published, articles written, ads sold, artwork chosen, and supportive letters from government officials requested. An artist was selected to create the official poster and a party organized for its unveiling. Sponsors and patrons were solicited. Performers, lectures, and the film series were scheduled. Theme exhibits were organized. There were stages, sound, and lighting equipment to be rented. Parking, shuttles, and trolleys had to be arranged, and guides were trained for walking, bicycle, boat, and bus tours. Media were contacted and interviews arranged. Merchandise was ordered and volunteers found to staff the information booth. Children's events were planned; vendors were contracted and booths assigned; and antique cars were found for the parade.

There was street theater with unicycles, acrobats, dancers, clowns, and jugglers, and three stages featuring jazz, swing, Dixieland, and big band music by more than twenty acts. The film series starred Fred Astaire and Ginger Rogers, Ray Milland, Irene Dunn, Joan Crawford, Carol Lombard, William Powell, and Jean Harlow. A fashion photography exhibit was installed at the Bass Museum, and a fashion tour featuring Armani, Kenneth Cole, and Versace was added to the activities. Vendors offered antiques, furniture, jewelry, clothing, books, toys, collectibles, posters, tee-shirts, glassware, lamps, and original art. People could walk down Ocean Drive grazing on gyros, shaved ice, frozen bananas dipped in chocolate, Jamaican food, Vietnamese dishes, Texas-style fajitas, baklava, souvlaki, funnel cake, ice cream, catfish on a stick, and a host of other calorie-laden foods. Eleven lectures were scheduled in conjunction with the fashion theme.[3]

Every year there was some last-minute crisis. Wind storms blew down tents and light poles; people didn't show up for their scheduled shifts;

accidents happened. One year the league decided to have its Moon Over Miami Ball on Collins Avenue. Literally. Guests would enter through the Ritz Plaza and work their way to the dining and dancing area under a tent in the middle of the street. When the tent people arrived, they discovered that the police department had failed to ban parking. The street was lined with cars. The tent man was going to leave; the ball would collapse. Eventually they got the tent up and worked late to get everything ready by the time the guests began arriving.[4]

The veterans sighed with nostalgia for the tranquil charm that was gone even as they marveled at the scope of the explosive activity around them. They loved the exposure for the district and the income they got at their souvenir booth, but some felt the event had turned into a "street zoo." The weekend had become too much about fun and not enough about educating people about the Art Deco district.

The amount of money to produce the event had soared. The league had paid $6,000 for police to direct traffic and provide security in its first years; now it was $47,000. Adding the rental for the parking meters along the eight blocks of Ocean Drive that would be closed for the weekend and other required city services and permits, the league deposited $80,000 in the city's treasury for the event. Originally they didn't have to pay for the parking meters. No one was parking there so the city didn't lose any money by closing the street.[5]

The rising cost of putting on Art Deco Weekend was indicative of the rising cost of everything on South Beach. The oceanfront hotel room that Rose Abrams of Brooklyn rented for $235 a month in 1982 was going for $350 a night in season in 1998. South Beach had matured beyond neon lights and fancy paint jobs and was making a full-court press to be incredibly cool. It still was a bargain compared to many other tourist destinations. A travel research firm found that the average rate for hotel rooms for all of Miami Beach in 1997 was $94.25, compared to $105.00 for New Orleans, $111.52 for Honolulu, and $104.67 for San Diego.[6]

The agonizingly chic Delano cost from $400 to $2,000 a night. At the Tides, guests could relax on the broad keystone terrace with an overpriced piña colada before retiring to their terribly understated room with a view of the blue Atlantic and a chalkboard near the door for leaving messages for $335 a night, plus tax and minibar charges. The National went online with a $225 rate for a room with a view of Miami and as much as $570 for a suite. The Astor on Washington Avenue underwent a $5 million renovation and reopened with stylish rooms featuring queen-sized beds, marble bathrooms, and double-insulated windows to muffle the racket outside for $210 a night.[7]

Hotels banked on unusual amenities or decor to attract customers. One had a communal dining room and allowed guests to bring their dogs to pal around with the Maltese who supervised the front desk. One had fresh flowers in each room, another had telescopes to gaze out at the ships sailing across the horizon or get a closer view of the goings-on across the street in Lummus Park. By 1998 there were approximately four thousand hotel rooms in the district between Twenty-first Street and Government Cut. A Ritz Carlton was on the way, a Regent was being discussed; there were rumors of several yet-to-be-named independent boutique hotels.

The loudest buzz in the hospitality industry, though, was something the city had planned and fantasized about for almost twenty years. In 1994 the city had offered a dowry of a five-and-a-half-acre oceanfront site three blocks from the convention center to the developer that came up with the best proposal to build an eight-hundred-room hotel. It wasn't the first time that Miami Beach made such an overture. An earlier invitation included six hundred feet of oceanfront property plus "special inducements and liberal terms to parties who will erect the class of hotel desired." That overture was made by Carl Fisher in an advertisement in the *Miami Metropolis* on March 21, 1914.

Hotel developers lined up like fans waiting for World Series tickets to go on sale. Marriott International was interested. Hyatt Hotels picked up a packet. Bally Hotels indicated it might take a gamble on the deal. H. Ross Perot was rumored to be preparing a proposal. The prestigious Tisch and Ratner families planned to bid under their Loews Hotels flag. Even "The Donald" was in the crowd of more than sixty interested investors who paid $250 for an official bid packet.[8]

It would be the second largest hotel in Dade County, outsized only by the venerable Fontainebleau. It was a sweet deal. The winner would get the first five years of the land lease for free. The city would pitch in with more than $45 million in bond-backed financing and possibly a new parking garage. An additional $10 million was set aside for a smaller hotel to be built by an African-American developer, a response to a 1993 black tourism boycott. Investors would need about $100 million in private financing.[9] Preservationists gnashed their teeth when they thought of what such a massive project would do to the visual rhythm of Collins Avenue. The new hotel would sit north of Sixteenth Street on the former sites of the demolished Poinciana, Sands, and New Yorker.

On March 7, 1994, at 5:01 p.m., proposals from six viable competitors were opened. Each was accompanied by a $25,000 deposit.[10] It took four months for the city and its consultant to review the plans and make a decision. When it was over, Loews Hotels was the winner. Its chief executive was Jonathan Tisch. The powerful Tisch family had developed the Americana Hotel, since renamed the Sheraton Bal Harbour, a few miles north of Miami Beach and had other real estate investments in Dade County. Partner Bruce Ratner's uncle had built the Clevelander Hotel on Ocean Drive, and Ratner companies owned several properties on Lincoln Road. Both families had the kind of prestige and financial clout that made city officials swoon.

The new 830-room hotel would be sixteen stories of updated Art Deco luxury bearing the insignia of the Loews chain, third in the top-ten list of luxury hotel chains by the Zagat U.S. hotel guide. The St. Moritz Hotel was one that the league really wanted to save, and they successfully lobbied to have it incorporated into the new design. The St. Moritz looked like the younger brother of the Havoline thermometer from the 1933 Chicago World's Fair. Kinerk, serving in 1994 as vice chairman of the league, called it "one of the most outstanding buildings in the historic district." Morris Lapidus, in his split with the league, said the St. Moritz was worthless and should be demolished.[11]

The second hotel would be the four-hundred-room Royal Palm Crowne Plaza to be developed by the minority-owned company. Art Unger and the league were relieved when it was announced that a renovated Royal Palm would be part of the Crowne Plaza project. Unger had struggled to hold on to his grandfather's hotel, but the city had to have the property to complete its land package.

Work finally got under way on the Crowne Plaza in 1998. The Royal Palm had deteriorated during the city's stewardship. Water seeped into the building through the walls and around windows. The reinforcing rods corroded and the concrete was dropping off the building. Engineers diagnosed the hotel's condition and pronounced it terminal.[12] The city commission would have to approve the demolition permit.

Nancy Liebman strode into the city commission meeting armed for combat. Other buildings in similar condition had been saved. The engineering reports were presented. Even the city's preservation coordinator said that saving the Royal Palm was hopeless. A promise was made by the developer that the new building would faithfully echo the Royal Palm's original design. Liebman, steeling herself, made the motion to issue a demolition permit for the Royal Palm and said, "It is indeed a dark day when I have to sit here and do this."[13]

Plenty of visitors were arriving to fill up all the new and renovated hotel rooms. Diners sitting at a Lincoln Road café would see a parade of families with children, young singles, grandparents, honeymooners, drag queens, and businesspeople strolling past. Cultural and heritage tourism had become a huge industry. The Travel Industry Association of America had just added cultural tourism as a measurable sector in its 1997 report to its members. Almost half of U.S. states had established or were developing heritage and cultural tourism programs where none had existed ten years earlier. The National Trust for Historic Preservation's listing of "Historic Hotels of America," which had started in 1989 with only thirty-two properties, was soaring past one hundred members, including Tony Goldman's Park Central.[14]

The gay community on South Beach had grown from a few individuals who were interested in the Art Deco district to being a major economic force. There was a gay business guild and gay guest houses were doing a brisk business. Gay nights at the dance clubs were wildly popular. The White Party, started in 1985 as an AIDS fundraiser, had grown into five days of club nights, tea dances, and beach parties. It was considered a "must" event on the social circuit. City leaders, recognizing the importance of gays in the revitalization of the city, had adopted in 1992 the city's own equal rights ordinance banning discrimination based on sexual orientation.

There was a lot more than an interest in Art Deco buildings and glorious weather that was drawing people to South Beach. The entertainment industry was occupying South Beach like a victorious army. Office space was becoming as much in demand as parking space. Sony Music International's Latin American division was headquartered on Lincoln Road. Producers of the nationally syndicated fashion show *Main Floor* were down the road. Lincoln Road became a magnet for the Latin American headquarters of several entertainment corporations. *MTV Latino* was filmed and edited there. The same company was transmitting the Discovery Channel to Latin America, Spain, and Portugal. They followed a tradition dating from 1925, when the Western Union office on Fifth Street was opened to relay all U.S. messages headed for South America.[15]

Two television series, *Grapevine* and *The 100 Lives of Black Jack Savage*, made the network schedule but failed to repeat the success of *Miami Vice*. A pilot cleverly named *South Beach* didn't make it that far. Production companies were scattered all over South Beach. It was not unusual to see a cameraman backing down a South Beach sidewalk being followed by a singing star mouthing his latest single. Residents became adept at figuring out how to avoid filming locations jammed with equipment trucks, motor homes, lights, cameras, a catering tent, extras, wardrobe and makeup and hair stylists, and crew members. Police directing traffic and crowds of onlookers, distanced behind barricades, stood and talked among themselves while they waited for something exciting to happen.

The movie industry was not new to Miami. Film crews had been using Florida's lush backdrops since 1914. Theda Bara was on South Beach in 1921, making a motion picture set in the South Pacific. Irene Castle followed in 1922, picnicking on a Miami Beach golf course between scenes. The Firestone mansion served as a location.[16] The industry never became firmly established, though, partly because of the lack of support facilities in South Florida. A few movies still were filmed in the area. Andrew Capitman's first hotel, the Cardozo, was used as a set for the Frank Sinatra movie *A Hole in the Head* in the late 1950s. The *Flipper* series was filmed in North Miami in the 1960s. Most locals preferred to ignore the filming of the *Porky's* movies at the Fienberg-Fisher school or a breakdance movie filmed on Espanola Way in 1984. By 1999, though, Florida had become the number-three filming destination in the United States. Production companies flourished. They hired police for security, obtained permits, paid property owners to use their porch or lobby, rented space to park trucks, wrangled generators, lights, and the thousand other details that made it all look real on screen.

With the productions came celebrities. Visitors wanted to drop by the News Café, where the cast of MTV's *Real World* regularly stopped in for burgers, camera crew in tow. A block or so south, Cindy Crawford had jogged by for a scene in the movie *Fair Game*. They could dance at the club where Will Smith learned the moves for his *Miami* video. They were hoping to spot Lenny Kravitz at a Washington Avenue restaurant, or bump into Jennifer Lopez or Ricky Martin at a club on Pennsylvania Avenue, or see Hugh Grant in the elevator at his Washington Avenue hotel. They wanted to stay at the Cardozo Hotel, which had been bought by Emilio and Gloria Estefan, who were making South Beach their base of operations. Everyone from Courtney Love to Bobby Brown, from Sylvester Stallone to Dennis Rodman was being seen on South Beach.[17] Harrison Ford was there filming *Random Hearts*; Robin Williams and Nathan Lane came to town to film *Birdcage*. Visitors wanted to see where Whitney Houston and Kevin Costner filmed *My Bodyguard* and where Cameron Diaz walked when shooting *There's Something About Mary*. They wanted to check out where Al Pacino strolled in *Any Given Sunday* and where George Clooney stood on the beach in *Out of Sight*.[18] Some dedicated *Miami Vice* fans still were looking for Don Johnson's old hangouts. On any given day there could be an alligator strolling on Ocean Drive for a documentary, a woman riding on a horse for a soft drink ad, a lion lounging on the beach surrounded by models, stunt people throwing themselves through windows, and naked men being photographed while frolicking on a hotel terrace in direct view of the offices next door, a bit of a distraction for those involved in more mundane work and who brought binoculars the second day.[19]

Burt Reynolds and Richard Dreyfuss came to town to film *The Crew*. The story was familiar to some older South Beach residents. A landlord was threatening to evict his elderly tenants so he could renovate his run-down hotel and cash in on the tourism revival. An old, dilapidated but livable Ocean Drive hotel was needed in which to set the film. There weren't any suitable ones left. The producers chose Tony Goldman's Park Central. Set decorators raided salvage yards and thrift shops to find old furniture, stuck a fake Moorish facade across the front and dirtied up the lobby. Goldman's daughter Jessica looked around and confirmed that it looked just as bad as it did when her dad bought it in 1986.[20]

April Fool

For April Fool's 1987, the days when the slightest spark of activity gave hope to the Beach pulling itself out of the doldrums, *Miami Herald* writer Rick Hirsch penned a tongue-in-cheek report from the future. Dateline: Miami Beach, March 26, 2015. He "predicted" that on the 100th anniversary of the resort city, South Beach would be the center of Miami Beach's tourist industry and that a depressed Middle Beach would be the target of preservationists' desperate calls to rescue its rundown 1950s hotels. The power players of the twentieth century would have been consigned to fringe status, and the idealistic preservationists would be running the show. The Art Deco district would have become an international destination.[21]

In Hirsch's world, Ellie Schneiderman was elected mayor. Gerry Sanchez was president of the chamber of commerce. Former Miami Beach power brokers were standing on a sidewalk soliciting signatures to revive the Saturday night dances in the ballroom of a former luxury condominium, now a public elderly housing project. Alex Daoud Park had been dedicated next to South Pointe Tower. Demonstrators were marching up and down sidewalks carrying signs to "Save the Fontainebleau," which was scheduled for demolition.

It gave many people a good chuckle with the morning bagel and coffee. It turned out that Hirsch was right. He was just sixteen years off. It happened by 1999.

Well, not everything was on the money. Schneiderman had moved to Homestead to establish a new art center in what Hurricane Andrew left of the city's historic downtown. Gerry Sanchez had left South Beach. By 1992 he was burned out. He was a developer, not an innkeeper. He was trying to ride herd on hired managers who were in charge of 650 rooms in his menagerie of hotels. He lost a key person in his 250-employee Brooklyn operation, so more of his attention was needed there. He sold the house on Key Biscayne but worked out the deal of a lifetime for a fabulous mansion on Pine Tree Drive until his lawyer fouled up the lease. Sanchez had come to Florida to take it easy and was working seven days a week. His wife said enough was enough. They went back to New York.[22]

The Miami Beach Architectural District was celebrating its twentieth anniversary on the National Register of Historic Places in 1999. The Art Deco district was the cynosure for tourism in all of South Florida. Six thousand international tour operators gathered at the convention center to be wined, dined, and dazzled at the annual tourism "Pow-Wow," the event's first meeting on Miami Beach in five years. They were entertained at lunches, cocktail parties, and performances that drew rave reviews for the Art Deco district.

Hirsch's prophecy about a shift in leadership also proved correct. After a nasty election campaign filled with allegations of fraud, corruption, and hypocrisy, long-time preservation advocate Neisen Kasdin was reelected as mayor in 1999. Nancy Liebman, halfway through her second term on the city commission, was joined by Matti Bower, who was elected on her third try. For the first time, the commission had a Hispanic majority.

One familiar name was missing from the cast of characters. Abe Resnick was diagnosed with leukemia in 1992. He didn't let his illness slow him down. He secured the site for his Holocaust Memorial at Meridian and Dade Boulevard, over the opposition of garden club ladies. He was appointed by President Ronald Reagan to serve on the council in charge of building the U.S. Holocaust Memorial Museum in Washington, D.C. His leukemia was in remission, but after a six-hour operation in August 1998 he suffered a stroke and died.[23]

It was unlikely that anyone still remembered Hirsch's prediction that the kitsch of Middle Beach would be the target of preservation debate when developers applied for a demolition permit for the Royal York Hotel, built during the booming resort days of the 1950s. The Royal York had unexpected conical columns, a corrugated stucco facade and a curvy porte cochere that would seem at home to George Jetson. Two other 1950s hotels also were being threatened by the wrecking ball.[24]

The resorts that had been built in the 1950s were sprawling, self-contained tourist destinations. Every year a new one had opened, more flamboyant than the one before it. On opening nights, searchlights washed the night sky, a red carpet was unfurled, and limousines worthy of a Hollywood premiere appeared. Hotels with exotic names like the Marseilles, the Monte Carlo, the Casablanca, Algiers, and Bombay filled in the empty lots along the waterfront. The finer hotels had prize fights, house orchestras, and expensive shops stocked with beach attire that only tourists would be caught dead wearing. The showrooms at the big hotels starred Frank Sinatra, Dean Martin and Jerry Lewis, Liberace, Tony Bennett, Tom Jones, Johnny Mathis, Don Rickles, Vaughan Monroe, Patti Page, and Tony Martin, and glittery production numbers by leggy showgirls in feathered headdresses, sequins, stiletto heels, and often not much else. They had huge sweeping driveways leading to elaborate entrances where uniformed doormen welcomed the Cadillacs and Lincolns and the occasional Buick. Architectural critics of the day dismissed them for defying the sleek, clean, stripped-down designs that were taking over furniture showrooms, appliance stores, and streetscapes across the country.

Through the 1970s, local families would go together in groups of three or four and rent a cabana for the summer at one of the big hotels, soaking up the luxury for a quarter of the price that snowbirds from Toronto paid for the same accommodations in February. Young ladies held their bridal showers in the crystal- and gold-trimmed banquet rooms. Parents booked ostentatious ballrooms for their sons' bar mitzvahs. Kids from Beach High who could pass for eighteen sneaked into the dark, smoky showrooms and mixed with the couples in beaded evening gowns and tuxedos.

These were the hotels that the country knew as Miami Beach, the ones that were built the second time Miami Beach was an international tourist destination. By 1999, Middle Beach seemed outdated as a 1972 Plymouth. The Algiers and Bel Aire were demolished. The bird cages disappeared from the Sans Souci's lobby. When one hotel was demolished in a dramatic implosion, its roof was carpeted for the event and film of the demolition was used in a television commercial for the carpet company to prove the durability of its product.

The hotels were old enough to have become passé, but too young to meet traditional historic preservation standards. An incipient movement had begun in cities such as Los Angeles and Las Vegas to acknowledge the authority of postwar architecture. Original McDonald's restaurants, roadside motor courts, and tract housing became targets for the preservation faithful.

The idea that Middle Beach had any long-term architectural value first came from Robert Venturi and Denise Scott Brown. In a letter sent to the president of the Southern Florida chapter of the American Institute of Architects in 1973, Scott Brown said, "The progression from (south) to (north) along Miami Beach is also a progression through recent American architectural history from the 1930s to the 1970s. We feel that this progression is an important part of the architectural and cultural heritage of this country and should be seen as such by those who control its survival."

A new term was coined: *MiMo*, short for Miami Modernism, to describe the Middle Beach hotels. The public scoffed at the idea and said that the preservationists had gone too far this time. But the MiMo hotels were the same age in 1999 as the Art Deco buildings were when the league started in 1976. The league had been offering tours of "Magnificent Mid-Beach" and started beating the publicity drum. They were following the same steps to build public interest and support that worked for the Art Deco district. They hoped it would work again.

A change already was being seen. The Eden Roc restored its lobby to its original design and hoped to capitalize on the retro-appeal of 1950s swank. Glossy white paint was stripped off of the original rosewood columns. Partitions, installed during an impulsive effort to reconfigure the lobby, were removed. The floating staircase was spiffed up with a new glass railing. The Eden Roc's original architect, Morris Lapidus, now ninety-six years old, was guest of honor at the reopening. It had been almost twenty-five years since his unrestrained designs were the subject of a major exhibit at the Architectural League of New York. He was delighted with the restoration.[25] He had both the good fortune and the good genes to have outlived most of his critics.

Before the preservation board could act, the owner of the Royal York obtained a demolition permit and brought down the building to make room for a twenty-one-story luxury hotel. The attorney for the owner explained, "My client doesn't want this old thing. My client wants to build a new beautiful lavish hotel. It will bring a nice class of people to the city."[26] The class that was paying $2,000 a night for a suite at the Delano probably would have taken exception to his characterization.

The city commission, now laden with preservation votes, flexed its muscle to try to contain development in the city both to protect the older but not yet historic hotels and to limit another explosion of high-rises in a robust economy. It redrew the city zoning map and down-zoned much of the city. Developers would be limited to building smaller structures than before. It reduced the build-out capacity of the city by sixty-four hundred units.[27] The city quickly was reaching concurrency when the roads, water supply, and sewer system simply couldn't handle any more. The action did not affect a number of mammoth projects that already had been approved under the old rules and were about to dramatically change the Miami Beach skyline. Three condominiums—the White, Blue and Green Diamonds—would rise forty-six and forty-eight stories in Middle Beach, boldly claiming the status of being the tallest ocean-front condos in the world.

Thomas Kramer's Portofino Group already had made a similar architectural statement at the southern tip of the island. He built a forty-four-story condominium tower with one of the most spectacular views on the planet. On one side was the Atlantic Ocean that met the sky just west of Nassau. On a clear day, it seemed as if residents of the penthouse could see all the way to Cuba. The sun set beyond the glittering office towers of downtown Miami. To the north were the rooftops of the sizzling Art Deco district, whose success had created an economic environment that made the new high rises possible.

The Portofino Tower was joined by the thirty-seven-story Murano and the forty-story Continuum. They all were frightfully expensive, many of the units bought as second or third homes by people who could afford to pay someone to water their houseplants. With the new buildings in place, little apartments on Commerce Street, where the sun used to arrive on the front sidewalk along with the morning newspaper, were still in shadow at 11:00 a.m. Residents on Ocean Drive and Collins Avenue who used to watch the marine traffic in Government Cut while they lunched could no longer see the smokestacks on even the largest cruise ships.

South Beach had become glitzy and commercialized. The significance of the historic district was being overshadowed by its entertainment, restaurants, shopping, and high-priced real estate. More than 80 percent of the buildings had been improved to some extent, almost half had been renovated, some of them two and three times.[28] Even hotels outside South Beach were trying to capitalize on the success. Radisson Hotels spent $20 million renovating the Deauville at Sixty-seventh Street and Collins Avenue, a full forty-five streets north of the district, and promoted it on its web site as being "nestled in the Art Deco district."[29] The neighborhood had become famous. The hotel names, emblazoned in neon on spires and towers, were splashed across movie screens, travel posters, fashion layouts, television screens, and tour brochures.

The Tiffany was a jewel box of a hotel on Collins Avenue. Tony Goldman hired designer Todd Oldham to give it a cosmopolitan makeover. New York jeweler Tiffany & Co. sued, arguing in federal court that its name could be tainted by the South Beach hotel, despite the fact that the jeweler managed to have had a noticeable measure of success during the previous fifty-nine years that its name sat on the roof of the Collins Avenue hotel.

It wasn't the first time a South Beach hotel was taken to court over its name. The Ritz Plaza was named the Grossinger until that famous Catskills resort family objected. It changed the name to the Ritz Carlton, which led to a suit by its counterpart in New York in 1946. Goldman lost the Tiffany's challenge and had to rename the hotel. He sassily dubbed it "The Hotel" but the name on the historic spire remained in place.[30]

CHAPTER 15

Epilogue

Richard Moe, president of the National Trust, said, in a May 2000 speech, "My definition of a preservationist is someone who is concerned about the rootlessness and erosion of community that threatens the very foundations of our society, someone who wants to maintain a connection with the past, who feels the need for a tangible link with something real, something solid and meaningful."[1]

South Beach had created a lot of preservationists. The impact of the Art Deco district, combined with the attention to the preservation movement initiated by the county's sweeping 1982 ordinance, created an atmosphere that stamped enormous changes on the city. The preservation board had created eight historic districts, with plans for more. All of the oceanfront south of The Fontainebleau at Forty-fourth Street was under some form of protection. Another dozen sites, including bridges, fire stations, and the old city hall had been designated as historic landmarks. Legislation was being considered that would effectively prohibit demolition of any structure built before 1942 whether it was in a historic district or not. Allowable height and density for new construction had been reduced dramatically. Critics complained that the city had gone too far and was suffocating investment, that there were too many regulations too inflexibly applied.

Preservation had become an effective tool wielded by those wanting to maintain the city's scale and character and put a stop to runaway development that blocked off the ocean and blocked out the sun. The Art Deco district had not become a picture-perfect restored 1930s-themed enclave, nor had it been able to retain affordable housing for the elderly Jews who had called it home. Its unique architecture had, instead, become the basis for an unprecedented economic turnaround. Like San Diego's Gaslamp District, Ybor City in Tampa, and New Orleans's French Quarter, South Beach had become the habitué of the young.

South Beach remained a walkable, human-scaled neighborhood with many qualities touted by new urbanism. It appealed to both those who had tired of suburban sprawl and long commutes and those who enjoyed the glamor and hedonistic nightlife. Many new arrivals couldn't explain why they liked it except to say that it felt comfortable. The transformation of South Beach probably could have been achieved with more grace and less pain, but a change was inevitable. Disagreement on what direction it would take put its elderly residents in the middle of a tug of war. Lack of a cohesive vision supported by legislation left the transition in the hands of individual developers during the most fragile years. In the end, capitalism threatened to demolish South Beach; capitalism saved the hotels and apartments, and capitalism had wrought its extreme makeover.

The story is still being written every day on the streets of South Beach. At the turn of the millennium, its Mediterranean and Art Deco buildings became something built "last" century. South Beach had become a rebellious teenager—too mature to do what it was told without an argument, but not mature enough to make responsible decisions on its own.

By 2000, the median age on Miami Beach had dropped to thirty-nine, and less than 20 percent of its residents were over the age of sixty-five. Even with all the new arrivals, the population of Miami Beach had risen to only a few hundred more residents than there were in 1970.[2] Rents in the Flamingo Park area had doubled in ten years. Renovated four-hundred-square-foot apartments were renting for $1,200 a month.

The National Trust for Historic Preservation listed the New Yorker as one of the twenty-five greatest losses and the designation of the Art Deco district as one of the twenty-five greatest gains in historic preservation in the past fifty years.[3]

The city was still trying to put the area south of Fifth Street back together with a $27 million program to repave streets and add landscaping, street lighting, a fountain, and a pedestrian plaza based on a master plan by noted Miami-based designers Andres Duany and Elizabeth Plater-

Zyberk. Smitty's old Rolls Royce garage survived, after all. It was gutted, rebuilt, and converted first into a nightclub, then into retail shops for the gold card set. Hungry patrons still lined up every evening at Joe's Stone Crab on Washington Avenue, with a second line at the new take-out window.

The site of the Biscaya, demolished in 1987, became the home of a new thirty-three-story condominium, called The Floridian after the old hotel's original name. The Nemo Hotel, which had been a magnet for drug dealers, prostitutes, and crime, was renamed the Mercury. The renovated four-star boutique hotel featured golden oak paneling, Italian furniture, recessed lighting, imported linens, goose down pillows, marble baths, and black stretch limousines out front. It paid tribute to its past with the Nemo restaurant, featuring herb-seared sea bass, Australian organic free-range lamb, and tobiko caviar. On Ocean Drive the Beacon Hotel, which Benjamin Levy had seen every afternoon when he sat for a couple of hours to smoke a cigarette and people-watch, was redone with Heywood Wakefield furniture on the mezzanine, blue poodle chairs, papaya-colored walls, and Harrison Ford's name on the guest register.

The Ocean Beach Hotel that plumber William Brown built in 1915 as the Beach's first hostelry had survived hurricanes, redevelopment, and the moratorium. It was barely recognizable. It had been shuttered by the city for code violations. The building had a new owner who was going to restore it as a luxury boutique hotel. There was one problem, though. The street had been widened over the years and the hotel's front porch had been lopped off. The general contractor gathered up fifty tons of steel beams and fifteen fourteen-ton hydraulic jacks, lifted the hotel two feet off the sand, and moved it fifteen feet west. The owner planned to spend $1 million restoring the hotel, which had cost $10,000 to build new. Suites would start at $250 a night. They still were looking for the shipwreck that Mr. Brown had discovered and left under the foundation.[4]

The Bass Museum, after numerous delays and a three-year closure, opened its new Arata Isosaki-designed wing, smaller than originally proposed but striking. Across the street, the fifty dancers of the Miami City Ballet were taking their morning classes. Carpenters still were hammering in the finishing touches, and the air smelled of new paint. The new

$7.5 million facility, designed by Arquitectonica, was only the second state-of-the-art building ever constructed specifically for a dance company; the first was in San Francisco. Edward Villella, artistic director of the ballet, was ecstatic. "Before, when I would ask them to move, move, move, they would run into poles and walls. Now they run into space, space, space!"[5] The new library would be built to its east.

Books and Books opened a bookstore in the Sterling Building on Lincoln Road and named its café named after the Russian Bear restaurant that was there in the fifties. Hoffman's Cafeteria, which later became the Warsaw Ballroom, then a series of nightclubs, had returned to its roots as Jerry's Deli with a spectacular renovation that was as close to an original 1930s Art Deco deli as any Hollywood set designer could imagine.

Mrs. Joya still was selling fine linens at Moseley's. She arrived by 7:30 a.m. and often fixed breakfast for everyone. Mrs. Joya was placing orders for the granddaughters and great-granddaughters of her first customers. Now they were getting customers from the new luxury condos and from Fisher Island, an exclusive enclave built around the former mansion of William Vanderbilt. It was becoming more difficult to get the intricate handwork done, but you still could get a nice set of sheets for $4,000 or a six-piece towel set for $700.[6]

The kids who grew up on Miami Beach were raising their kids on the Beach. Active in the community, they now gave speeches in the same auditoriums where they had delivered their sixth-grade valedictory address. Another generation was playing ball at Flamingo Park. Newer arrivals and the media had adopted the "SoBe" abbreviation for the neighborhood, which proved highly profitable for a beverage manufacturer from Connecticut.

Tony Goldman turned over his South Beach operations to his daughter Jessica. While he remained based in New York, he expanded his interests to Philadelphia and hired Don Meginley and Gary Farmer to work with him there. Gerry Sanchez was trying to work his magic in Newburgh, New York. No slouch in the self-promotion department, he allowed himself to be dubbed the "Duke of Deco" by the local newspaper. Craig Robins of Dacra had redirected his attention across the bay and was revitalizing the Miami Design District, where the league had been born. He also hired architects Andres Duany and Elizabeth Plater-Zyberk

to design a "modernist neighborhood" based on their new urbanist theo-
ries, to be built on the site of the old Saint Francis Hospital. It was forty
blocks north of the Deco district, but it was being publicized as part of
South Beach.[7]

Lynn Bernstein went to work for the city. Richard Hoberman and Ivan
Rodriguez were still working for the county, although in different jobs,
and Michael Kinerk was still at the *Miami Herald*. Dennis Wilhelm was
doing archive work for Arquitectonica, a firm that was designing future
landmarks. Diane Camber still was at the Bass Museum, and Linda Polansky was greeting hostelers at the Clay Hotel. Dona Zemo was working
for the chamber of commerce. Her former roommate, Jane, stayed in
Miami Beach and married Saul Gross, an early South Beach developer,
who joined Matti Bower on the city commission in 2001; Dona was maid
of honor in their wedding. Denis Russ was heading the Miami office
of an organization involved in raising private funds for neighborhood
redevelopment. Maria Pellerin was president of Carrfour Corporation, a
project founded by the Greater Miami Chamber of Commerce to build
affordable housing for the homeless. John Capitman was a college professor in Massachusetts. Andrew Capitman and Margaret Doyle lived
and worked in New York. After two busy terms on the city commission,
Nancy Liebman ran for mayor of Miami Beach in 2001. Her campaign
was unsuccessful. Ernie Martin immediately recruited her to become
president of the Urban Environment League of Greater Miami. The
seven-member Miami Beach City Commission was evenly split with
three Jews, three Hispanics, and one Hispanic Jew.

Jimmy Resnick still had his offices above the hardware store and
beauty shop on Alton Road. He acknowledged that the district had been
good for the city but simply wanted nothing to do with historic preservation in general. The city commission named a street for Abe Resnick.
They chose Dade Boulevard, the street where the Boulevard Hotel had
stood until he demolished it in 1980. The lot still was vacant.

Abe Resnick and a friend took a trip to Europe a few years before he
died. The family became frantic when he disappeared for about ten days.
When he contacted them again, he disclosed that he had gone to his old
hometown in Lithuania. He met the mayor and saw his grandmother's
gravestone. The house where he grew up was still there. He wanted to go

back to Cuba, but he never did. He wanted to know what happened to his beautiful home. While he was in the hospital, the man who built the house for him went to Havana and took pictures of it. Jimmy took them to him in the hospital. Resnick, who didn't believe in saving old buildings smiled and seemed pleased that someone had saved the ones that meant the most to him.[8]

The young boy who stood on the deck of the SS *St. Louis* and watched the skyline of Miami Beach recede as he and his family were being taken back to Nazi Europe survived to keep his promise. Herbert Karliner had finally stepped on the sands of Miami Beach in 1954 and was living in North Miami Beach.[9]

There were a sad number of people missing from the South Beach scene. Architect and former league chairman Andres Fabregas died in 1985. Carl Weinhardt passed away a year later. Randy Sender, who designed the renovations of the Clay Hotel, the Clevelander, and the Waldorf Towers, committed suicide in 1990. Richard Rickles, a city planner who authored the design plans for Ocean Drive and Espanola Way, was lost in 1994. Almost all the elderly Jews who made South Beach a culturally unique neighborhood had passed away. None were buried on Miami Beach. There never has been a cemetery in the city. Other people who passed through South Beach were fondly remembered and sorely missed.

Locals were tiring of clubs and restaurants that were overpriced and had bad service. Some club owners, complaining that South Beach had become oversaturated and that new regulations aimed at cleaning up the district were too restrictive, began looking to downtown Miami as the next stop for party central. That would be fine with a lot of the longtime Miami Beach residents.

Tourists still were coming to see the Art Deco district for its buildings. Tour business was brisk at the league's Welcome Center, now housed in the Tenth Street Auditorium. Instead of waiting for a volunteer guide, visitors could rent a recorded tour and follow a map around the district at their own pace. Its gift shop was in the former lobby and offices were upstairs. A museum occupied the hall where seniors used to dance the foxtrot and cha-cha. It sat on Ocean Drive at the end of Barbara Capitman Way.

People jostled each other as they tried to make their way along the crowded sidewalks on the other side of Ocean Drive. Eager, fresh-faced employees at the sidewalk cafés greeted each one, thrusting flyers and menus into passing hands. The regulars sat with each other and bragged about what celebrities had dropped in the night before. They spent each day within view of the streets named Barbara Capitman Way and Leonard Horowitz Place. No one at the sidewalk cafés knew who they were.

In his presidential address to the 1998 American Institute of Architects convention, John Belle stated, "Preservation and the reuse of older buildings has long been synonymous in the United States with fringe groups, saving a building to which they have an emotional attachment. It is time that the true value of renovation, restoration and reuse take center stage, for they are the front line of sustainable design."[10] But that lesson was hard to learn. Miami Beach was still allowing demolition of historic buildings that were considered unsalvageable. Historic structures were being torn down in the name of ridding numerous cities of blight or crime. New Orleans demolished more than 350 buildings in the eighteen months ending May 1997, and 75 buildings in its National Register districts were slated for demolition after being declared public nuisances.[11] Paducah, Kentucky, demolished hundreds of vacant historic homes. New Jersey Governor Christine Todd Whitman climbed in a front-end loader to knock down the first of thirty-five houses built in the 1880s before she left for her new job as head of the Environmental Protection Agency in Washington.[12]

Those who had been on South Beach since the beginning of the league missed the days when you always could find a parking space, and the only music was the rustle of the palm fronds and the soft percussion of the waves on the beach. They knew it was about more than buildings and color schemes. It was about a living, breathing neighborhood and the people who lived and worked there. They appreciated the economic miracle but missed the excitement of possibilities. They wondered if the people who had come to South Beach because it was the hot place to be would put down roots and be concerned about something other than the rising cost of parking. The sense of having an allegiance to the community seemed to have been lost. People still smiled to strangers on the street, but they remained strangers. Many new arrivals were there to be seen rather than to become involved. People who bought the high-rise apartments as vacation getaways were involved in their communities back home. They had come to South Beach to escape responsibilities, not assume new ones.

South Beach is more than architecture or preservation or historic eras. This constantly evolving neighborhood includes one of the most popular tourist destinations in the United States. It must serve the needs of the vacationer from New Jersey alongside the daily requirements of the accountant and his wife who live on Euclid Avenue and the retiree who walks his dog every morning. It is the renovated apartments and the new high-rise condominiums, the remodeled hotels and the sparkling new ones. It shares in the responsibility of contributing to the city's cultural and economic vitality, not just with hotels, restaurants, and nightclubs but also with copy shops, art galleries, doctors' offices, drugstores, banks, and new investment in its buildings. It cannot be thought of as having a single identity. It is part of a municipality, not a specimen in a plastic bubble.

Most of what happened on South Beach in the 1970s and 1980s was done without the involvement, or even the consent, of many people who lived and worked there. Economics dictated that it would not stay the same. Those who sought redevelopment and those who sought to preserve what existed both did so thinking that it was best for South Beach, best for its residents, and best for the city. The neighborhood lived through thirty rocky years during which its future was uncertain. Those who now live there, who govern there, who do business there make new decisions every day that will affect South Beach for the next thirty years.

South Beach still has its special magical appeal, the feel of a warm, silky breeze softly scented with the sea cooling the apartments of Flamingo Park by day and warming the front porches of Ocean Drive at night. Sitting at a sidewalk café at midnight in January just because you can sit at a sidewalk café at midnight in January. Most people strolling along Lincoln Road and shopping at the boutiques on Washington Avenue don't know anything about the old Jews and the Yiddish newspapers, the kosher hotels and the cafeterias, the card games and impromptu concerts in Lummus Park. The quiet little seaside vacation village, the tuxedo and evening-glove resort, and the old Jewish *shtetl* are only memories. The sightseers taking pictures of the colorful buildings and the carefully dressed people standing in line at the clubs and the guests in the four-hundred-dollar-a-night rooms feel that South Beach was invented just for them. They're right.

Notes

Chapter 1

1. Michael Kranish, "These are people who emigrated . . . their whole life and this is how it ends," *Miami Herald*, August 29, 1982.

2. Ibid.

3. Laura Owens, "Concord still favorite spot at noontime," *Miami Herald*, October 21, 1982.

4. Kranish.

5. Ibid.

6. John Capitman, interview with the author, Waltham, Mass., March 30, 2001.

7. Christopher Alexander, "A City Is Not a Tree," *Architectural Forum*, 1965, as published in *The City Reader*, ed. by Richard T. LeGates and Frederic Stout, 119.

8. Debbie Sontag, "The colors of Lenny's life," *Miami Herald*, March 13, 1988.

9. Arva Moore Parks, *Forgotten Frontier*, 139. The Biscayne station was located at about today's 71st Street. It was one of five stations along the southeast coast built by the U.S. government in 1876 to aid shipwreck victims.

10. Howard Kleinberg, *Miami Beach: A History*, 12.

11. Parks, 67.

12. Gay Nemeti, "Snapshots of a century," *Miami Herald*, January 1, 2000.

13. Arlene Olsen, *A Guide to the Architecture of Miami Beach*, 4.

14. Charles Edgar Nash, *The Magic of Miami Beach*, 86–92; Kleinberg, 20, 24.

15. Kleinberg, 24–25.

16. J. N. Lummus, *The Miracle of Miami Beach*.

17. At that time, casinos were recreational and entertainment facilities. There was no gambling.

18. Fishbaugh, State of Florida Photographic Archives, published in Kleinberg, 29.

19. Kleinberg, 28–30.

20. Ibid., 30–31.

21. Advertisement, *Miami Metropolis*, 1913.

22. Nash, 99.

23. Kleinberg, 31.

24. Lummus.

25. Kleinberg, 37–40, 58. The state required three hundred registered voters for an area to become a city and Miami Beach had only thirty-three. It became a city two years later.

26. Michael Greenwald, "The road to restoration," *Miami Herald*, March 14, 2001.

27. "Build a hotel on Ocean Drive at once," *Miami Herald*, April 24, 1915. Throughout the years, Brown's Ocean Beach Hotel operated under several names, including the Star Hotel.

28. Kleinberg, 48, 52.

29. Charles Whited, "Miami rocked by turbulence from the start," *Miami Herald*, December 31, 1989.

30. Kleinberg, 55. Construction of the causeway resulted in Miami Beach becoming an island. It effectively dammed Biscayne Bay, which prevented tidal flushing. Residents of the north bay area lobbied for creation of a new inlet from the Atlantic at a narrow spot called Baker's Haulover, north of today's town of Bal Harbour. The new cut, completed in 1925, severed the peninsula from the mainland.

31. "Double Barrier Now Blockades Harbor," *Miami Daily News*, January 11, 1926. The *Prins Valdemar* was an old Danish naval training ship brought to Miami for use as a floating night club. After salvage, it was towed to Miami Harbor, where it was given a permanent land berth and briefly used as the Miami Aquarium. The remains of the *Prins Valdemar* were found in 1999 during construction of the American Airlines Arena.

32. Kleinberg, 125–26. Once worth $20 million, Fisher's estate at his death in 1939 was only $40,000. However, his circle of friends had not diminished. Honorary pallbearers included Walter Chrysler, Bernard Gimbel, Frank Sieberling, and William K. Vanderbilt.

33. Advertisements for the Shelborne Hotel, San Marino Hotel, and Cubana Airlines, *Miami Beach Sun*, March 25, 1955.

34. Olsen.

35. Molly Arost Staub, "Miami Beach: Everything old is new again"; Kleinberg, 70.

36. Ivan Rodriguez and Margot Ammidown, *From Wilderness to Metropolis*, 69.

37. "Apartment Association Protests Hot Plates," *Miami Beach Sun*, March 25, 1955.

Chapter 2

1. John Guinther, *Direction of Cities*, 219–22.

2. Barbaralee Diamonstein, *Remaking America*, 16.

3. Tony Wrenn and Elizabeth E. Mulloy, *America's Forgotten Architecture*, 25.

4. Richard T. LeGates and Frederic Stout, *The City Reader*, 119.

5. Diamonstein, 18.

6. Resolution No. 75-14624, City of Miami Beach, adopted February 19, 1975.

7. Michael Kranish, "South Beach: Where dreams die," *Miami Herald*, August 29, 1983.

8. "Chronology of Early Development Patterns on Miami Beach up to 1930," prepared by fifth-year students of the School of Engineering and Environmental Design, University of Miami, under the supervision of Professor Aristides J. Millas.

9. Frederic Tasker, "Asked for a hotel, Muss offered a community," *Miami Herald*, September 24, 1978.

10. Ibid.

11. Jewel Bellush and Murray Hausknecht, eds., *Urban Renewal, People, Politics & Planning*, 8–9.

12. Joan Wulff, "Old-fashioned design: Shy but determined," *Miami Herald*, July 22, 1982.

13. Dennis Wilhelm, interview with the author, Miami, August 3, 2002.

14. Diamonstein, 16.

15. Marty Stofik and Emily Perry Dieterich, "Dade County's National Register Landmarks."

16. Since 1976, three areas have incorporated as municipalities, which brings the current total to thirty-one.

17. Philip Johnson became one of the most influential figures in American design and architecture by creating landmarks, including his own "Glass House" in New Canaan, Conn.

18. John Capitman, interview with the author, Waltham, Mass., March 30, 2001.

19. Keith Root, *Miami Beach Art Deco Guide*, 84.

20. Terrazzo is a mixture of marble chips and concrete, ground to a polished finish. Usually it is tinted and poured within brass strips to create geometric or floral motifs. It is inexpensive and cool to the touch, a popular flooring choice in South Florida.

21. Barbara Capitman, *Deco Delights*, 86–90.

22. Barbara Wulff.

23. Betty Friedan, *Fountain of Age*, 391–93.

24. Roberta Brandez Gratz, *Cities Back from the Edge*, 295–301.

25. Barbara Capitman, 86–90.

26. "Designers organize to restore theaters," *Miami Herald*, February 27, 1977; Sam Boldrick, interview with the author, Miami, July 31, 2002; John Capitman, interview.

27. Michael H. Raley, et al., *Old Miami Beach*, 32.

28. Diane Camber, interview with the author, Miami Beach, August 2, 2002.

29. J. N. Lummus, *The Miracle of Miami Beach*.

30. Ernest Martin, Ph.D., interview with the author, Miami, August 8, 2002.

31. Ivan Rodriguez, interview with the author, Miami, August 6, 2002.

32. Michael H. Raley et al., *Old Miami Beach*, 47.

33. The HCRS was abolished in 1981, and responsibility for the National Register was taken over by its successor, the National Park Service.

34. Chris Delaporte, Foreword to Capitman, Kinerk, and Wilhelm, *Rediscovering Art Deco USA*, x.

35. Jo Werne, "Art deco buildings worth saving," *Miami Herald*, May 7, 1978.

36. Adler, a high-profile leader of Historic Savannah, later became widely known through his part in the events that were recounted in the book *Midnight in the Garden of Good and Evil*.

37. Elan Zingman-Leith, telephone interview with the author, October 3, 2002.

38. Statement of Significance, National Register of Historic Places Inventory-Nomination Form, Miami Beach Architectural District, Section 8, Florida State Archives.

39. Raley et al., 59.

40. Zachary Weiss, "Mechanisms for Citizen Participation in the Planning Process."

41. Carol Glinn, "Bent on Destruction," *Preservation* 17, no. 4 (July/August 1995), 16.

Chapter 3.

1. Debbie Sontag, "Paradise at bargain rates," *Miami Herald*, October 17, 1985.

2. Barbara Capitman, *Deco Delights*, 55, 64.

3. Dennis Wilhelm, e-mail to the author, August 14, 2002.

4. Michael Kinerk, interview with the author, Miami, August 2, 2002. Kinerk and Wilhelm coauthored a book about the topic, *Popcorn Palaces, The Art Deco Movie Theater Paintings of Davis Cone* (New York: Harry N. Abrams, 2001).

5. Joan Fleischman, "Remodeling stirs fears for Art Deco," *Miami Herald*, August 5, 1978; Morris S. Thompson, "Art Deco theater gets reprieve," *Miami Herald*, August 17, 1978.

6. Diane Camber, interview, August 2, 2002.

7. Christopher Boyd, "Old Glories . . . can Deco, disco and developers salvage a city?" *Miami Herald*, May 31, 1987.

8. Barbara Baer Capitman, "Yesterday and Tomorrow Meet Today," *Miami Design Preservation League Art Deco Week Program*, October 13, 1978, 3.

9. Diane Camber.

10. Lynn Bernstein, interview with the author, Miami Beach, October 29, 2002.

11. Michael Rothe, "Firestone Estate," *Miami Herald*, March 23, 1950.

12. Howard Kleinberg, *Miami Beach: A History*, 161.

13. Patrick Riordan and Barry Bearak, "Forced sale tumbles a high roller," *Miami Herald*, October 21, 1977.

14. Ibid.

15. Theodore C. Link, "Beach gambling will reopen under Costello, writer finds," *St. Louis Post Dispatch*, reprinted in *Miami News*, January 5, 1950.

16. Ibid.

17. Milt Sosia, "Paid on Beach: 500 bookies give cash to syndicate," Agnew Welch Scrapbooks, Florida Collection, Miami-Dade Public Library, Volume 10, 88.

18. Haines Colbert, *Miami Daily News*, November 3, 1950.

19. Michael H. Raley et al., *Old Miami Beach*, 63.

20. Bill Wisser, *South Beach, America's Riviera*, 126.

21. Raley et al., 63.

22. Ibid., 59.

23. Robert Liss, "Art Deco foes come out of woodwork to protest size of preservation area," *Miami Herald*, February 2, 1979.

24. Sara Rimer, "Victory for Art Deco proves that the past has a future," *Miami Herald*, May 15, 1979.

25. Letter from L. Ross Morrell to Liz Cloud, Division of Elections, January 4, 1978, Florida State Archives.

26. Minutes, National Register Review Committee Meeting, February 8, 1979.

27. Rimer.

28. Ibid.

Chapter 4.

1. Andrew Capitman, telephone interview with the author, March 5, 2002.

2. Michael H. Raley et al., *Old Miami Beach*, 27–28.

3. Andrew Capitman.

4. Barbaralee Diamonstein, *Remaking America*, 11.

5. Andrew Capitman.

6. Ibid.

7. Roberta Brandez Gratz, *Cities Back from the Edge*, 49–50. Dana Crawford was the winner of the 1995 Louise duPont Crowninshield Award, the highest honor bestowed by the National Trust for Historic Preservation.

8. Woody Vondracek, "Know your Art Deco," *Miami Herald*, January 3, 1993.

9. Dona Zemo, interview with the author, Miami Beach, October 29, 2002.

10. Linda Polansky, interview with the author, Miami Beach, August 1, 2002.

11. Diane Camber, interview, August 2, 2002.

12. Polansky.

13. Ibid.

14. Joan Wulff, "Old-fashioned design: Shy but determined," *Miami Herald*, July 22, 1982.; John Capitman, interview with the author, March 30, 2001.

15. Frederic Tasker, "Asked for a hotel, Muss offered a community," *Miami Herald,* September 24, 1978.

16. Maura FitzGerald and Willie Fernandez, "Elderly find relocation near reality," *Miami Beach Sun Reporter,* September 27, 1979.

17. Rick Abrams, "Sisters still waiting for demolition crews," *Miami News,* February 16, 1976.

18. Roberto Fabricio, "S. Beach butcher sharpens his ax to fight Redevelopment Agency push," *Miami Herald,* February 6, 1977.

19. Gay Nemeti, "The legacy of Mariel; Timeline," *Miami Herald,* April 18, 2000.

20. Ricardo Alsonso-Zaldivar, "No matter the origin, the dream remains the same," *Miami Herald,* April 14, 1985.

21. Guillermo Martinez, "Forgotten in the Peru Embassy," *Miami Herald,* April 5, 1985.

22. Alex Larzelere, *The 1980 Cuban Boatlift,* 3–6.

23. Ibid., 6–8.

24. Ana Veciana, "It was hell, refugee says of long wait," *Miami News,* April 19, 1980.

25. Heather Dewer, "692 Haitians land here," *Miami News,* April 14, 1980. The cases of Cuban and Haitian refugees still are handled differently by the State Department, a situation that continues to cause conflict within the exile communities.

26. Larry Wippman and Ana Veciana, "New fleet of rescue boats ready to set sail for Cuba," *Miami News,* April 22, 1980.

27. Marilyn A. Moore, "I leave my house for Castro . . . We have our freedom," *Miami News,* May 15, 1980.

28. Terry Williams, "Jones, LaFleur, Adams, McDuffie: time bombs that finally exploded," *Miami News,* May 19, 1980.

29. Ferdie Pacheco, M.D., interview with the author, Miami, October 29, 2002.

30. Jack Knarr, "Deadly tide of violence recedes after worst riot in Dade history, "*Miami News,* May 19, 1980.

31. Michael Kranish, "The domino effect," *Miami Herald,* August 29, 1982.

32. Michael Kranish, "Where dreams die," *Miami Herald,* August 29, 1983; "The domino effect."

33. Linda Polansky, interview, August 1, 2002.

34. Cynthia Bevans, "Ex-prisoners cause crime increase," *Miami Beach Sun-Reporter,* August 8, 1980.

Chapter 5.

1. Bill Wisser, *South Beach: America's Riveria,* 33–35.

2. Jimmy Resnick, interview with the author, Miami Beach, August 7, 2002.

3. Christopher Wellisz, "Abe Resnick: Always the outsider," *Miami Herald,* July 31, 1986.

4. Ibid.

5. Wisser, 33–35.

6. Ibid.

7. Resnick.

8. Henry Alan Green and Marcia Kerstein Zerivitz, *MOSAIC*, 55. The SS *St. Louis*, a ship of the Hamburg-American lines, left Germany on May 15, 1939, with 936 Jews trying to escape Hitler's regime. Most had applied for American visas but planned to stay in Cuba while waiting for approval. As they sailed, the Cuban president changed the country's immigration rules. Only twenty-two passengers with approved visas were allowed to disembark in Cuba. The United States denied pleas to accept the rest of the passengers. The captain reluctantly followed orders to return to Germany. At the last minute, the refugees were accepted by Belgium, Netherlands, France, and England. Germany conquered three of those countries, and it is estimated that six hundred of the St. Louis refugees died in Nazi concentration camps. See http://www.watchmen.org for more information.

9. "Eyewitness describes ship burning off Miami," *Miami Daily News*, May 15, 1942.

10. Stephen Trumbull, "Awed soldiers move into Gold Coast hotel," *Miami Herald*, February 21, 1942.

11. "$12 Beach Hotel Rooms Fairy Land to Soldiers," *Miami Daily News*, February 22, 1942.

12. Howard Kleinberg, *Miami Beach: A History*, 142–46; Sonji Jacobs, "Vets renew hold on Beach," *Miami Herald*, December 13, 1999.

13. Jacobs, "Vets renew hold"; Kleinberg, 144–48; Ivan Rodriguez and Margot Ammidown, *From Wilderness to Metropolis*, 148–49; "The Volunteer," www.mccormackmedia.com.

14. Kleinberg, 144–48; "The Volunteer."

15. Stanley Arkin, interview with the author, Miami, February 28, 2002.

16. Rodriguez and Ammidown, 148–49; Kleinberg, 146.

17. Resnick; Wisser, 33–35.

18. Resnick.

19. Ibid.

20. Michael Kranish, "Is future in the past? Deco advocates think so," *Miami Herald*, August 29, 1982.

21. Ellen Bartlett, "Art deco demolitions draw protests," *Miami Herald*, January 13, 1980.

22. Barbara Brundage, "League calls for demolition moratorium," *Miami Beach Sun-Reporter*, March 1, 1980.

23. Michael H. Raley et al., *Old Miami Beach*, 83.

24. Janis Johnson, "Good times and bad for Art Deco on Miami Beach strip," *Smithsonian*, December 1982.

25. "Destruction of the Boulevard," *Miami Beach Sun-Reporter*, June 17, 1980.

26. Resnick.

27. Nancy Liebman, interview with the author, Miami Beach, May 9, 2002.

28. Matti Bower, telephone interview with the author, Miami Beach, August 13, 2002.

29. Debbie Sontag, "The colors of Lenny's life," *Miami Herald,* March 13, 1988.

30. Ibid.

31. Isaac Bashevis Singer, *My Love Affair with Miami Beach,* 5.

32. Anders Gyllenhaal, "To hotel wrecker, beauty is in the eye of deco defender," *Miami Herald,* January 8, 1981.

33. Mitch Lubitz, "Condo Mania: 2 Art Deco hotels rezoned," *Miami News,* December 23, 1980.

34. Larry Perl, "Art Deco plan to get further study," *Atlantic Journal,* January 28, 1981.

35. "New Buildings Replacing Landmarks," *Miami Daily News,* June 25, 1950.

36. "Beach's First Building Bows to March of Time," *Miami Daily News,* May 2, 1941; Kleinberg, 176, 179, 199, 236.

37. Ellen Bartlett, "Both sides agree; We love New Yorker hotel deal," *Miami Herald,* February 19, 1981.

38. Mitch Lubitz and Kathy McCarthy, "Treasure or trash, hotel is gone," *Miami News,* April 24, 1981.

39. Ellen Bartlett, "Art Deco New Yorker tumbles," *Miami Herald,* April 24, 1981.

40. Lubitz and McCarthy.

41. Metropolitan Dade County Ordinance 2-17-81.

42. Public Law 89-665; 80 STAT. 915; 16 U.S.C. 470.

43. Dwight Young, "The Back Page," *Preservation* 51, no. 5 (September/October 1999), 144.

44. Michael Kranish, "Art Deco supporters assail Beach officials opposing preservation," *Miami Herald,* March 27, 1982.

45. Ibid.

46. Gay Nemeti, "Snapshots of a century," *Miami Herald,* January 1, 2000.

47. Charles Whited, "An era's echo, that's Art Deco," *Miami Herald,* November 5, 1977.

48. Dory Owens, "Preservationists: Developers rule board," *Miami Herald,* October 24, 1981.

Chapter 6.

1. Dona Zemo, interview, October 29, 2002.

2. Ronald Lawson, ed., *The Tenant Movement in New York City, 1904–1984.*

3. Janis Johnson, "Good times and bad for Art Deco on Miami Beach strip," *Smithsonian,* December 1982.

4. Liz Balmaseda, "Revamped hotel debuts with Deco fantasy ball," *Miami Herald,* December 15, 1980.

5. Michael Kinerk, interview with the author, Miami, August 2, 2002.

6. Dennis Wilhelm, e-mail to the author, February 13, 2003.

7. Michael Kranish, "Gambling on a design," *Miami Herald*, December 9, 1982.

8. Ibid.

9. Ibid.

10. Barbara Capitman, unpublished notes, Barbara Capitman Archives, Miami Design Preservation League; Barbara Capitman, *Deco Delights*, 73.

11. Capitman, *Deco Delights*, 9, 72–73.

12. Dory Owens, "Summer of 1982," *Miami Herald*, September 9, 1982; Michael Kranish, "From boom to bust," *Miami Herald*, September 9, 1982.

13. Kranish, "From boom to bust."

14. Alison Bass, "Neglect of elderly found at S. Beach hotel, state says," *Miami Herald*, August 12, 1982.

15. Ibid.

16. Louis Trager, "Officials threaten prosecution," *Miami Herald*, August 22, 1982.

17. Michael Kranish, "By city order, nothing flows and nothing flowers," *Miami Herald*, August 29, 1982.

18. Michael Kranish, "All South Beach suffers," *Miami Herald*, August 29, 1982.

19. Larry Perl, "Redevelopment ad hoc group put on hold," *Miami Beach Sun-Reporter*, July 22, 1982.

20. Michael Kranish, "Development votes delayed," *Miami Herald*, September 2, 1982.

21. Lawson.

22. Douglas W. Rae, *City: Urbanism and its End*, 336.

23. Eric Reider, "Dade's year; more scars than stars," *Miami Herald*, January 1, 1983.

24. Michael Kranish, "South Beach: Where dreams die," *Miami Herald*, August 29, 1983.

25. Michael Kranish, "These are people who emigrated," *Miami Herald*, August 29, 1982.

26. Edna Buchanan, "Caretaker, 79, slain trying to protect woman," *Miami Herald*, August 15, 1982.

27. Kranish, "These are people who emigrated."

28. Charlotte Hildebrand Harjo, "Ghosts on the Beach," *Jewish Journal of Greater Los Angeles*, June 16, 2000.

29. Michael Kranish, "Renewal ruins block, then locks some residents in," *Miami Herald*, August 29, 1982.

30. Jane L. Marcus, "Those were the days," *Miami Beach Sun-Reporter*, September 16, 1984.

31. Linda Polansky, interview with the author, August 1, 2002.

32. Lizette Alvarez, "A worldly gathering: travelers flock to S. Beach hostel," *Miami Herald*, June 17, 1988.

33. Gratz, 259.

34. Donna Wares, "A hostel takeover," *Miami Herald*, July 4, 1985.

35. Michael Kranish, "Beach officials may be sued, high court rules," *Miami Herald*, March 22, 1983. A civil court jury later found in favor of the mayor and commissioners in a 1984 decision on the merits of the case.

36. Michael Kranish, "The domino effect," *Miami Herald*, August 29, 1982.

37. Joan Wulff, "Escorts give residents safe feeling," *Miami Herald*, August 5, 1982.

38. Kranish, "These are people who emigrated."

39. Michael Kranish, "Abandoned streets suit the people of the night," *Miami Herald*, August 29, 1982.

40. Kranish, "The domino effect."

Chapter 7

1. Laura Misch, "He's Leaving," *Miami Herald*, April 21, 1983.

2. "1983: Bleakness tinged with hope," *Miami Herald*, January 1, 1984.

3. Isaac Bashevis Singer, *My Love Affair with Miami Beach*, viii.

4. Denis Russ, interview with the author, Miami Beach, October 27, 2002.

5. Michael Kernan, "All Hands on Deco!" *Washington Post*, January 19, 1983. The building earned the cover of the November 1982 issue of *Progressive Architecture*.

6. Christo and Jeanne-Claude, "Surrounded Islands, Miami, Florida 1980–1983," http://www.christojeanneclaude.net/christo/xtojc/si.html.

7. Christo and Jim Stingley, "Art Deco district also basks in pink glow of Christo," *Miami News*, May 4, 1983.

8. Dona Zemo, interview with the author, Miami Beach, October 29, 2002.

9. Barbara Capitman, *In the Pink, a Barbara Capitman Publication*, no. 2, September 1983 Pd. Political Adv.

10. Capitman, *In the Pink*.

11. Ibid.

12. Ibid.; David Hughes, "Exclusive One-on-Two Interview with Betty Comden and Adolph Green," *Stage and Screen*, www.stagenscreen.com; "Village Vanguard; The House that Jazz Built," www.gvny/content/history/van.htm.

13. Steve Sonsky, "Hollywood just sent its 'Vice' squad to Miami," *Miami Herald*, March 7, 1984.

14. Mike Sante, "TV Show will hurt S. Florida tourism, travel agents warn," *Miami Herald*, January 9, 1985.

15. Dennis Wilhelm, interview, Miami, August 27, 2002.

16. Andrew Capitman, interview, March 5, 2002; Michael H. Raley et al., *Old Miami Beach*, 47.

17. The author was the Dade Heritage Trust officer who served on the conference planning committee.

18. Program, Ocean Drive Developers' Conference, April 11–14, 1985.

19. Larry Perl, "MacArthur residents shuffle out," *Miami Beach Sun-Reporter*, September 13, 1980.

20. Dory Owens, "Fifth Street developers unveil their statement," *Miami Herald*, January 17, 1985.

Chapter 8.

1. Michael Kranish, "City won't help renters on police site," *Miami Herald*, May 5, 1983.

2. Paul Shannon, "After a week's notice, tenants evicted," *Miami Herald*, May 19, 1983.

3. Ibid.

4. Ibid.

5. Michael Kranish, "Diamond-in-the-rough dreams," *Miami Herald*, November 17, 1983.

6. Jane Marcus Yaffe, "New era dawns," *Miami Beach Sun- Reporter*, March 21, 1985.

7. Debbie Sontag, "Sudden eviction sparks tenants' resentment," *Miami Herald*, December 1, 1985.

8. Ibid.; Jimmy Resnick, interview with the author, Miami Beach, August 7, 2002.

9. Jackie Potts, "Lights . . . Camera . . . Pay Dirt," *Miami Herald*, January 4, 1997. The time capsule was found in 1997 by a construction crew. The items were given to Wometco heir Micky Wolfson for his Wolfsonian Museum.

10. Joel Achenbach, "The road to nowhere," *Miami Herald*, April 27, 1986.

11. Jeanette Joya, interview with the author, Miami Beach, August 7, 2002.

12. Michael Kranish, "It's more than a five 'n dime," *Miami Herald*, February 24, 1983.

13. The Miami Beach Woolworth's closed in 1997 when the Woolworth Corp. closed all four hundred of its F. W. Woolworth stores nationwide.

14. Michael Kranish, "Merchants fight the road to ruin," *Miami Herald*, December 22, 1983; David Morton, "Miami Beach: Yesterday, today and tomorrow," *Progressive Architecture*, August 1980, 61–64.

15. Debbie Sontag, "What's New on Beach? Plenty," *Miami Herald*, December 4, 1986.

16. Gratz, 289.

17. Ellie Schneiderman, interview with the author, Miami, February 20, 2002.

18. Craig Gilbert, "Will artists save the mall?" *Miami Herald*, March 10, 1985.

19. Debbie Sontag, "New proprietor of Waldorf has families in mind," *Miami Herald*, August 3, 1986.

20. Dory Owens, "Developers rush for Beach's gold," *Miami Herald*, December 20, 1984.

21. Ibid.

22. Ibid.

23. Christopher Boyd, "Beach fantasy proves seductive," *Miami Herald*, May 31, 1987.

24. Donna Wares, "Small developers say loans are hard to get," *Miami Herald*, November 3, 1985.

25. Dory Owens, "Beach seeks new blood: Kendall yuppies," *Miami Herald*, February 4, 1985.

26. "60 More evicted in crackdown," *Miami Herald*, February 9, 1986.

27. Gerry Sanchez, speech to Ocean Drive Developers' Conference, Miami Beach, January 9, 1986.

28. Gerry Sanchez, interview with the author, Newburgh, N.Y., May 5, 2002.

29. Program, Developers' Conference on Historic Ocean Drive, January 8–12, 1986.

30. Sanchez, interview; Debbie Sontag, "For S. Beach, he's the man with the golden touch," *Miami Herald*, July 13, 1986.

31. Sanchez interview. Spanish singer Rafael bought the house from him a few years later for almost two and a half times what Sanchez paid.

32. Linda Polansky, interview with the author, Miami Beach, August 1, 2002.

33. Sanchez, interview.

34. Dory Owens, "New Yorker gambles on reviving South Beach," *Miami Herald*, September 15, 1986.

35. Ibid.

36. Melissa Dribben, "Renaissance Man," *Philadelphia Inquirer Sunday Magazine*, May 21, 2000.

37. Debbie Sontag, "Ocean Drive: New and old a world apart," *Miami Herald*, December 15, 1985.

38. Debbie Sontag, "South Beach developers unite for lobbying effort," *Miami Herald*, October 26, 1986.

39. Debbie Sontag, "Buying wave hits Ocean Drive," *Miami Herald*, September 2, 1986; "Partners turn slum into condo," *Miami Herald*, September 11, 1986.

40. Debbie Sontag, "What's new on Beach?"

41. Boyd, "Old glories."

42. Sanchez, interview.

43. Debbie Sontag, "Developer cashing in on S. Beach restoration," *Miami Herald*, July 31, 1986.

44. Rick Hirsch, "Hold your nose if you like Deco," *Miami Herald*, June 1, 1986.

Chapter 9.

1. Irene Lacher, "A slice of life," *Miami Herald*, July 11, 1985.

2. Ibid.

3. Fred Tasker, "Organizing benefit bash is a real zoo," *Miami Herald*, June 12, 1985.

4. Christopher Wellisz, "War declared again: Capitman, Resnick dissolve peace pact," *Miami Herald*, June 5, 1986.

5. Christopher Wellisz, "Beach OKs Deco historic districts," *Miami Herald,* June 10, 1986.

6. Beth Dunlop, "The preservation battle goes to court," *Miami Herald,* January 13, 1985. Metropolitan Dade County later acquired the Deering Estate and restored it as a public historic and environmental resource.

7. *Penn Central Transportation Co. v. New York City,* 538 U.S. 104 (1978).

8. *Maher v. New Orleans,* 516 F.2D 1051 (5th Cir, 1975).

9. Christopher Boyd, "Old Glories . . . can Deco, disco and developers salvage a city?" *Miami Herald,* May 31, 1987.

10. Christopher Boyd, "Beach fantasy proves seductive," *Miami Herald,* May 31, 1987.

11. Paul Shannon, "It's demolition derby time for Rolls Royce mechanic," *Miami Herald,* February 9, 1984.

12. Boyd, "Old glories."

13. Jo Werne, "Deco condo: Broadway producer expects a hit with revival of 1936 building," *Miami Herald,* May 31, 1987.

14. Ibid.

15. Ibid.

16. Stephen Smith, "Builder putting love back into the Beach," *Miami Herald,* May 7, 1987.

17. Gratz, 51.

18. Christopher Wellisz, "Code board sticks to its guns on fine," *Miami Herald,* November 20, 1986.

19. Debbie Sontag, "Deco district's guiding force resigns from job," *Miami Herald,* February 19, 1987.

20. Rick Hirsch, "Director lost job on gamble," *Miami Herald,* March 1, 1987. Sanchez later offered a more substantial guarantee and got the loan.

21. The corporation operated under supervision while its accounting problems were cleared up and then was restored to full funding.

22. Marlene Sokol, "Bankers still tiptoe on beach," *Miami Herald,* May 31, 1987.

23. Ibid.

24. Gelareh Asayesh, Andres Viglucci, "Old and Young: Only poverty unites older Jews, younger immigrants," *Miami Herald,* May 31, 1987.

25. Christopher Wellisz, "Crime rate holds steady, but crack creates new problems," *Miami Herald,* May 31, 1987.

26. Christopher Wellisz, "Empty, but full of trouble," *Miami Herald,* March 8, 1987.

27. Ibid.

28. Debbie Sontag, "Tidy up boarded buildings, city asked," *Miami Herald,* November 20, 1986.

29. Wellisz, "Empty, but full of trouble."

30. Debbie Sontag, "Family, friends struggle to restore hotel," *Miami Herald,* April 10, 1986.

31. Ibid.

32. Wellisz, "Empty but full of trouble."

33. Ibid. The owners of the Poinciana demolished the hotel in February 1988.

34. Christopher Wellisz, "Court order halts razing of old hotel," *Miami Herald*, February 12, 1987.

35. Advertisement, Howard Kleinberg, *Miami Beach: A History*, 131.

36. Phil Kuntz, "Al Capone's onetime refuge may tumble," *Miami Herald*, November 28, 1985.

37. Ibid.

38. Ibid.

39. Donna Wares, "Cats find home as court postpones Biscaya demolition," *Miami Herald*, December 22, 1985.

40. Historic Preservation Certification Application, Floridian (Biscaya) Hotel, Project No. 0232-86-FL, Florida State Archives.

41. Gerry Sanchez, interview with the author, Newburgh, N.Y., May 5, 2000.

42. Wellisz, "Court order halts razing."

43. Ibid.

44. Ibid.

45. Christopher Wellisz, "Meginley: I'm no do-gooder," *Miami Herald*, February 15, 1987.

46. Wellisz, "Court order halts razing."

47. Sanchez, interview.

48. Ibid.

49. Patrick May, "Demolition crew puts old hotel to rest," *Miami Herald*, March 16, 1987.

50. Ibid.

Chapter 10.

1. Lynn Bernstein, interview with the author, Miami Beach, October 29, 2002.

2. Stephen Smith, "Delay razing Deco buildings, planner urges," *Miami Herald*, August 6, 1987.

3. Keith Root, *Miami Beach Art Deco Guide*, 20.

4. Smith, "Delay razing Deco buildings."

5. David Hancock, "Deco area gets new protection," *Miami Herald*, January 19, 1988.

6. Barbara Capitman, *Deco Delights*, 5.

7. David Nickell, "A Senator's turbulent campaign," *Miami News*, July 25, 1987.

8. Mary Ann Esquivel, "Owner says Senator will fall," *Miami Herald*, July 17, 1988.

9. Mary Ann Esquivel, "Art Deco backers lose fight for hotel," *Miami Herald*, October 13, 1988.

10. Ibid.

11. Michael Kinerk, interview with the author, Miami, August 2, 2002. As of publication, the lot where the Senator stood still was being used as a surface parking lot.

12. Lizette Alvarez, "Pop star Elton John films video in Art Deco district," *Miami Herald*, September 4, 1988.

13. Jane Wooldridge, "On location," *Miami Herald*, February 19, 1986.

14. David Kidwell, "Fashion biz brings bucks to the Beach," *Miami Herald*, October 10, 1990.

15. Lizette Alvarez, "Picture perfect," *Miami Herald*, November 6, 1988.

16. Michael Tilson Thomas, videotape interview, "NWS—The First Ten Years," www.nws.org.

17. Stephen Smith, "Symphony checking into the Plymouth," *Miami Herald*, January 8, 1988; Debbie Sontag, "Where anything goes," *Miami Herald*, May 31, 1987.

18. Stephen Smith, "Sale of South Beach hotel hits a sad note," *Miami Herald*, November 20, 1987.

19. David Hancock, "Residents of hotel beat drum for musicians as they check in," *Miami Herald*, February 19, 1988.

20. David J. Phillips, e-mail to the author, January 6, 2003; Ted Arison, videotape interview, "NWS—The First Ten Years."

21. Thomas, interview.

22. Marty Merkley, e-mail to the author, November 19, 2002.

23. Program, October 12, 1989, New World Symphony, Miami Beach.

24. Nancy Liebman, interview with the author, October 25, 2002.

25. Kinerk, interview, August 2, 2002.

26. Barbara Capitman, *Deco Delights*, 43.

27. Ibid.; Bernstein, interview; Liebman, interview.

28. Sontag, "The colors of Lenny's life."

29. Ernest Martin, Ph.D., interview, August 8, 2002.

30. Sontag, "The colors of Lenny's life."

31. Dennis Wilhelm, interview, August 3, 2002.

32. Ibid.; Kinerk, interview, August 2, 2002.

33. David Kidwell, "10th Street named for Capitman," *Miami Herald*, December 23, 1990.

Chapter 11.

1. Richard Hoberman, interview with the author, Miami, August 3, 2002.

2. Bonnie Weston and Cindy Ycaza, "Fire inquiry focuses on hotel," *Miami Herald*, October 11, 1990.

3. Bonnie Weston and Cindy Ycaza, "Deco hotel beyond hope after blaze," *Miami Herald*, October 10, 1990.

4. Bonnie Weston, "Hotel fire was preservationist's nightmare," *Miami Herald*, October 11, 1990.

5. Christopher Boyd, "Art Deco figure indicted for fraud involving loan," *Miami Herald*, June 24, 1989.

6. Judge Lewis, writing for the court, United States Court of Appeals for the Third Circuit, Nos. 95-1829 and 95-1856, *United States of America v. Leonard A. Pelullo*, appellant, filed January 9, 1997.

7. Boyd, "Art Deco figure indicted." In 1991, a jury convicted Pelullo of forty-nine counts of wire fraud and one count of racketeering. The convictions on wire fraud were reversed on appeal. Pelullo was retried and convicted a second time. (U.S. Court of Appeals for the Third Circuit, *USA v. Leonard A. Pelullo*, Nos. 93-1261, 93-1284, 14F.3D88L, 1994 U.S. App. LEXIS 1138, filed January 13, 1995, Circuit Judge Cowen.)

8. Christopher Boyd, "Deco units for sale; Beach hotels to be auctioned off," *Miami Herald*, November 28, 1989.

9. Gregg Fields, "Royale Group's hotels auctioned," *Miami Herald*, November 20, 1990.

10. Fred Tasker, "A battle lost, Deco fans vow to win war," *Miami Herald*, October 17, 1988.

11. Nancy Liebman, interview with the author, Miami Beach, October 25, 2002.

12. David Kidwell, "Battle within," *Miami Herald*, September 19, 1991.

13. Jimmy Resnick, interview, August 7, 2002.

14. Richard Wallace, "Another old hotel bites the dust," *Miami Herald*, February 25, 1992.

15. David Kidwell, "Wall's collapse ends restoration effort," *Miami Herald*, November 10, 1992.

16. Beatrice E. Garcia, "Developers set sights on oceanfront gem," *Miami Herald*, December 30, 1991.

17. Barbaralee Diamonstein, *Remaking America*, 14.

18. Beatrice E. Garcia, "South Beach developers win Deco hotels," *Miami Herald*, April 10, 1992.

19. Preliminary Report, Hurricane Andrew, Ed Rappaport, National Hurricane Center, National Oceanographic and Atmospheric Administration, 10 December 1993.

20. Seth Borenstein, "A Mike Tyson storm," *South Florida Sun-Sentinel*, August 24, 1992.

21. Heather Dewar, "Scenes of destruction for miles," *Miami Herald*, August 25, 1992.

22. Preliminary Report, Hurricane Andrew.

23. U.S. Department of Commerce News, NOAA press release, "Hurricane Andrew," August 21, 2002. Hurricane Andrew originally was designated as a category 4 storm, but final evaluation of the data upgraded it to a category 5 storm.

24. Compiled from reports in the *Miami Herald*, August 23–26, 1992; the *South Florida Sun-Sentinel*, August 23–25, 1992; NOAA press release, August 21, 2002. The koalas were taken to Busch Gardens in Tampa temporarily.

25. Ibid.

26. Anne Moncreiff Arrarte, "Frustration, rates soar in rental search," *Miami Herald*, September 4, 1992.

27. Dwight Young, "The Back Page," *Historic Preservation News*, October 1992.

28. David Kidwell, "Three votes planned for preservation," *Miami Herald*, October 25, 1992.

29. Liebman, interview, October 25, 2002.

Chapter 12.

1. Ferdie Pacheco, M.D., *Fight Doctor*, 14–15.

2. Ferdie Pacheco, M.D., interview with the author, Miami, October 29, 2002.

3. Ibid.

4. Ibid.

5. Ibid.

6. Robert Lohrer, "Olden Gloves; Fifth Street Gym takes its shot at a comeback," *Miami Herald*, May 31, 1987.

7. Ibid.

8. Greg Cote, "Historic knockout; 5th Street gym leveled with little care, fanfare," *Miami Herald*, May 4, 1993.

9. Dr. William R. Bouknight, "Short Cuts to the Top," Sermon, Christ United Methodist Church, Memphis, Tenn., http://cumcmemphis.org.

10. Bonnie Weston and Alfonso Chardy, "Beach mayor indicted for racketeering, U.S. says," *Miami Herald*, October 30, 1991.

11. Carl Hiaasen, "Daoud, Sheik: Where's the laugh track," *Miami Herald*, November 3, 1991.

12. David Lyons and Luis Feldstein Soto, "Acquittals," *Miami Herald*, September 14, 1992; Luis Feldstein Soto, "Daoud guilty on one count," *Miami Herald*, September 26, 1992.

13. David Lyons, "Told of his alleged tampering, judge blocks Daoud plea bargain," *Miami Herald*, April 20, 1993.

14. Tom Dubocq, "Daoud going free early—for helping to nail pals," *Miami Herald*, April 13, 1995. The waterfront mansion where the original meeting occurred was sold in 1998 for $2.9 million and immediately torn down to make room for an $18 million villa for a Swiss media mogul.

15. Howard Kleinberg, *Miami Beach: A History*, 190.

16. Ibid., 18.

17. Bonnie Weston, "Spitting incident could draw reprimand," *Miami Herald*, November 4, 1990.

18. "Post taps Hirschfeld as chairman," *Miami Herald*, February 23, 1993.

19. Jimmy Resnick, interview, August 7, 2002.

20. Christopher Wellisz, "Abe Resnick: Always the outsider."

21. Nancy Liebman, interview with the author, Miami, November 21, 2002.

22. Lynn Horsley, "Family Affair: Siblings Keep the Clevelander Going," *Miami Herald*, March 13, 1988.

23. John Lantigua, "South Beach revelers can't stop dancing," *Miami Herald*, July 21, 1995.

24. Liebman, interview, November 21, 2002. Eventually she was able to pass legislation to require more security to control underage drinking.

25. Ada Louise Huxtable, *Goodbye History, Hello Hamburger*, 125.

26. John Pastier, "Uncommon Market," *Historic Preservation* 48, no. 1 (January/February 1996), 102–3.

27. Brad Edmonson, "Road trips to history," *Preservation* 52, no. 5 (September/October 2000), 20.

28. Neil Alexander, "Big Gamble in the Big Easy," *Historic Preservation* 46, no. 4 (July/August 1994), 26.

29. Joan Fleischman, "Architect Lapidus erases League from his blueprint," *Miami Herald*, August 31, 1995.

30. Beatrice E. Garcia, "Development returning to South Pointe area," *Miami Herald*, December 9, 1991.

31. Peter Whoriskey, "Miami Beach's very big deal," *Miami Herald*, July 23, 1995.

32. Isaac Bashevis Singer, *My Love Affair with Miami Beach*.

33. Peter Whoriskey, "Luxury homes rise after cheap abodes razed," *Miami Herald*, March 8, 1999.

34. Peter Whoriskey, "As S. Pointe moves up, some are forced out," *Miami Herald*, March 27, 1994.

35. Peter Whoriskey, "A demolition derby?" *Miami Herald*, November 16, 1995.

36. Fran Brennan, "South Pointe worth preserving?" *Miami Herald*, February 7, 1996.

37. Rick Jervis, "The Beach's needy hang on to their hopes," *Miami Herald*, November 10, 1996.

38. Dan Foomkin, "Farewell to Homes," *Miami Herald*, March 2, 1989.

39. Michael Kranish, "A Tower in Trouble," *Miami Herald*, March 17, 1983.

40. Denis Russ, interview with the author, Miami Beach, October 27, 2002.

41. Jervis, "The Beach's needy."

42. Ibid.

43. Matti Bower, interview with the author, Miami Beach, August 13, 2002.

44. Russ, interview. The name of the organization was changed to the Miami Beach Community Development Corporation in 1997.

45. Jervis.

46. Andres Viglucci, "Old building makes comeback, so does tenant," *Miami Herald*, March 23, 1996.

47. Ibid.

48. Elaine De Valle, "Advocates say Beach ignoring homeless," *Miami Herald*, September 21, 1995.

49. Ibid.

50. Gail Epstein Nieves, "When they were kings," *Miami Herald*, August 6, 1999.

Chapter 13.

1. Mark Robichaux, "Amsterdam Palace," *Miami Herald*, January 2, 1989.
2. Ibid.
3. Gerry Sanchez, interview with the author, Newburgh, N.Y., May 5, 2002.
4. David Kidwell, "Versace delays demolition plans," *Miami Herald*, April 15, 1993.
5. Ibid.
6. Ibid.
7. "New Buildings Replacing Landmarks," *Miami Daily News*, June 25, 1950.
8. Rafael Lorente, "Designing a plan for the future," *Miami Herald*, September 16, 1993.
9. Rafael Lorente, "Demolition begins at Beach hotel," *Miami Herald*, September 10, 1993. The Flambeau was demolished a few years later without protest.
10. Peter Whoriskey, "Versace's villa," *Miami Herald*, July 20, 1997.
11. Ibid.
12. Martin Metzer, "Two roads to a fatal encounter," *Miami Herald*, July 20, 1997.
13. Ibid.
14. Ibid.
15. Ibid.
16. Miami Beach police offense incident report 97-24687, July 15, 1987.
17. Ibid.
18. "Journey to sorrow," *Miami Herald*, July 19, 1997. Versace's Ocean Drive mansion was purchased in September, 2000, for $19 million by North Carolina telecommunications magnet Peter Loftin, who had plans to turn it into a boutique hotel.
19. Barbaralee Diamonstein, *Remaking America*, 9.
20. Peter Whoriskey, "Survey: Beach is losing historic buildings," *Miami Herald*, May 17, 1997.
21. John Forester, "Planning in the Face of Conflict," *The City Reader*, 434–36.
22. Les Beilinson, interview with the author, Miami, October 27, 2002.
23. Dale K. DuPont, "High-end risk for an Art Deco gem," *Miami Herald*, April 21, 1997.
24. Ibid.
25. Peter Whoriskey, "History ignored . . . and embraced," *Miami Herald*, June 22, 1997.
26. Diamonstein, 23.
27. Peter Whoriskey, "Deco debate: What are its true colors?" *Miami Herald*, December 3, 1993.
28. Howard Kleinberg, *Miami Beach: A History*, 129.
29. Allen Freeman, "The compatibility question," *Historic Preservation* 49, no. 1 (January/February 1997), 24–25.
30. Peter Whoriskey, "Not chic enough?" *Miami Herald*, August 11, 1998.

31. Gail Meadows, "The Wolfsonian," *Miami Herald*, November 5, 1995.

32. Cliff Yudell, "Of the road," *Miami Herald Tropic Magazine*, December 22, 1996.

33. Helen Cohen, "Collection at heart of Bass dispute," *Miami Herald*, November 21, 1993.

34. Rafael Lorenta, "Museum battle ends," *Miami Herald*, June 9, 1994.

35. Gail Meadows, "Beach proposal unites artistic visions," *Miami Herald*, June 24, 1997.

Chapter 14.

1. Ernest Martin, Ph.D., interview, August 8, 2002.

2. Michael Kinerk, interview with the author, Miami, August 2, 2002.

3. *Impressions* 15, no. 1 (January 1998), Special Program Issue, Miami Design Preservation League.

4. Nancy Liebman, interview with the author, October 25, 2002.

5. Kinerk, interview, August 2, 2002.

6. Lydia Martin, "Neon South Beach grows up, tones down," *Miami Herald*, January 18, 1996.

7. Ibid.

8. Anthony Faiola, "Developers vie for 'free' hotel site on Beach," *Miami Herald*, March 6, 1994.

9. Ibid. The boycott was called by the NAACP after a 1990 visit to Miami by South African leader Nelson Mandela. Miami's Cuban-American officials refused to meet with Mandela because of his statements of support for Cuban President Fidel Castro. The boycott ended in 1993 after county officials agreed to a program to encourage black participation in the hospitality industry.

10. Ibid.

11. Joan Fleischman, "Architect Lapidus erases League from his blueprint," *Miami Herald*, August 31, 1995. Before his death in January 2001, Lapidus said, "I am not a preservationist of the art deco junk on Ocean Drive. For one thing, it doesn't bear a resemblance to what it was. It had been highly colored and neonized. To me, that's billboard stuff. The Fontainebleau and the Eden Roc were the great hotels that made Miami Beach world famous."

12. Nancy Liebman, interview, November 21, 2002.

13. Barbara De Lollis, "Beach commission votes for Royal Palm demolition," *Miami Herald*, November 19, 1998.

14. "Heritage Tourism," www.nthp.org and "Partners in Tourism, nasaa-arts.org.

15. Howard Kleinberg, *Miami Beach: A History*, 102.

16. "Actors picnic between scenes at Miami Beach," *Miami Herald*, April 6, 1922.

17. Allison Klein, "Anything goes during filming in S. Beach," *Miami Herald*, August 2, 1999.

18. Liz Doup, "Follow famous footsteps to South Fla. history," *Miami Herald*, August 29, 1999.

19. Tara Solomon, "Make ours au natural," *Miami Herald*, March 7, 1999; Klein, "Anything goes."

20. Howard Cohen, "Hanging with the crew," *Miami Herald*, August 28, 1999.

21. Rick Hirsch, "Beach's Days of future past," *Miami Herald*, March 29, 1987.

22. Gerry Sanchez, interview with the author, Newburgh, N.Y., May 5, 2003.

23. Elinor J. Brecher and Allison Klein, "Ex-Beach Commissioner Abe Resnick dies," *Miami Herald*, September 4, 1998.

24. Peter Whoriskey, "Beyond Art Deco," *Miami Herald*, July 13, 1999.

25. Peter Whoriskey, "Hotel restored to '50s glamour," *Miami Herald*, February 13, 1999.

26. Peter Whoriskey, "Bell tolls for classic '50s hotel," *Miami Herald*, August 21, 1999.

27. Allison Klein, "Commission downzones some parts of Beach," *Miami Herald*, November 8, 1998; Allison Klein, "Commission completes downzoning, part II," *Miami Herald*, July 25, 1999.

28. Frederic Tasker, "Dilutions of grandeur," *Miami Herald*, July 10, 1999.

29. www.radisson.com/miamibeachfl, December 28, 2002. The language had been changed as of publication date.

30. Sara Olkon, "Trademark change too late for SoBe's Tiffany," *Miami Herald*, December 3, 1999.

Chapter 15.

1. Richard Moe, speech, May 4, 2000, printed in *The Commonwealth*, May 15, 2002, 9–12.

2. U.S. Census Bureau, Census 2000, Table DP-1, Miami Beach.

3. Compiled by Arnold Berka, "Memorable losses and gains in American preservation during the past 50 years," *Preservation* 51, no. 5 (September/October 1999), 24.

4. Michael Greenwald, "The road to restoration," *Miami Herald*, March 14, 2001.

5. Jordan Levin, "Great leap forward," *Miami Herald*, January 23, 2000.

6. Jeanette Joya, interview with the author, Miami Beach, August 7, 2002. At the end of 2004, after seventy years on Lincoln Road, Moseley's closed its doors. Joseph Moseley's sons, who had inherited the business, were ready to retire and their sons were not interested in running the linen store. An offer for the property that was "too good to refuse" also contributed to the decision.

7. www.aqua.net.

8. Jimmy Resnick, interview with the author, Miami Beach, August 7, 2002.

9. Henry Alan Green and Marcia Kerstein Zerivitz, *MOSAIC*, 55.

10. Gratz, 346.

11. Sudip Bose and Jason Berry, "Demolition Derby in New Orleans," *Historic Preservation* 49, no. 5 (September/October 1997), 14.

12. "Out with the old," *Historic Preservation* 48, no. 6 (November/December 1996), 16.

Selected Bibliography

Books

Bacon, Edmund. "New World Cities." In *American Civilization*, ed. by Daniel Boorstein. Thames & Hudson, 1972.

Bellush, Jewel, and Murray Hausknecht, eds. *Urban Renewal: People, Politics Planning*. New York: Doubleday Anchor, 1967.

Capitman, Barbara Baer. *Deco Delights*. New York: E. P. Dutton, 1988.

———, ed. *Portfolio—Art Deco District*. Miami Beach: Miami Design Preservation League, 1980.

Capitman, Barbara, Michael Kinerk, and Dennis Wilhelm. *Rediscovering Art Deco, U.S.A.* New York: Penguin Books, 1994.

Cerwinski, Laura. *Tropical Deco: The Architecture and Design of Old Miami Beach*. New York: Rizzoli International Publications, 1981.

Chase, Charles Edwin. *Resourceful Rehab: A Guide for Historic Buildings in Dade County*. Miami: Metropolitan Dade County, 1987.

Diamonstein, Barbaralee. *Remaking America*. New York: Crown, 1986.

Duany, Andres, Elizabeth Plater-Zyberk, and Jeff Speck. *Suburban Nation: The Rise of Sprawl and the Decline of the American Dream*. New York: Farrar, Straus and Giroux, 2001.

Dunlop, Beth. *Florida's Vanishing Architecture*. Englewood, Fla.: Pineapple Press, 1987.

Friedan, Betty. *Fountain of Age*. New York: Simon and Schuster, 1993.

George, Paul. *Visions, Accomplishments, Challenges: Mount Sinai Medical Center of Greater Miami, 1949–1984*. Miami Beach: Mount Sinai Medical Center, 1985.

Gratz, Roberta Brandez, with Norman Mintz, *Cities Back from the Edge*. New York: John Wiley & Sons, 1998.

Green, Dr. Henry Alan, and Marcia Kerstein Zerivitz. *MOSAIC: Jewish Life in Florida*. Coral Gables, Fla.: MOSAIC, Inc., 1991.

Guinther, John. *Direction of Cities*. New York: Viking, 1996.

Howell, Sandra C. *Designing for Aging: Patterns of Use*. Cambridge, Mass.: MIT Press, 1980.

Huxtable, Ada Louise. *Goodbye History, Hello Hamburger*, Washington, D.C.: The Preservation Press, 1986.

Kleinberg, Howard. *Miami Beach: A History*. Miami: Centennial Press, 1994.

Larzelere, Alex. *The 1980 Cuban Boatlift: Castro's Play—America's Dilemma*. Washington, D.C.: National Defense University Press, 1988.

Lawson, Ronald, ed. *The Tenant Movement in New York City, 1904–1984*. New Brunswick, N.J.: Rutgers University Press, 1986.

LeGates, Richard T., and Frederic Stout. *The City Reader*. New York: Routledge, 1996.

Lennox, Chad, and Jennifer Revels. *Smiling Faces, Historic Places*. Columbia, S.C.: Palmetto Conservation Foundation, 2002.

Liebs, Chester H. *Main Street to Miracle Mile: American Roadside Architecture*. Boston: Little, Brown and Co., 1985.

Lummus, J. N. *The Miracle of Miami Beach*, Miami: Miami Post Publishing, 1940.

Maddex, Diane, ed. *Master Builders: A Guide to Famous American Architects*. Washington, D.C.: The Preservation Press, 1985.

Moore, Deborah Dash. *To the Golden Cities: Pursuing the American Jewish Dream in Miami and L.A.* New York: The Free Press, 1994.

Mormino, Gary R., and George E. Pozzetta. *The Cradle of Mutual Aid Immigrant Cooperative Societies in Ybor City*. Ybor City: Ybor City Chamber of Commerce, 2002.

Munroe, Gary. *Life in South Beach*. Miami: Forest + Trees, 1988.

Muir, Helen. *The Biltmore*. Miami: The Pickering Press, 1987.

Nash, Charles Edgar. *The Magic of Miami Beach*. Philadelphia: David McKay Co., 1938.

Olsen, Arlene. *A Guide to the Architecture of Miami Beach*. Miami: Dade Heritage Trust, 1978.

Pacheco, Ferdie, M.D. *Fight Doctor*. New York: Simon and Schuster, 1977.

Parks, Arva Moore. *The Forgotten Frontier*. Miami: Banyan Books, 1977.

Peters, Thelma. *Miami 1909*. Miami: Banyan Books, 1984.

Rae, Douglas W. *City: Urbanism and Its End*. New Haven: Yale University Press, 2003.

Raley, Michael H., Linda G. Polansky, and Aristides J. Millas. *Old Miami Beach, A Case Study in Historic Preservation, July 1976–July 1980*. Miami Beach: Miami Design Preservation League, 1994.

Redford, Polly. *Million Dollar Sandbar*. New York: E. P. Dutton, 1970.

Rodriguez, Ivan, and Margot Ammidown. *From Wilderness to Metropolis; The History and Architecture of Dade County (1825–1940)*. Metropolitan Dade County, 1982.

Root, Keith. *Miami Beach Art Deco Guide*. Miami Beach: Miami Design Preservation League, 1987.

Rotella, Carlo. *October Cities*. Los Angeles: University of California Press, 1998.

Rymer, Russ. *American Beach: A Saga of Race, Wealth, and Memory*. New York: Harper Collins, 1998.

Sanford L. Ziff Jewish Museum of Florida. *Building a Place in the Sun: The Jews of Miami Beach 1913–1945*. Miami.

Scheinbaum, David. *Miami Beach: Photographs of an American Dream*. Miami: Florida International University, 1997.

Singer, Isaac Bashevis. *My Love Affair with Miami Beach*. New York: Simon and Schuster, 1991.

Ueda, Reed. *Postwar Immigrant America: A Social History*. Bedford: St. Martin's Press, 1994.

Venturi, Robert, Steven Izenour, and Denise Scott Brown. *Learning From Las Vegas*. Cambridge, Mass.: MIT Press, 1972.

Wisser, Bill. *South Beach: America's Riviera, Miami Beach, Florida*. New York: Arcade Publishing, 1995.

Wrenn, Tony, and Elizabeth E. Mulloy. *America's Forgotten Architecture*. Washington, D.C.: National Trust for Historic Preservation, 1976.

Yudel, Mark. "The Shtetl." In *Jewish Heritage Reader*, ed. by Lily Edelman. New York: Taplinger Publishing, 1965.

Collections

Agnew Welch Scrapbooks, Florida Collection, Miami-Dade Public Library
Barbara Capitman Archives, Miami Design Preservation League
Miami News Photographs, Historical Museum of Southern Florida
Sanborn Maps of Florida, State University System of Florida
University of Texas Libraries Map Collection

Periodicals and other published material

Advertising Age
American Preservation
Atlantic Journal
Chicago Tribune
Greenwich Village Gazette
Miami Beach Sun-Reporter
Miami Herald
Miami News
Miami Today
New York Times
Sarasota Herald-Tribune
South Beach Magazine
South Florida Sun-Sentinel
Tampa Tribune
USA Today
Wall Street Journal
Washington Post

Historic Preservation, the magazine of The National Trust for Historic Preservation.

Impressions. Miami Beach: Miami Design Preservation League, 1997, 1998, 1999, 2000, 2001.

Allman, T. D. "Nights in the Sun," *Esquire*, September 1988.

Capitman, Barbara Baer. *In the Pink*, no. 2, September 1983, Pd. Political Adv., Miami Beach.

The Center of the World; New York: A Documentary Film. Steeplechase Films and WGBH Educational Foundation, 2003.

Dribben, Melissa. "Renaissance Man," *Philadelphia Inquirer Sunday Magazine*, May 21, 2000.

Friedman, Alice T. "The Luxury of Lapidus," *Harvard Design Magazine*, no. 11 (Summer 2000).

Gralnick, William A. "Café Cardozo: It's 'old Miami Beach' but it's 'in' today," *Miami Today*, July 14, 1983.

Jackson, Bob. "The Deco Decade: Then and Now, There and Here," Art Deco Week in Old Miami Beach Program, Miami Design Preservation League, October 1978.

Johnson, Janis. "Good times and bad for Art Deco on Miami Beach strip," *Smithsonian*, December 1982.

Keeps, David. "The Last Resort: Miami," *The Face*, May 1987.

Levy, David, and Clark Malcolm. "Design and Problems of Aging," National Resource Center on Supportive Housing and Home Modification, www.homemods.org.

Perrault, John. "Report from Miami," *Art in America*, November 1981.

Ralston, Jeannie. "Making Miami Nice," *Venture*, October 1988.

Ross, Jane. "Miami Beach's Art Deco revival," *Florida Trend*, November 1979.

Rothchild, John. "What can historic preservation mean in such a place?" *Marquee*, April/May 1983.

Sandusky, Jay. "Beach's deco district to lure hotel investors," *Miami Review*, January 8, 1986.

Selby, Nick. "Gay Influence in Miami's Rebirth," Reuters News Service, 1995.

Stapp, Mary. "Why does South Beach still suck?" *New Times*, December 2–8, 1987.

Staub, Molly Arost. "Miami Beach: Everything Old Is New Again," *Women's World*, April/May 1988.

Stofik, Marty, and Emily Perry Dieterich, "Dade County's National Register Landmarks," *Preservation Today* 2, no. 1 (Winter 1987/1988).

Weiss, Zachary. "Mechanisms for Citizen Participation in the Planning Process," *Planning*, 1971, American Society of Planning Officials, 152.

Wilhelm, Dennis. "25 Sterling Years of Preservation," Art Deco Weekend program, Miami Design Preservation League, January 2002, 5.

Index

Cameo Theater, 29

Cape Florida Lighthouse, 26

Capitman, Andrew, 5, 54, 56, 178, 252;
and Cardozo hotel, 54–55, 57, 88–89,
240; and Miami Design Preservation
League, 27, 53; as owner of Art Deco
hotels, 54–55, 86–89, 96, 103–4, 109,
164–65, 175

Capitman, Barbara, 5, 24, 31, 57–58, *120*;
and Art Deco hotels, 54, 56; and creation of Art Deco district, 5, 6, 18, 24,
31, 175; criticism of, 59, 84, 101, 175; and
family, 5, 31, 54, 56, 178; health of, *120*,
169, 178–79; and historic preservation
ordinance, 84–85; legacy of, 175, 179,
195, 253–54; and Miami Design Preservation League, 25, 27, 31, 34, 109, 184;
and National Register nomination, 37–
40, 49, 53; and politics, 105–6, 147–48;
and promotion of Art Deco district, 34,
43, 45–46, 176, 178; and protests of
demolitions, 43, 82, 166–69; as writer,
31, 33, 167, 178

Capitman, John, 5, 54, 56, 178, 252; involvement in the Art Deco district, 18,
24, 25, 27, 30

Capone, Al, 48

Cardozo hotel, 44–45, *115*, 234, 240–41;
under Capitman ownership, 54–57, 86,
88–89, 188; under Royale Group ownership, 109, 111

Caribbean islands, 19, 48, 219, 246

Carib theater, 132

Carlyle hotel: under Capitman ownership,
79, 86, 88–89, 104; under Royale
Group ownership, 111, 139

Carter, President Jimmy, 2, 133

Carver hotel, 198

Casablanca hotel, 243

Casa Casuarina, 218–24, 275n18. *See also*
Amsterdam Palace

Casinos, bathing, 9–12, 15, 81, 95, 257n17

Castle, Irene, 240

Castro, Cuban President Fidel, 36, 61–66,
72, 141

Causeways, 106, 137, 166; County Causeway, 13, 258n30; MacArthur Causeway,

112, 158, 161, 163, 165, 191; Venetian
Causeway, 195. *See also* Collins Bridge

Cavalier hotel, 86, 171

Cavanaugh Communities. *See* Royale
Group

Celebrities, on South Beach, 104, 132, 134,
150, 199; broadcasting live from, 34,
107; filming movies, 107, 240–41; filming music videos, 169, 240–41; filming
TV series, 106–9, 240; as hotel guests,
13, 226, 241, 250; musicians, 2, 58, 87,
104, 157, 198, 227, 244; as property
owners, 147, 188, 206, 241; seen at
nightclubs, 206–7, 210, 241, 254

Center Theater (New York), 28

Central Beach Elementary School. *See*
Fienberg-Fisher School

Cermak, Mayor Anton, 95

Charles Deering estate, 148, 195–96,
269n6

Charleston, S.C., 20, 52; preservation
ordinance, 27, 83–84

Chatov, Ramon, 172

Chautauqua Institution, 110

Cheezem, Charles, 129–30

Chicago, Ill., 20, 48, 95, 196, 206; architects and architecture, 28, 36, 39, 142,
229, 238

Chiles, Governor Lawton, 190

Christo. *See* Javacheff, Christo and Jeanne-
Claude

Chrysler Building (New York), 28, 30, 38

Churches, 26, 131, 133, 142, 224

Ciment, Mayor Norman, 100, 106

Cincinnati, Ohio, 25

Cinema Theater, 32–33, 42–43, 71, 112

Claire apartments, 29

Clarkson, Mrs. Philip, 36

Clay, Cassius. *See* Ali, Muhammad

Clay hotel, 58, 67–68, 97, 141, 266n35;
renovations of, *122*, 142, 253; as youth
hostel, 96, 252

Clevelander hotel, 152, 206, 238; owned by
Gerry Sanchez, *121*, 141–42, 145, 253

Clooney, George, 241

Club 1235, 112

Club Ovo, 144

Club Z, 112

Coast Guard. *See* United States Coast Guard

Cobain, Kurt, 227

Cochise County Courthouse, 28

Coconut Grove, 25, 58, 66; historic, 7, 26, 30; price of real estate in, 135, 139, 143

Coconut plantation, 8, 10, 39, 213

Code enforcement. *See* Miami Beach, City of

Cohen, Mona, 217

Collins, John, 8, 228, 231; as developer, 9, 10, 17; as farmer, 8, 9, 17, 39–40

Collins, Phil, 107

Collins Avenue, 16, *113*, 181, 206, 231, 236; character of, 58, 142, 164, 194, 196, 238; demolitions on, 80–84, 164–69, 185, 224; historic districts and, 110, 145–46, 148, 182–83; vacant property on, 44, 90. *See also individual hotels by name*

Collins Bridge, 9–12, 39

Collins Canal, 9, 39–40, 71, 106

Collins Park, 172, 183, 231–33

Colonial Williamsburg, 43–44, 224

Colony hotel, 7, *114*

Colony Theater, 71, 136, 142, 231

Columbus, Christopher, 218–20

Comden, Betty, 106

Community and Economic Development. *See* Metro-Dade County

Community Reinvestment Act of 1977, 86–87

Concord Cafeteria, 1–2, 100

Condominiums, 3, 19, 73, 137–38, 205; collapse of market for, 89–90, 149, 155; conversion of hotels and rentals to, 138, 151, 215, 216; high-rise, 76, 81–82, 246, 250

—in redevelopment area: existing, 6, 21, 24, 36, 61, 92, 93, 211; new construction of, 23, 129, 211–12, 246

Continuum, the, 246

Convention center. *See* Miami Beach Convention Center

Convention hotel, 47, 183, 194, 205, 237–38

Cook, Sandra, *126*

Cooney, Gerry, 200

Cooperstown, N.Y., 209

Coral Gables, 27, 158, 160, 188, 191; historic preservation ordinance of, 26, 84

Corruption, political, 48, 201–2

Costello, Frank, 48

Costner, Kevin, 241

County Causeway, 13. *See also* MacArthur Causeway

Court orders, 47, 157, 182, 247; against City of Miami Beach, 46, 159–60, 162, 212

Courts at South Beach, 212

Crawford, Cindy, 241

Crawford, Dana, 56, 261n7

Crawford, Joan, 235

Crime, 68, 98–99, 153, 181–82, 205; arson and fires, 68, 90, 180–81, 226; assault, 67–68, 133; burglary, 68, 93, 97, 133, 157; drugs, 68, 93, 107–8, 155; effects of, 61, 97, 133, 145, 155, 214, 254; homicide, 68, 93–94, 108, 157, 223–24; increasing rate of, 68, 93, 95, 107, 138; robbery and muggings, 68, 93, 133; vagrancy, 155, 158. *See also* Corruption; Gambling; Organized Crime

Cruise ships, 22, 104, 177, 189, 246

Cuba, 36, 72, 204, 253, 263n8; Havana, 16, 80; Mariel boatlift, 61–69

Cuban community: and discrimination, 27, 262n25; growing on South Beach, 37, 88, 101–2, 134, 140, 154; involved in Art Deco district, 36, 52, 72–73, 77, 141, 152; and Miami Beach politics, 131, 203–4, 243, 252; in redevelopment area, 95, 199. *See also* Mariel boatlift

Cultural and heritage tourism. *See* Tourism

Cultural center, 231–33

Cunanan, Andrew, 223–24

Dacra Companies, 187, 227–29, 251–52. *See also* Robins, Craig and Scott

Dade Boulevard, 39, 90, 145, 155, 252; as site of Holocaust Memorial, 204, 243

Dade County. *See* Metro-Dade County

Dade County School Board, 76–77
Dade Heritage Trust, 27, 161, 195, 204, 229; and Miami Design Preservation League, 27, 204, 229; and Ocean Drive Developers Conference, 110, 266n17
Dallas, Tex., 20, 34
Daoud, Mayor Alex, 126, 201–2, 242
David Allen, 131
Deaths, 5, 181, 192, 223–24, 243; of people involved with the Miami Design Preservation League, 178, 253, 276n11
Deauville hotel, 34, 246
Deco Plaza, 111–12, 141
Deering Estate. See Charles Deering estate
Delano hotel, 132, 183; after renovation, 226–27, 236, 245
Delaporte, Chris, 37–38
Delicatessens, 134, 147, 251; kosher, 3, 17, 140, 147
Demolitions, 74, 83, 100, 225; laws to prevent, 42–43, 74; in Middle Beach, 16, 46, 243, 245, 252; before National Register district, 74–76, 80–81, 221; in National Register district, 116, 128, 185, 186–87, 238–39, 254, 275n9; in other states, 23, 40, 49, 56, 254; partial, 83, 166, 221, 248; in redevelopment area, 92, 119, 128, 200–201, 213–14; threatened, 26, 76–77, 149–50, 156, 183, 243. See also Biscaya; New Yorker; Revere; Senator
Denver, Colo., 56
Depression Moderne. See Architectural styles
Depression of 1929. See Great Depression
Design standards, 154, 187–88, 225–30
Detroit, Mich., 20
Developers: of new construction, 76, 89–90, 229, 252; in National Register district, 90, 130, 185, 225; of hotels, 50, 183, 237–38; and politics, 50, 60, 130; in redevelopment area, 21–22, 61, 91–93, 129, 158, 211–13. See also Muss, Stephen; Resnick, Abe
Developers, original Miami Beach. See Collins, John; Fisher, Carl; Lummus, J. E. and J. N.

Developers, renovation and restoration, 110–11, 138–41, 219, 229, individual, 112, 138–41, 150–52, 177, 216; on South Beach before 1986, 144, 176, 225, 249; outside South Beach, 20, 158, 229. See also Dacra Companies; Goldman, Tony; Royale Group; Sanchez, Gerry
Diamonstein, Barbaralee, 188
Diaz, Cameron, 241
Discovery Channel, 240
Discrimination: anti-Semitism, 12, 17, 142; by age, 19, 58; by ethnicity, 37, 64, 262n25; by race, 17, 198–99, 214; by sexual orientation, 239
Dixon, L. Murray, 39, 164
Dixon apartments, 140
Dog track. See Miami Beach Kennel Club
Dominican Republic, 218
Douglas, Marjorie Stoneman, 84
Douglas Entrance, 26
Doyle, Margaret, 55–56, 85, 101, 252; renovating hotels, 55–56, 87, 89
Dreyfuss, Richard, 241
Drucker, Sam, 2, 94
Drugs, 65, 68, 90, 107–8, 202; impact on neighborhood of, 68, 93, 98, 155, 158, 213; neighborhood recovery from, 138, 187, 250
Duany, Andres, 249, 251–52
Dunaevsky, Dov, 84, 146
Dundee, Angelo, 198–99
Dundee, Chris, 197–200
Dunn, Irene, 235
DuPont Building, 30, 148
Duran, Roberto, 199

Economic Recovery Tax Act, 85
Economics of historic preservation, 21, 51, 55, 224; doubts about, 89, 105; as revitalization tool, 20, 107, 135, 138, 255; return on investment, 138–39, 142–43, 145, 150, 152; tax incentives, 26, 56, 85, 162. See also Renovation costs
Economy (Miami Beach), 15–18, 94, 249, 255; economic development efforts, 101, 154; effect of historic preservation on, 138, 144–45, 239, 245; local businesses

Hialeah, 103, 142, 202

Hibiscus Island, 13

High rises, 90, 191, 209, 245–46, 255; in redevelopment area, 23, 129, 211, 246, 255; replacing historic buildings, 19, 29, 76, 80, 82, 238, 243–45, 250

Hilton hotels, 47

Hirsch, Rick, 242–43

Hirschfeld, Abe, 203

Hispaniola, 218

Historic American Building Survey, 37

Historic building surveys, 28–31, 224; in Metro-Dade County, 36–37, 83; for National Register, 34–37, 39, 221

Historic districts in Miami Beach, 83, 149, 154, 182–83, 204, 225; Espanola Way district, 146, 148, 182; Flamingo Park district, 182; Lincoln Road/ Museum district, 183, 188, 194, 196; Ocean Beach district, 213–14; Ocean Drive/Collins Avenue, 110, 146, 148, 165–66, 182, 221

Historic districts outside Miami Beach, 83, 110, 196; in other states, 40, 56, 85, 165, 209, 254

Historic preservation board. See Miami Beach, City of

Historic preservation law, 26, 83–84, 105, 148–49

Historic preservation movement, 248; MiMo, 244; national, 20–21, 51; opposition to in Miami Beach, 65, 81, 105, 252; other groups involvement in, 186, 231; state and county, 26–27, 36, 109, 195. See also Economics of historic preservation; Historic preservation law; Historic preservation organizations

Historic preservation ordinances, 27, 83– 85; Metro-Dade County, 83, 104–5, 249

—Miami Beach, 83, 104–5, 145–46, 182, 187, 196; amendments, 166–67, 221– 22; opposition to, 83–85, 213, 248

Historic preservation organizations, 20, 26, 73–74, 84. See also Dade Heritage Trust; Miami Design Preservation League; National Trust for Historic Preservation

Historic Sites Act of 1935, 83

Hoberman, Richard, 101–3, 126, 180, 190– 92, 252; and demolitions, 161, 166, 168; and Miami Design Preservation League, 174, 221–22, 235

Hoffman's Cafeteria, 29, 251

Hohauser, Henry, 39, 73

Hole in the Head, A, 240

Holland, Robert, 138, 140–41, 225

Holliday, Judy, 106

Hollywood, Fla., 150

Holocaust, 2, 59, 69–70, 94, 147, 253, 263n8; memorials, 204, 243

Holt, Officer Tony, 155

Holtz, Abel, 126

Homeless, 98, 125, 216–17, 252; after Hurricane Andrew, 192, 194; using vacant buildings, 155, 160, 181

Home Mortgage Disclosure Act of 1975, 86–87

Homestead Air Force Base, 191, 193

Homicides, 68, 93–95, 108, 157, 223–34

Honolulu, Hawaii, 107, 236

Horowitz, Leonard, 78–79, 85, 126, 169, 254; and Capitman family, 5–7, 18, 24, 55; and demolitions, 79, 81, 165; health of, 175–78; and Miami Design Preservation League, 25, 27, 33, 46

—and South Beach color palette, 78–79, 102–3, 108, 176, 228; and individual buildings, 102, 112, 176, 266n5

Hospitals, 66, 76, 252; in Miami Beach, 3, 169, 189–90, 252; during World War II, 71, 158

Hostels. See Clay hotel; Youth hostels

Hotel, The. See Tiffany hotel

Hotel owner-operators, 17, 35, 44, 61, 141, 193; of boarded-up buildings, 90, 181; opposed to Art Deco district, 34, 50, 52, 84, 110–11, 144; in redevelopment area, 11–12, 22, 67, 93, 95, 129–30, 250; of residential hotels, 35, 90–91; after South Beach turnaround, 225–26, 228–29. See also Art Deco hotels; Dacra Companies; Goldman, Tony; Muss, Stephen; Novak, Ben; Polansky, Linda; Royale Group; Sanchez, Gerry; *individual hotels by name*

litions, 42–43, 221–22, and Miami Design Preservation League, 52, 79, 184, 221, 238
King David Deli, 147
Kipnis, Samuel, 136
Kitt, Eartha, 87
Klein, Calvin, 170
Knickerbocker Village, 24
Kohn, Dorothy, 149–50
Kosher: bakeries, 17, 41, 102, 266n5; delis, 3, 140, 147; hotels, 18, 95, 156–57, 255; markets, 17, 41, 94, 105, 139, 200; restaurants, 5, 17
Kramer, Thomas, 211–13, 246
Krause, Hans-Joachim, 226
Kravitz, Lenny, 241

LaGorce, John, 17
Land sales: in early years, 10–11, 13, 17, 29; in redevelopment area, 129, 212
Land use: in Art Deco district, 76, 83, 128, 220–21, 245–46; and development patterns, 16, 30, 41; in Middle Beach, 16, 46; in redevelopment area, 6, 21–23, 59–60, 91, 128–29
Lane, Nathan, 241
Lansky, Meyer, 49
LaPan, Earl, 87
Lapidus, Morris: as architect, 46–47, 132, 245; as critic of Art Deco district, 210–11, 228, 238, 276n11
Larimer Square (Denver, Colo.), 56, 261n7
Las Vegas, Nev.: architecture of, 47, 244; as competition for tourism, 19, 49, 199
Lauren, Ralph, 230
Lawsuits (against Miami Beach), 46, 212; involving code enforcement, 97, 156, 159, 221–22, 266n35
Leonard hotel, 95
Leslie hotel, 86, 141
Levin, Lillian, 130, 180–81
Levy, Benjamin, 1–7, 24, 93, 100, 208, 250
Lewis, Jerry, 244
Liberace, 244
Liberty City, 65–66, 198
Library. See Miami Beach, City of
Liebman, Nancy, 76–77, 110, 177, 183, 191; as city commissioner, 120, 203–5, 208,

243, 252, 273n24; and demolitions, 161, 163, 168, 185, 221, 239; and Miami Design Preservation League, 109, 126, 174–75, 184–85, 222, 235
Limited partnerships, 54, 58, 88, 109
Lincoln, Officer Calvin, 223
Lincoln Building, 29, 131
Lincoln hotel, 131
Lincoln Plaza apartments, 216
Lincoln Road: and the arts, 135–36, 141–42, 171–74, 231–32; decline of, 133–34; history of, 17, 29, 41, 71, 81, 113, 131–32; as part of historic district, 135, 182, 205, 229; retailers on, 2–3, 133–34, 251, 267n13, 277n6; revival of, 134–36, 144, 210, 231, 239, 255
Lincoln Theatre, 44, 144, 173–74
Liston, Sonny, 199
Lithuania, 69–70, 81, 204, 252
Loews hotel, 237–38
Lombard, Carole, 235
Lopez, Jennifer, 241
Los Angeles, Calif., 244
Louis, Joe, 199
Love, Courtney, 241
Low-income housing. See Housing, affordable and low-income
Lum, Henry, 7–8, 39
Lummus, J. E. and J. N., 9–12, 17, 29, 81, 211
Lummus Park, 6, 107, 114; as gathering place, 4, 78, 237, 255; relationship to Ocean Drive, 6, 110, 206, 220, 223; after storms, 180, 192

MacArthur Causeway, 165, 191; as County Causeway, 13; as entrance to South Beach, 112, 158, 161, 163
MacArthur hotel. See Deco Plaza
Magazines: articles about Art Deco district, 33–34, 132, 138, 170, 195; fashion shoots, 170–71; articles about renovations, 226, 266n5; articles about South Florida, 68, 151
Magnum, PI, 107
Maher v. New Orleans, 149
Main Floor, The, 240
Majestic hotel, 73

South Shore. *See* Miami Beach redevelopment area
Spanish Colonial architecture. *See* Architectural styles
Spanish Monastery, 26
Sports, 3, 137; professional, 107, 197–201, 209
Spring break, 205–6
SS *Normandie*, 16
SS *St. Louis*, 70, 253, 263n8
Stallone, Sylvester, 241
Stanley Myers Health Center, 135
Starck, Phillipe, 226–27
Star hotel. *See* Ocean Beach hotel
Star Island, 13, 149
State Historic Preservation Officer. *See* Florida, State of
St. Augustine, Fla., 8, 53
Stein's Hardware, 210
Sterling Building, 131, 134–35, 141, 251
Stewart, Jimmy, 132
St. Francis Hospital, 169, 252
St. Moritz hotel, 29, 181; as part of convention hotel site, 183, 185, 238
St. Patrick's Catholic Church, 224
St. Petersburg, Russia, 32
St. Paul, Minn., 50
Strand restaurant, 151, 154
Streamline Development, 154. *See also* Gross, Saul
Streamline Moderne architecture. *See* Architectural styles
Streets of San Francisco, 107
Structural failure, 74, 156, 186–87, 238–39, 254
Subsidized housing. *See* Housing
Suburbs: inner ring, 13, 15, 31; outer, 137, 153; in hurricanes, 191–93; preservation in, 26, 84, 158, 160–61, 196
Suislaw River Bridge, 28
Sullivan, Ed, 34
Super Bowl, 107
Surrounded Islands. *See* Javacheff, Christo
Surveys. *See* Historic building surveys
Sutton, Max, 98
Sweetwater, 202
Swimming pools: demolished, 79, 81, 168;

private, 201, 220, 222; public, 137, 189. *See also* Casinos, bathing
—on hotel property: Ocean Drive, 152, 226; Collins Avenue, 45, 226; others in Miami Beach, 35, 47, 173
Symphony. *See* New World Symphony
Synagogues: in South Beach, 4, 17, 139, 178–79; in Miami Beach, 204, 217. *See also* Beth Jacob Congregation Hall

Tallahassee, Fla., 40, 49, 53, 101
Tampa, Fla., 65, 272n24; historic districts, 53, 209, 249
Taradesh, William, 81
Taxes, 13, 23; city resort taxes, 109, 138, 167; other city taxes, 49, 76, 89–90
Tax incentives for historic preservation, 26, 55, 85, 162
Tax Reform Act of 1978, 26
Teich, Gertude, 131
Television shows: live from Miami Beach, 34, 107; *Miami Vice*, 106–9, 112, 169, 220, 240; others set in South Beach, 108, 240–41
Temple Beth-Jacob, 6, 95
Temple Beth Sholom, 217
Temple Emanu-el, 178–79
Temple Menorah, 204
Tenth Street Auditorium, 4, 98, 253
Tepper, Lillian, 155
Theater of the Performing Arts, 136, 178, 232
Theaters, movie, 29, 132, 173. *See also* Cinema Theater; Colony Theater; Lincoln Theater; Radio City Music Hall
Thomas, Merrie and Dick, 139, 143
Thomas, Michael Tilson, 171–74
Thomas, Philip-Michael, 106–7, 220
Thrift stores, 41, 210
Tides hotel, 7, 111, 144, 164; after renovation, 122, 236
Tiffany hotel (The Hotel), 113, 226, 247
Time magazine, 68
Tisch, Jonathan, 238
Tonight Show, 34, 107
Tourism boycott, 237–38, 276n9

M. Barron Stofik was active in city, county, and state historic preservation groups in Florida for more than a decade. The former newspaper reporter has been a magazine writer and editor, and has worked on numerous publications about historic preservation. Three cats allow her and her family to share a home with them in Connecticut.